INSURGENT UNIVERSALITY

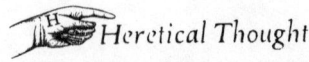 Heretical Thought

HERETICAL THOUGHT

Series editor: Ruth O'Brien, The Graduate Center, City University of New York

Assembly
Michael Hardt and Antonio Negri

The Rise of Neoliberal Feminism
Catherine Rottenberg

INSURGENT UNIVERSALITY

An Alternative Legacy of Modernity

MASSIMILIANO TOMBA

UNIVERSITY PRESS

Oxford University Press is a department of the University of Oxford. It furthers the University's objective of excellence in research, scholarship, and education by publishing worldwide. Oxford is a registered trade mark of Oxford University Press in the UK and certain other countries.

Published in the United States of America by Oxford University Press
198 Madison Avenue, New York, NY 10016, United States of America.

© Oxford University Press 2019

All rights reserved. No part of this publication may be reproduced, stored in a retrieval system, or transmitted, in any form or by any means, without the prior permission in writing of Oxford University Press, or as expressly permitted by law, by license, or under terms agreed with the appropriate reproduction rights organization. Inquiries concerning reproduction outside the scope of the above should be sent to the Rights Department, Oxford University Press, at the address above.

You must not circulate this work in any other form
and you must impose this same condition on any acquirer.

CIP data is on file at the Library of Congress
ISBN 978-0-19-088308-9

9 8 7 6 5 4 3 2 1

Printed by Sheridan Books, Inc., United States of America

CONTENTS

	Preface	vii
	Acknowledgments	xi
1.	Introduction: Decolonizing Modern History	1
2.	1793: The Neglected Legacy of Insurgent Universality	30
3.	1871: The Institutions of Insurgent Universality	71
4.	1918: An Insurgent Constitution	120
5.	1994: Zapatistas and the Dispossessed of History	186
	In Lieu of a Conclusion: Trajectories of Possession	223
	Notes	235
	Index	281

PREFACE

Insurgent Universality: An Alternative Legacy of Modernity embodies Heretical Thought, and not just because Massimiliano Tomba is a heretic himself. He advances a heretical body of work that challenges Hegel, Kant, and early Marx in addition the library of political theorists and scholars they influenced. He shows how we must bring in from the margins of the modern canon of political theory a group of passionate early advocates for the commons as an alternative to making private property sacrosanct. By so doing, Tomba presents readers with a highly original notion of universality, one that advances through insurgencies that interrupt the nation-state by undermining state sovereignty. These insurgencies are not the libertarian fantasy of "a mass of atomized individuals" banging down the doors of the state. Instead, by participating in the social sphere outside the reach of the state, they have erected a "rich multiplicity of institutions." In questioning whether individuals are organized or housed within colliding social spheres, Tomba advances an inherently democratic argument that they are, and can continue to be organized within social institutions that precede political and economic institutions.[1]

To create a sweeping argument that privileges society, and recognizes a global capacity for democratization, not advancing self-interested individuals, individualism, or the state, Tomba jettisons the idea that time is an arrow—rejecting "linear development" and opting for a "historical multiverse" instead of a "uni-verse." He breaks free from the 17th-century Enlightenment notion of *terra nullius*, on which European colonialists relied to deny Indigenous peoples the right to stay on their land, and from the assumption that this arrangement was the inevitable consequence of developments in European societies.

The English and Scottish Enlightenment principle that the state should protect private property as an individual right was not foreordained, not an "anthropological constant that is reproduced in every human grouping at different levels of development." Universalizing the idea that private property was a necessary component of civilization gave European colonialists the means to strip Indigenous peoples of their lands—and modern-day scholars the means to strip alternative views, old and new, from their reading lists.

Tomba focuses on how John Locke rejected the common possession of lands, calling Indigenous peoples "uncivil" and "wild." Yet more than forty years before Locke's *Second Treatise*, Gerrard Winstanley published *A Declaration from the Poor Oppressed People of England* that challenged what he called "Particular Propriety." Winstanley, an English Protestant religious reformer, founded the Diggers (or the True Levellers), who protested enclosures by occupying public lands that had been privatized.

Tomba wants us to read, for instance, this line-by-line:

> The power of enclosing land and owning property was brought into the creation by your ancestors by the sword; which first did murder their fellow creatures, men, and after plunder or steal away their land, and left this land successively to you, their children. . . . And therefore, though you did not kill or thieve,

yet you hold that cursed thing in your hand by the power of the sword; and so you justify the wicked deeds of your fathers . . .

Winstanley, like Jacques Roux and François-Noël Babeuf, has been peremptorily excluded from the modern political theory canon.

Tomba asks us to read these heretical thinkers closely because they dispute the idea that property is an individual right, like freedom and equality. From peasants to sans-culottes, Communards, and Zapatistas, he writes, Indigenous peoples have "experimented with democracy as a practice that concerns taking care of both the community and the land they worked." Looking back to the medieval era, the idea of the commons existed under the Teutons, the Romans, and the Celts. There is no reason that land must be private, or that power must be "monopolized by the state."

Specific moments within history effect change, but these moments are not necessarily sequential. Ideas zig-zag or ping-pong over time. The Dark Ages did not promise the Enlightenment; it was only during the Enlightenment that we could congratulate ourselves about the light coming on. Not pursuing "the arrow" allows Tomba to give us alternative trajectories, and to him the years 1793, 1871, 1918, and 1994 provide instructive case studies.

For example, the idea of the commons reappeared during the French Revolution with the publication of *The Manifesto of the Enragés* and *The Manifesto of the Equals*. And in contemporary society we have seen this type of insurgent universality among the Zapatistas in the Mexican region of Chiapas, as well as at Standing Rock in the United States and Canada:

> Chiapas, the Zapatista insurgency, is not for peasants' ownership of the land; it stands against its individualization and for common possession, democratically regulated in the forms of local self-government.
>
> In this [system], the relation between the land and those who use it is not one of unilateral exploitation but of mutual

assistance: "The concept of property is redefined as usufruct on the part of human generations, which use the land as *boni patres familias* [good family fathers]. Not only does this concept denote an attitude towards common land, but it is spatially and temporally broadened: no subject, individual or collective, even the entire humanity, that is of one's own epoch, is "owner of the earth."

If we start with the priority of the territory, not of its occupant, the network of property relations changes profoundly, becoming defined and delimited. The individual subject ceases to be at the center of these relationships, replaced by "the connective fabric and . . . the groups that an individual was part of." In similar fashion, Europe ceases to be considered the center of the world, and a single linear, teleological narrative no longer defines our understanding.

Tomba's book corrects notions not just of ownership, democracy, and natural rights but of causality, linearity, and individuality. He connects such seemingly disparate histories that Hegel, Kant, and, later, Marx "missed," such as the Russian *obshchina*, the Paris Commune, and the Andean *ayllu*, all with erudition, wit, passion, and boundless imagination. *Insurgent Universality* alters our way of thinking about insurgency and democracy, and thus makes an outstanding addition to the Heretical Thought series at Oxford University Press.

Professor Ruth O'Brien
The Graduate Center, CUNY

ACKNOWLEDGMENTS

The maturation of this book profited from my long stays in the United States. At times, to refresh one's thoughts, there is nothing better than to move your life into a new environment and let yourself go through a change of spaces and times. *Insurgent Universality* benefited from conversations with many new and old friends and with colleagues of the New and Old Worlds. Special thanks go to all my friends at the Advanced Research Collaborative and the Committee on Globalization and Social Change at The Graduate Center, CUNY. To everyone in these conversations, I extend my collective thanks. I do want to distinguish those with whom I have continued a rich and long dialogue, like Susan Buck-Morss, Duncan Faherty, Uday Mehta, Julie Skurski, and Gary Wilder. I have been fortunate to draw on conversations with all of them, and I am very grateful for their comments on parts of my book. Uday has become an indispensable interlocutor, and I am sure he will find pieces of our common conversation in this book.

A special thank-you goes to Fadi Bardawil, Didier Fassin, Bernard Harcourt, David Kazanjian, Joan Scott, and Linda Zerilli for comments on an earlier draft of this book at the Institute for Advanced Study in Princeton, where most of this book was written.

Joan Scott encouraged this work from the beginning and helped me to make it more robust with her remarks. Andrew Arato, Gopal Balakrishnan, Mauro Farnesi Camellone, Andrea Cengia, Paulina Ochoa Espejo, Giovanni Fiaschi, Carlos Forment, Jason Frank, Ferruccio Gambino, Asad Haider, Harry Harootunian, Fernando Leiva, Robyn Marasco, Robert Meister, Dmitri Nikulin, Anne Norton, Kristin Ross, and Paul Roth contributed with their comments to make the book clearer to me and, I hope, to the reader, too. My thanks also go to Angela Chnapko and Ruth O'Brian for their support, comments, and enthusiasm. Rafaella Capanna helped me make this book accessible to the English-speaking public, and Patrick King helped me with the editing of the book, especially with his comments.

Finally, a special thank-you goes to my beloved partner Banu Bargu and my sons Carlo and Teo. To Carlo, for his curiosity and patience. To Teo, who was born as this book went to print. To Banu, my deepest love for always standing by me and helping me to stay on course whenever I needed it. To her, my gratitude for convincing me to abandon my project on Kant and to work on insurgent universality instead. This book is dedicated to her.

An early version of chapter 2 was published as "1793: The Neglected Legacy of Insurgent Universality," *History of the Present. A Journal of Critical History* 5, no. 2 (2015): 109–36, and an early version of chapter 4 appeared as "Politics Beyond the State: The 1918 Soviet Constitution," *Constellations* 24, no. 4 (2017): 503–15.

Santa Cruz
February 2019

INTRODUCTION

Decolonizing Modern History

> To treat the past (better: what has been) in accordance with a method that is no longer historical but political.
> —WALTER BENJAMIN[1]

IN THE TWENTIETH CENTURY, ONE of the many revolutionaries who has been removed from the dominant canon compared all human history to a huge river bounded by two dikes: on one side, that of the guardians of the state and conservation; on the other, that of the reformists with their faith in progress. The two groups, on opposite sides of the river, hurl insults at each other, but they fully agree that the river should remain in its channel. Sometimes, however, the river floods over the dikes and "jumps" onto an unexpected trajectory. It engulfs the banks and gives the landscape a new physiognomy. Insurgent universality can be compared to this river when the practice of democracy exceeds the constitutional shell of the state.

In *Insurgent Universality*, I reinterpret the history of some revolutionary events through those collective endeavors that are the declarations, manifestos, and constitutions. As any activist well knows, writing a manifesto, declaration, or political document is always a collective endeavor. There are different drafts, sentences cut out and paragraphs added. A declaration is a battlefield on which different positions temporarily converge. For each of them, there correspond not only proper names of people but also, and above all, social forces. The author of a declaration, if and when one can speak of a single author, is only the pen in which tensions, conflicts, agreements, and disagreements converge.

When I discuss the French Revolution, it is not through the writings of Robespierre or Saint-Just that I reinterpret it. In the same way, when I discuss the Russian Revolution, the names of the great leaders and their writings remain in the background. Building an alternative canon of modernity, as an appendix to an *Alternative Legacy*, requires a double move. The first move requires abandoning the privileged point of view of both great theorists and leaders, but not to substitute them with other leaders or figures marginalized by the dominant historiography. Rather, and this is the second move, it is about considering the practice of insurgents as theory in action that goes to constitute the collective ink with which the political documents of an insurgency are written. Insurgent universality is mainly anonymous, because when democracy is real, its practice does not need great personalities or leaders.

The universality that I call insurgent is an experiment with time, space, and politics. If one casts off the dogma of the philosophy of universal history, the enormous political and economic material that constitutes the present ceases to be organized in terms of advanced, backward, or residual forms. It instead becomes an interweaving of temporalities that recombine in the moment of an insurgency. As happened in Russia, with the rural commune when populists and Socialist Revolutionaries tried to combine the forms of local self-government and collective ownership of the peasant communities with the workers' councils. As was the case during the Paris Commune, when the Communards referred to medieval forms of local self-government to reconfigure them in a socialist sense. As it is the case in Chiapas, where the Zapatistas recall the true spirit of the 1917 Constitution and the self-government of indigenous communities. These experiments must be investigated not in the abstract but, rather, by digging through the temporal layers of existent historical material. Universality is not a mere problem of scale but also of relationships and bridges between temporalities that can be both coeval and dislocated in other historical layers.

CHRONOTONES

One can date the beginning of modernity with the capitalist era (sixteenth century) or with the birth of the modern state (seventeenth century), or even with the industrial revolutions of the late eighteenth century. In any case, in accordance with self-representation of modern (Western) history, these events would catapult Europe into a vanguard position in world history, on the tip of the vector of a unilinear conception of historical time. What we call "modernity" corresponds to a certain conception of history, or rather to its singularization, which in the German language took place in the late eighteenth century and coincided with the semantic change of the word *Geschichte* that changed from the plural "histories" to the collective singular "history." The latter is the prerequisite of the modern Western idea of universal history (*allgemeine Weltgeschichte*).[2]

This term is anything but neutral. The prefix *Welt* does not simply mean "world"; it has a strong unifying and ordering significance. Universal history is presented as a line along which events take place from the origins to the present, and the universal historian works backward toward the origins in order to find the meaning of those events.[3] When Hegel made use of the concept of universal history, he placed the modern state at the tip of the historical-temporal arrow and worked backward, ordering every age in relation to the modern Western conception of freedom. From Hegel's perspective, teleological directionality was bound to the past more than to the future. Teleology served to justify the historical trajectory that led to a certain configuration of the Western modernity. It was the Hegelian-Fichtean philosopher August Cieszkowski who would project teleology toward the future.[4] In both cases, the teleology of history is based on the assumption that historical time is an arrow, against which it would be possible to lay out qualitative differences in quantitative terms. Thus, non-state political forms become pre-state and non-capitalist economic forms become pre-capitalist. In this way, the enormous range of possibilities offered by the countless non-capitalist forms is subsumed in the definition of backward or pre-capitalist forms as if their future were enclosed in that "pre": becoming capitalist forms. In the historiographical approach I propose here, I intend to keep open the potentiality that those forms hold as alternative trajectories of modernity.

The dominant Western representation of historical time presumes a certain conception of time and space as metahistoric universals valid everywhere that enable comparison. It was Kant who elevated space and time to "pure" forms of intuition, preceding any experience and able to order each experience into coherent representations. This time, as a condition of possibility of any representation, "cannot be made representable to us except under the image of a line, insofar as we draw it."[5] Indeed, Gottfried Herder rebelled against this absolute conception of time, strictly stating, in contrast to Kant, that "every changing thing has in itself the measure of its own time. . . . There are not two things in the world that have the same measure of time. The beat of my pulse, the course or the sequence of my thoughts are not the measure of time for others; the course of a stream, the growth of a tree are not the measure of time for all streams, trees and plants. . . . Therefore, (we can say with a daring but nevertheless exact expression) there exists an infinite multiplicity of temporalities in the universe at the same time; the time that we imagine to be the measure of everything is only a proportion made up of our thoughts, . . . an illusion."[6] For us, it is not a question of choosing, in a more or less arbitrary manner, Herder's *Metakritik* instead of Kant's *Kritik* but, rather, asking ourselves what conception of time is appropriate to our present and the duties of politics today.

Reinhart Koselleck and, before him, Ernst Bloch, Walter Benjamin, and Karl Marx in his later days pluralized historical temporalities. For Koselleck, historical research is "not of one historical time, but rather of many forms of time superimposed one upon the other."[7] Koselleck, by paying attention to the simultaneity of multiple historical times, observed that the spatializing metaphor has the advantage of pluralizing the concept of time: "temporal strata" (*Zeitschichten*) refer, as in the geological model, to multiple layers of time (*Zeitebenen*) of different lengths and from different places, but which are nonetheless simultaneously present and active.[8] According to Koselleck, "history contains many differentiable strata, each changing faster or slower, anyhow each of them with different paces of change."[9] But these different paces of change (*Veränderungsgeschwindigkeiten*) still refer to a historical temporality against which one can measure the greater or lesser speed of the changes. Instead, what I want to address is the art of pluralizing the historical times in such a way as to transform a quantitative difference (the speed of the change) into a qualitative difference (temporality).

In the 1950s, looking at anti-colonial struggles, Ernst Bloch developed an idea, counter to the unilinearity of historical time, of a "broad, flexible and thoroughly dynamic 'multiverse.' . . . A unilinear model must be found obsolete if justice is to be done to the considerable amount of non-European material. It is no longer possible to work without curves in the series; without a new and complex time-manifold (the problem of 'Riemannian time')."[10] Walter Benjamin introduced the idea of the "differential of time." What the dominant historiography considers deviations, which "disturb the main line of inquiry," are for Benjamin the basis of his conception of history.[11] According to Benjamin, the task of the real historical materialist is not just about explaining the past, reconstructing it from its dark side, but also turning it into something incomplete.[12] From this perspective, it is about working with the roads not taken, or repressed, which, from the past, can shed light on the possibilities that were left unfinished but remain vital to re-imagine our present.

Finally, Marx, in his later years and in dialogue with the Russian populists, devised a geological conception of history in which different layers overlap. In a letter to Vera Zasulich, Marx writes that it would be a mistake to consider the different forms of "primitive" communities as belonging to the same historical stratum: "as in geological formations, these historical forms contain a whole series of primary, secondary, tertiary types, etc."[13] In this new vision, as Marx learned from Nikolay Chernyshevsky, historical jumps were possible and Russia did not have to go through the process of capital accumulation that had taken place in Europe. On the contrary, as we will see in chapter 4, the Russian agrarian commune could have been the basis for new collective forms of land ownership.[14] In the 1860s, Marx had already investigated the relationship between industrial capital and archaic and new forms of social relations. He observed that the capitalist mode of production incessantly encounters preexisting forms and it "encounters them as antecedents, but not as antecedents established by itself, not as forms of its own life process."[15] The result of this encounter, as Harry Harootunian points out, gives rise to "a heterogeneous mix rather than the destruction of one made by another."[16] This "heterogeneous mix" of temporalities, in which archaic forms coexist and overlap with new forms, gives rise to social and political conflicts, whose outcomes are not predefined by any law of history. These unpredictable results are demarcated by the political struggle for the orientation of new historical trajectories.

In the examples given, the modern conception of universal history is rearticulated into a plurality of historical temporalities interwoven and in friction with each other. A new conception of history as multiverse requires a different conception of time, which I develop in these pages by including myself in the tradition that goes from Benjamin and Bloch to latter-day Marx. There is need for an elastic time, as Ernst Bloch suggested, borrowing the idea of space conceived by mathematician Bernhard Riemann;

or, borrowing another concept from mathematics, a topological time, thus as a circle drawn on a handkerchief, then crumpled and wrinkled, and in which the distance between points becomes variable and the past can overlap the present.[17] In other words, there is no longer need for a time that is absolute and Newtonian. Rather, a time that, just as in relativistic physics is bent by gravity, so too, in history is bent by the density of events.

There exists a chronological time that always goes by the same, without quality and indifferent to any qualitative change. Its absolutism leads one to say that if a civilization has remained "backward" it is because it has used its time poorly. But there is no such thing as having used time well or poorly. Time is used in different ways, and this qualitative difference impresses upon time a rhythm and a direction: a *temporality*. Global, social, and political space must be interpreted as entirely temporalized: there are different rhythms, speeds, and legacies that run parallel, intersect, and conflict when one temporality imposes itself as dominant and tries to synchronize the others. These conflicts act as prisms that refract the white light of universal history in the colors of the different temporalities.

The pluralization of historical temporalities responds today to the need to understand and intervene in a globalized world that requires, beside provincializing Europe,[18] also overcoming the provincialism of time, "one for which," wrote T. S. Eliot, "history is merely the chronicle of human devices which have served their turn and been scrapped, one for which the world is the property solely of the living, a property in which the dead hold no shares."[19] In order to de-provincialize time, one needs to reconfigure the discourse on history. The modern conception of history, and the historical time that underlies it, has become untenable today, for several reasons. First, the singularization of the concept of history is ideological, since it processes historical ruptures, absorbing them in the historical continuum or transforming them into deviations with respect to the normative trajectory of modernity based on the state, private property, and the capitalist mode of production.

In light of this concept of history, Tocqueville and the young Hegelians could only draw a single line that went from the Ancien Régime to the French Revolution to Napoleon, the meaning of which was an enormous process of concentration of power in the new state machine.[20] The same conception of history could also lead to reading the Terror, or anything that spills over from a supposed normative-liberal course of Western history, as *dérapage* or, as in Benedetto Croce's interpretation of fascism, a historical "parenthesis."[21] Second, the singularization of history in universal history is intrinsically Eurocentric and colonial. It puts European civilization at the top of the historical-temporal vector, judging the enormous variety of non-European political and economic forms as pre-capitalist or premodern. This conception of history allowed for John Stuart Mill's colonial liberalism, which, by operating in the disjuncture between universalism and its actualization, considers despotism the appropriate political form for backward states of society populated by "nonage" races.[22] The concept of universalism, not unlike other "isms" such as nationalism, liberalism, and even socialism, operates as a temporalized and temporalizing arrow concept. Modern political concepts are presented as universal, operating as temporal vectors that, as bearers of a unifying need, produce historical-temporal differentiations and gradations of historical time that become stages along the arrow of unilinear historical time.

The modern conception of history has produced the image of history as an inevitable development passing through necessary phases. Thus, on the one hand, there arose, on opposing political sides, the image of the "underdeveloped" or "developing" countries, heading toward the unequivocal development model of free-market economics and a liberal democratic state. On the other hand, the same conception of history gave rise to an image of economic development in phases, so that the transition to socialism should have required passage through the capitalist mode of production and the development of its intrinsic contradictions. Movements for decolonization reacted against this conception

INTRODUCTION: DECOLONIZING MODERN HISTORY | 9

of history. In a letter of October 24, 1956, that Aimé Césaire wrote to Maurice Thorez, at that time the secretary of the French Communist Party, Césaire denounced the paternalism of the Communist Party members: "their inveterate assimilationism; their unconscious chauvinism; their fairly simplistic faith, which they share with bourgeois Europeans, in the omnilateral superiority of the West; their belief that evolution as it took place in Europe is the only evolution possible, the only kind desirable, the kind the whole world must undergo."[23] Finally, denouncing the "emaciated universalism" that suppresses the multiplicity of particular and alternative paths of development, Césaire presented an alternative vision of universalism based on a solidarity that respects the particulars.[24] With that letter, Césaire announced his resignation from the party.

There is a third reason that makes the modern conception of historical time untenable. Empty and homogenous time is purely abstract, but it has real effects. It is the time of capital or, more precisely, it is the time of socially necessary labor that, through the world's stock markets, marks the rhythm of the production of commodities in the world market. Its real effects can be observed in the differentiation of levels of exploitation around the globe. What I want to emphasize is the co-presence of trajectories not synchronized by the dominant temporality of socially necessary labor time and the nation-state.[25] If the former imposes the rhythm, discipline, and intensity of labor time regulated in the competition between capitals, the latter synchronizes the different local temporalities with the homogeneous time of the juridical-administrative machine of the nation-state. The synchronization of temporalities characterized by rhythms of life and different cultural and juridical traditions generates friction that the nation-state constantly tries to neutralize by channeling, with greater or lesser amounts of violence, into the normative trajectory of the nation-state, the regime of private property, and capitalist production. Indeed, the empty and homogenous time works in the violent processes of construction and reproduction of national homogeneity. It regulates the disciplining of a nation through the regulation of the rhythms of life, from school to retirement, from work to national holidays.

It is not a matter of contrasting the traditional temporality of the communitarian forms to that of the nation-state and the capitalist mode of production. This opposition remains abstract or romantic. Rather, it is a matter of working in the tension between temporalities, where they flow over each other like different geological layers, increasing temperature and pressure to bring about metamorphic phenomena of an entire society. Continuing this geological metaphor, one could speak of subduction phenomena in which metamorphic rocks are formed and, in our case, new and unprecedented configurations of preexisting juridical, political, and economic material are generated.[26] Indeed, these new forms, as we shall see, are not the result of a *creatio ex nihilo*. They are generated in a field of forces full of conflict, where anachronistic elements are reconfigured in an original way. Such is the case of the medieval institution of the imperative mandate that reemerges in the experience of the *Sans-culottes* during the French Revolution (chapter 2), the Communards in 1871 (chapter 3), the soviets in the Russian Revolution (chapter 4), and the workers' councils of the twentieth century. The same experience, reactivated by the forms of self-government of the indigenous communities, reemerges in the Zapatistas' politics (chapter 5). The point is to examine the *chronotones*, from the Greek *chronos*, or "time," and *tonos*, or "tension"—that is, the friction generated by the sliding of different temporal layers.

RECONFIGURING THE PAST

My distinction between temporalities may bring to mind Chakrabarty's between History$_1$ and History$_2$ in his famous book *Provincializing Europe*. In fact, I owe Chakrabarty for the way he provincialized Europe and its conceptual self-representation. But what I intend to do is to pluralize the sometimes monolithic concept of Europe emerging from Chakrabarty's representation. Chakrabarty overlooks the field of possibility that opens up in the tension between temporalities. Showing European modernity as being crisscrossed by multiple conflicting temporalities allows me to raise the question of multiple possible bridges between European and non-European trajectories. In this way, the universal is not only placed on the abstract level of what Chakrabarty calls H_1, limiting H_2 in its particularity, but is also expressed in conflicts between different temporalities and, as in the cases we are examining, it builds unexpected bridges between alternative trajectories of modernity. For me, it is not a question of choosing between the dominant temporality of socially necessary labor or the nation-state and local temporalities anchored in traditional relationships. Rather, it is about considering the tension between those different temporalities as a field of possibility open to different political outcomes. It is in this tension that politics exposes itself to the risk of change and becomes truly political.

Abandoning universal history, because it is heavily compromised with the history of colonialism, remains a halfway-carried-out plan if Europe is not de-colonized as well, showing the multiplicity of alternative trajectories that the dominant historiography has deleted or placed in parentheses. Social and political change should be thought about and practiced in the tension of different temporalities and not as the goal of an inevitable historical development along the line of an empty and homogenous concept of time. Using an image of Benjamin's, revolutionary action coincides with the possibility of opening a "distinct chamber of the past,"[27] in which there is a future encapsulated and a past attempt at liberation to be redeemed. There are no waiting rooms in history but, rather, rooms that have remained closed and can be reopened. These rooms are the countless attempts at liberation tried repeatedly by the oppressed, but which were always interrupted by the violence of the ruling classes.

Opening these rooms is the task of politics. But we need an appropriate historiography for this task. The question of an ontological access to the past has been posed in different ways.[28] Leopold von Ranke's dream aspired to a position of objective neutrality toward the past—a dream that was shattered when Johann Gustav Droysen posed the question of the placement and the inevitable partiality of the historian. Subsequently, the linguistic turn, meaning the past as constituted by language, denied that there is something like historical objectivity. In essence, it denied the very existence of the past as an object, the reality of which is not given and cannot be given outside its textual representation. This perspective can easily lead to a multiplication of points of view and historical narratives where no single way of writing history is more realistic than any other. If one questions the assumption of the reality of the past, it is easy to break it up into a plurality of historical constructions that can be narrated from the perspective of a growing multiplicity of subjective points of view. Each point of view shows the ghostly side that is concealed in another perspective. In this way, the perspectives tend to potentially multiply indefinitely in what Hayden White called "the ghostly ballet of alternative 'meaning,'" but where there is no privileged position.[29] Koselleck puts a limit on this relativism of the points of view by stating that a historical event cannot be arbitrarily set up, since the "sources provide control over what might not be stated," though without prescribing what may be said.[30]

Paradoxically, the evaporation of "the past" into a multiplicity of points of view is the other side of the aproblematic assumption of the objectivity of the past when one seeks to capture it through the bombardment of big data. In both cases, a privileged point of view on reality is lacking and this qualitative loss is compensated by multiplying perspectives or data. There is a different way. We know that the historian, choosing a specific narrative strategy, determines emplotment and argument of the construction of the past and, therefore, can never be said to be neutral toward the past.[31] The point is to assume and develop the theoretical and political implication of this partiality. Benjamin provides a good starting point in his Thesis XII on the concept of history: "the subject of historical knowledge is the struggling, oppressed class itself."[32] Benjamin's Thesis XII, to be read as the ideal continuation of Marx's famous Thesis XI on Feuerbach,[33] opens up a crucial question: the incompleteness of the past.[34] It is from this assumption that we must start. The incompleteness does not concern only sources and archives. Nor does it concern the partiality of the point of view, which can never grasp history in its entirety. Nor is it a question of writing hypothetical or counterfactual histories. It is the past that presents itself as an arsenal of futures that have been blocked and that are allowed to reemerge by the subjects actually acting in the field of history, and not by the spectator or the historian.

It is not about presenting coherent interpretations of the many ways the past might or could not have been. It is the agency of insurgents in precise historical events that opens up ways that have remained blocked or repressed. In other words, it is not the historian but, rather, the insurgents who cite the past and make current that which might have been, transforming it into a critical arsenal for the historian and the present. The critical historian takes the insurgents' side and, with them, traces history not along the main course of a river but, instead, through the many underground rivers of a karst landscape. Concretely, as I show in chapter 2, it was the *Sans-culottes* who during the French Revolution reactivated the forms of local self-government and the imperative mandate from the political and juridical arsenal of the Ancien Régime; the Communards who cited 1793 and the medieval communal institutions to complete, in 1871, what was interrupted by the Terror and the nation-state (chapter 3); the Russian revolutionaries who referred to the tradition of *mir* and the Paris Commune to finish the work carried out there (chapter 4); and today the Zapatistas who cite the work of Emilio Zapata and the spirit of the Mexican Constitution of 1917 to complete the communal experiment of the peasants of Morelos, which took place from 1913 to 1917 (chapter 5).[35] The examples could go on. By borrowing the language of the Zapatistas,[36] the members of Occupy shared the same experiment in democracy and self-government with the Communards.

It is the historical approach of the Communards, the Zapatistas, and the Russian revolutionaries that teaches us how to look at the past as incomplete. What they practice recombines historical times by extracting from the past futures that have been blocked and which are alternatives to the present. These historians in action show us an image of history where the past flows alongside the present as different layers of a geological conformation. The task of critical historiography is twofold: to show how, in a given insurgency, anachronistic institutions are *reactivated* in a new configuration of the present; and to show how that reactivation makes it possible to trace an *alternative legacy of modernity*.

Those historical events, together with numerous other events, show us that there is no preordained historical trajectory that leads from the Middle Ages to the nation-state and the capitalist mode of production. In fact, teleology is not just faith in a preordained historical end. Teleology is above all the idea that history can be explained ex post facto as the development of certain principles through specific historical stages. For Hegel, it was the "progress of the consciousness of freedom," a perpetual progress through historical-geographical stages, according to which there would be "the Orientals, who knew only that One is free, then that of the Greek and Roman world, which knew that Some are free, and finally, our own knowledge that All men as such are free, and that man is by nature free."[37] The last stage is that of the nation-state, represented by the principles that emerged during the French Revolution. But Hegel overlooked the numerous revolutions within the revolution. In their practices and in their *Declarations*, the women, the slaves of Haiti, and the poor objected that the concept of "man" did not represent them. However, they did not claim inclusion in the order of national citizenship. This is how things are presented from the point of view of the teleological narration of the modern state and its juridical universalism. Women, the poor, and slaves have instead acted as the excess of the term "man" with respect to the law and to every essentialist definition of the human. In their praxis, the concept of "homme" has become a political operator capable of disordering the existing order.

What is at stake is not the problem of those excluded subjects and their stories but, rather, the tension generated when those political practices came into conflict with the juridical, political, and economic trajectory of the dominant modernity characterized by the nation-state, the capitalist mode of production, and private property. Western modernity has elevated these concepts to its own principles and enclosed them in the shell of the abstract subject of law. But freedom and equality are, above all, political practices that have emerged in the countless insurgencies that have undermined the existing order, opening it up to different outcomes. One could say, to simplify things, that when the servants rebelled against the authority of corporations, their purpose was not to become wage workers, formally free to sell their labor power. That is what became of them in the modern state and in the capitalist mode of production.

INSURGENCY: THE FACT OF UNIVERSALITY

In the second section of his book *The Contest of the Faculties*, Kant poses a crucial question for modernity and modern history: "Is humankind continually improving?"[38] Kant rejects the metaphysical option that bases three distinct conceptions of history on three respective anthropological conceptions: (a) from a pessimistic conception of man there would follow a *regressive* conception of the history of humanity, which Kant also calls terroristic; (b) from a way of looking at human nature as disposed to good, there would follow a progressive conception; and last, (c) from a conception of human nature that equally divides good and evil in the individual, there would follow a stalemate, which Kant calls "abderitism."[39] Kant also rejects the empirical hypothesis that would infer from the progress made so far by humanity a kind of law that would also guarantee progress for the future.

From these anti-metaphysical assumptions, Kant reformulates the whole question, asking himself about the possibility of a history a priori—that is, a history in which "the one divining the events himself brings about and arranges the events that he announces in advance."[40] For Kant, the human being is neither good nor bad, but is able to act freely. This does not mean that man always acts as a free being, but only that he can act freely and therefore, to be truly human, must also do so. The human being and the progress of humanity are practical tasks, not metaphysical laws of history. It is here that Kant makes his first exceptional juncture: theoretical philosophy meets a historical event and begins to speak its language. The same Kantian prose becomes lyrical:

> This event does not consist for instance in important deeds or misdeeds of human beings whereby what was great is made small among human beings or what was small made great, and, as if by magic, old and splendid states disappear and in their place others arise as if from the depths of the earth. No, nothing of the sort.... The revolution of a spirited people that we have witnessed in our times may succeed or fail. It may be so filled with misery and atrocities that any reasonable person, if he could hope, undertaking it a second time, to carry it out successfully, would nonetheless never decide to perform the experiment at such a cost. —Nevertheless, in the hearts of all its spectators (who themselves are not involved in the show), I assert, this revolution meets with a degree of participation in wish that borders on enthusiasm, a participation the expression of which is itself associated with danger. This participation can thus have no other cause than a moral capacity in the human race.[41]

The Kantian point of view is that of the spectator not directly involved in the revolution, but still ready to take the risk of making a partisan choice—that is to say, public participation in the ideas of the revolution. It is here that Kant makes his second juncture: he takes a partiality (*Parteilichkeit*) for the universality (*Allgemeinheit*) that that event, as a timely manifestation in history, represents the idea of freedom. The enthusiasm is enthusiasm for the universal, which is embodied in a certain historical event. Here freedom coincides politically with the right of a people to give themselves the constitution that they consider good. Nothing can be the same as before: the French Revolution expresses, for Kant, this republican principle that does not coincide with a certain constitutional architecture but, rather, with a way of thinking of and carrying out popular sovereignty—this new powerful concept that modernity has simultaneously freed and tried to put to rest.[42] One could say that modernity is still struggling with popular sovereignty and equality and, more importantly, with the articulation of these two concepts in an appropriate institutional framework. Kant is credited with having brought the universal into history and to have thought of it in the form of a new beginning. But at the same time, he has tamed it by laying it on the progressive course of universal history.

Kant has the merit of not judging the French Revolution from the point of view of its success or failure. For Kant, the revolution is not a military matter. Rather, the revolution is examined from the point of view of the field of possible experiences that it opens up in the present. However, this field of possibilities can and must now be spatially and temporally extended, not only repositioning the spectator's point of view but also assuming the "partiality" of the agents in the historical event and their ability to recombine historical times to make what is apparently archaic the most present and an anticipation of the not-yet.

It is possible to subject the Kantian gesture in the face of the French Revolution to a double shift in perspective. That is what I seek to do in looking at Paris from the Haitian Revolution and at the trajectory of the political and economic forms introduced there by the Bossale communities instead of at Toussaint Louverture.[43] The Haitian Revolution allows us to reconsider the conception of universal history and universalism.⁴⁴ The question that I intend to explore, and which constitutes the first change of perspective, is: What happens if instead of the event chosen by Kant, the revolution in Paris, we take as a starting point the revolution in Haiti? During the French Revolution, the uprisings of the slaves of Santo Domingo in 1791 and 1793 imposed the abolition of slavery by the colonies: "The French Republic wants all *men* without distinction of color to be free and equal."⁴⁵ In this way, the term "man" becomes the vector of a new universality. The Haitian Revolution realized the French Revolution by realizing its universality and postulating the full emancipation and citizenship of the African American slaves.⁴⁶ Article 3 of the Constitution of Haiti (1801) ratifies this new universality: "There cannot exist slaves on this territory, servitude is therein forever abolished. All men are born, live and die *free* and French."⁴⁷ It was not the ideals of the Enlightenment that placed the colonial question and the abolition of slavery on the order of the day but, rather, the uprisings of slaves that dictated a new political agenda and a new rhythm toward universal emancipation. This is the *fact of universality* that surpasses Kant's "Fact of Reason," a new universal that takes shape in the concrete "here" of Haitian territory, rearticulates the content of the Declaration of the Rights of Man, which, in principle in 1789, still referred only to white male landowners.⁴⁸ The new universality, which I have called "insurgent," encounters the uprising of women and the Declaration of the Rights of Woman and the Female Citizen of 1791, which in essence declares the existing French Constitution null and void; it encounters the peasant insurgency for defending rural communities as a third dimension between individuals and nation;⁴⁹ finally, it encounters the uprisings of the *Enragés* and the *Sans-culottes* who, in their assemblies, impose imperative mandates and the limitation of property rights. This universality is possible because the revolution combines the political and social dimensions. At stake there is not only the right of a people to give themselves the constitution that they consider best for themselves but also the disordering of a social order considered unjust, in that it reproduces the imbalances of power and the inequalities that republican politics would claim to have eliminated from the sphere of law.

The revolutionary rupture, which takes place in the uprisings of Paris and Haiti, is what constitutes insurgent universality: a whole order of property ownership in addition to gender and race relations is called into question and rendered open to new possible configurations. By suspending the present order and all means of belonging, anyone can be on the side of the insurgents, thereby running the risk of not belonging to one's own privileges.

New possible trajectories are tested, reactivating anachronistic temporalities and associative and community forms that are reconfigured into new institutions.[50] When the *Sans-culottes* and the Communards referred to medieval institutions and the Ancien Régime, they practiced, through their assemblies, a plurality of authority that challenged the monopoly of state power; they practiced a political citizenship whose universality was given by participation in the forms of local self-government, and not by the privilege of birth; they practiced a limitation and reconfiguration of the right to property; finally, they practiced a differentiation in the concepts of freedom and equality. The history of the long tradition of these insurgent institutions has yet to be written.

In the history of the French Revolution, these alternative political trajectories, which expressed different ways of using power, were violently synchronized by the dominant conception of the modern representative state and national sovereignty. This is the way in which the revolution is incorporated into universal history, reading ex post its progressive character in the path toward building the modern state and universal freedom. From this perspective, every step, from 1789 to the Napoleonic civil code, proves to be necessary with respect to the defeated anachronistic paths. Conservative historian François Furet deliberately ignored women and slaves in *A Critical Dictionary of the French Revolution*, which he drafted together with Mona Ozouf.[51] Similarly, progressive historian Albert Soboul defined the popular movement of the

Sans-culottes as "characterized by the pre-capitalist mentality . . . , a mentality that was essentially the same as that of the peasantry who were bitterly defending their common-land rights against the onslaught of capitalist agricultural methods."[52] Be it on either of opposing political and historiographical positions, in both cases there is an idea of universal history that either expunges alternative trajectories as deviations from a presumed normative course of modernity or characterizes them as backward—expressions of a "pre-capitalist mentality" with respect to a development of history that must pass through the destruction of community practices to give rise to the progress of capitalist agriculture with all its new contradictions. Instead, from our perspective, the mentality of the *Sans-culottes* was not pre-capitalist but, rather, represented another temporality and tried to give a different orientation to the process of modernization.

The Haitian Revolution challenged the universalism of the Declaration of 1789 because it challenged the Western categories that made the political action of the slaves unthinkable.[53] The universalism of the Declaration was taken from a political and legal level to a social level.[54] The universality practiced by these insurgents was of a different nature with respect to the universalism of 1789 and built a bridge between Haiti and the uprisings of women and the poor in Paris during 1792–93. The political agenda in 1793 had been updated by those subjects who did not claim recognition by, or inclusion in, an unjust order, but practiced the dis-belonging to that order by opening up new political and social configurations. These subjects took the floor and acted politically in their assemblies without seeking permission from the state. Indeed, the progressive inclusion of individuals in the realm of civil rights is not alien to the functioning of the modern state. However, what goes beyond this state logic is the collective agency of subjects that question social relations of domination, which are played at the level of gender, race and class. These relations are often hidden by formal juridical equality. Insurgent universality distinguishes itself from universalism through a different way of practicing politics, which is characterized by the exercise of power starting from communities, associations, assemblies, councils, and groups. Its range is neither the nation, nor the world, nor humanity. For this reason, its trajectory avoids both the conception of the universal as potentiality and the polemical conception of universalism.

The first universalism works as a temporalizing concept in which different populations have different roles to play in the development of universal history and, finally, they are configured as different stages toward the final goal of a universal civilization. This potential universalism has justified gradualism, according to which some populations may not yet be ready to enjoy the fruits of Western freedom. The polemical universalism is based on a common element (religion, nation, class) that is hypostatized in order to overcome and orient internal differences against another universal (another religion, nation, class). This universalism is political in the measure in which it is polemical. It remains reactive and its logic remains binary. Indeed, it always depends dialectically on an alterity toward which it must be possible to trace juxtapositions. Insurgent universality, instead, has freed itself from this obsession with totality, unity, binary opposition, and with -isms.

The universality that I call insurgent has to do with the democratic excess that dis-orders an existing order and gives rise not to chaos, like the theories of the social contract prescribe, but to a new institutional fabric. The democratic excess is such that it goes beyond the constitutional armor of the representative state and calls into play a plurality of powers to which citizens have access, not through the funnel of national citizenship but in daily political practice. This abandons the grounds of the politics of recognition; it does not ask for inclusion but, rather, practices a universal political citizenship that exceeds the limits of legal citizenship and calls into question the forms of dominion, not only in the political sphere but also in the social order. It is here that the deviation between 1789 and 1793 can be seen.

The discussion at the French Convention acknowledged this new level of universality, as shown by Guyomar's intervention: "Let us liberate ourselves rather from the prejudice of sex, just as we have freed ourselves from the prejudice against the color of Negroes."[55] In Paris just as in Haiti, women played an important role in the revolution.[56] And for having dis-ordered the natural order of society—that is to say, the patriarchal system which attributed only to white male landowners the ability to act politically in the public sphere—they were stigmatized as even more violent than men.[57] The irruption of this new insurgent universality also shook landowner relationships that were being delineated, starting from the new conception of individual private property. In Paris, the *Enragés* questioned the absolute right of property, claiming a maximum for prices and property so as to limit its concentration in a few hands; in Haiti, the insurgents put into practice redistributive measures that were defining a new system of property ownership. The cultivators limited the property rights of the owner through their work and use of the land. We can gather the owners' feelings through their complaints collected by Descourtilz: "We are masters of our property without being able to use it."[58] It was not the ownership of the property being called into question. Rather, the individual right of property was limited by the actual use of land by the cultivators. Something similar was happening in France, where the *Sans-culottes* considered the landowner a custodian (*dépositaire*) of goods belonging to the people, and by reconfiguring forms of the old regime, they subjected the property to popular control in view of the common good.[59] This was one of the possibilities opened up by the revolution in the tension between the temporality of the nascent nation-state and that of the local forms of self-government and collective use of property.

The revolution in Paris between 1792 and 1793 was divided between an individualistic conception of rights and the state based on the representation of the nation, and an articulation of clubs, sections, and districts that practiced freedom in institutional forms, which disseminated an imperative mandate over sovereignty in multiple assemblies. But the possibility of a plurality of authority was crushed. In Paris, Robespierre and the Terror made a clean sweep of the claims of the *Sans-culottes*. In Haiti, Toussaint laid the foundation for building the state on the model of the French state, and steered the plantation system toward the world market. This undertaking to standardize the course of dominant modernity was crowned, in France, by the Napoleonic Code Civil of 1804; in Haiti, by the Declaration of Independence of 1804 and the coronation of Jean-Jacques Dessalines as emperor. Haiti was thus aligned with the principle of the modern state with which the principles of national sovereignty and primitive accumulation of capital were put into practice. As we will see in chapter 2, the communitarian, egalitarian, nonindividualistic Bossale alternative had been suppressed, just as the sectional alternative of imperative mandates and the limitation of the absolute right of property had been suppressed in France.

There needs to be a second change in perspective, beyond a geographical shift, in the temporalities of the French Revolution. Kant works with a singular and singularizing concept of universal history, which is imposed as normative for all humanity that gradually has to channel itself into the course of modernity initiated by Europe. Kant, and Hegel after him, read the French Revolution through a conception of history that acts like a reverse optical prism. It merges a multiplicity of colors to bring out the white light of the progress of humanity. For this reason, we have to go beyond Kant, because in his modern Western conception of history the different histories are channeled into the evolutionary course shown by the event of the French Revolution, which becomes, by its universalism, *the event* that can show humankind's tendency toward progress. The different histories and temporalities of the revolution, or better, the *revolutions*, which passed through the revolution both in Europe and outside Europe, become streams whose measure of time is dictated by the river of universal history. However, the *dérapages* indicate possible trajectories of modernity and original reconfigurations of juridical and political material inherited from different historical layers. In order to see these trajectories, one should abandon the perspective of the spectator and embrace the ways in which the insurgents, in their practices, experiment with different times and cite the past.

The Kantian prism must be inverted in order to refract the light of progress into the different colors of the French Revolution, from the infrared of what-has-been to the ultraviolet of not-yet. To do this, however, it is not enough to go digging in the archives of forgotten histories. It is not enough to tell the history of those who were defeated and left without a voice. In essence, a bottom-up historiographical model is not enough, just as it is not enough to pluralize histories in a multiplicity of narratives. One has to work with the chronotones and trajectories that deviate from the dominant and normative course of modern history that we call modernity and pay attention to how the actors of an insurgency have reconfigured the relationships between the times. The difference between residue and anachronism is essential. The former is always at a crossroads: either it catches up and gets in sync with universal history, or it is crushed. Instead, the anachronism represents another possibility. The friction and tension between different trajectories can give rise to new configurations of political and economic modernity. But the condition for the possibility to travel along other trajectories is given by a new transcendental, in which time is plural.[60] And space is not homogeneous but, rather, streaked and temporalized by different temporalities.

TOWARD AN ALTERNATIVE LEGACY OF MODERNITY

The difference between the modern state and the alternative of insurgent universality can be represented by drawing upon an image suggested by Sieyès in his writings of 1789. Sieyès writes: "I imagine the law as if it is at the center of an immense globe. Every citizen, without exception, is at an equal distance from it on the circumference the globe, and each individual occupies an equal place. Everyone depends equally upon the law; everyone offers it his liberty and property to protect. This is what I mean by the common rights of citizens (*les droits communs de citoyens*), insofar as it is this that makes them all resemble one another. These private individuals all have dealings with one another. They make their arrangements and engagements with each other, always under the common safeguard of the law."[61] If equality is given by the equidistance from the center—that is, from the law and state power—the circumference may be more or less extensive, depending on the degree of universalism of the globe. But a circumference remains and, therefore, a dividing line between an outside and an inside remains. The space between the periphery and the center is wasteland because, according to Sieyès, the intermediate bodies have no reason to exist, as they would be a nation within the nation.

The difference between this image and insurgent universality can be represented as the difference between an entrenched center and a porous plurality characterized by units that are not subsumed into an omni-comprehensive unity. The plurality of powers redefines the semantics of universality, which is such because, unlike any national identity, it is not circumscribed by borders. The plurality of powers, with many centers but without circumference, denotes an alternative political trajectory to that of the modern political form based on the concept of unity and totality. The model is relational, a net-like shape, and not an area delimited by boundaries. If the state circumference described by Sieyès delimits a homogeneous space defined by the nation, the plurality of powers is open to a multiplication of relations in an uncircumscribed space. These units are not synchronized by a central power to the rhythm of the nation, the law, and the market but, rather, express different temporalities. This is why the paradigm of universality is both temporal and political at the same time.

An alternative political trajectory begins not by changing the measurements of the circumference described by Sieyès but, instead, with another idea of politics, which is not caged in a political form. In the experiences of insurgent universality, the plurality and autonomy of units can lead to their independence, or even to conflict. But this, rather than being feared and considered an element to be neutralized, must be understood as a dimension of politics. Alongside the dominant trajectory of Western modernity, there are other trajectories that disseminate sovereignty into units, constituted, in the history that we have reconstructed through the insurgent universality, of sections, departments, and districts. These alternative temporalities, which could appear as "a return of the archaic,"[62] reactivate existing structures in a new form rather than synchronizing them to the dogma of indivisible national sovereignty. Wherever these alternative traditions of modernity have been expressed, they have always articulated themselves in autonomous institutional forms and strained the dominant trajectory of modernity characterized by the dual primitive accumulation of political state power and capital. That alternative legacy would go as far as the Paris Commune, the soviets,[63] and the local authorities in the Zapatista experiment. By reactivating archaic institutions as democratic counterthrusts to statism, insurgent universality also builds historical bridges for an alternative legacy of modernity. In this way, the archaic ceases to be simply past and becomes a trail marker of possible futures—as long as we do not let the tremendous energy that springs from what-has-been fall into the hands of new reactionaries.

In European history, next to the trajectory of private property and the modern state, along whose course there arise the names of Hobbes, Cromwell, and Le Chapelier, there still runs the alternative legacy of the commons and the collective associations. The names that represent them are less known, as are generally the names of the defeated. In England, the Diggers with Gerrard Winstanley reactivated the original communion of goods and the right of the commons against the system of enclosures and the incipient system of private property;[64] in Germany, Thomas Müntzer evoked the original communion of goods to defend common property and agrarian communism,[65] also claimed in the Manifesto of the

German peasants in 1525, called the "Twelve Articles."[66] In France, Jacques Roux, in his Manifesto of the Enragés, denounced the absolute right of property in the name of the natural right to life and the concentration of wealth in the name of republican equality.[67] The defense of communitarian forms of life and collective possession took strength by reactivating the communist tradition of early Christianity.

These insurgencies allow me to open the past to its incompleteness, showing possibilities and alternative legacies. From a historiographical point of view, it is a question of breaking the dominion of the present over the past. My historical framework shows a modernity crossed by multiple temporalities as diverse rhythms and forms of life that conflict with each other, but that also intersect and overlap. In this historic-temporal multiverse, anachronistic temporalities cease to be remnants of the past, and huge masses of legal and political material, considered archaic within the unilinear conception of time, instead open up new possibilities for reconfiguring the present. Countless alternative temporalities not only stratify European history but also show possible bridges with the countless non-European temporalities. Thus, the anachronisms cease to be seen as a delay to be synchronized in accordance with a supposed tendency of modernity, and instead become full of energy, able to reorient modernity and construct new possibilities for a different communal life.

In this sense, the bridge between the Bossale communities and the *Sans-culottes* of Paris is instructive of a different way of looking at history. The insurgent universality of the *Sans-culottes* tried to put a limit on a modernity without measure through a maximum amount of property; it sought to limit the National Assembly's representative power through the restoration of the imperative mandate within the framework of a plurality of powers. Against an attempt to concentrate the entire political power in the hands of the government and establish the work of large-scale plantations for the world market, the Bossale communities reactivated community forms of balance able to set a measure and a limit to production and power. Their languages were different, but hardly untranslatable. Although the art of translation requires knowledge of the grammar of historical times, the anachronism can disclose possible futures.

There is a link between translatability and universality. In his notes on translation, Gramsci meant translation not only between languages but also between different paradigms and cultures.[68] The difference between social practices, cultures, and languages, in Gramsci's perspective, was to be understood as an articulation of different answers to fundamentally common historical problems. Translation, like politics, has the task of holding together theory and practice, and this would be possible only by identifying the common question to which a culture or social practice is the answer. At this point we must ask ourselves: what is our common problem?

Today, in an era when universalism risks becoming an empty shell, the concept of democracy risks becoming a procedure on the verge of devouring itself, and capitalism's creative destruction seems to be more and truly destructive, the alternative legacy of insurgent universality shows us another possibility for politics, economics, and property relations. Insurgent universality is an experiment with the democratic excess of the plurality of powers. It is the incompleteness of this experiment—not the experiment in itself—that is shared. This is the meaning of the beautiful image given to us by the Zapatistas in their 1996 Fourth Declaration: "The world we want is one where many worlds fit." Insurgent universality begins with this plurality of worlds, authority, and forms of self-government; it begins with equal access to politics in the form of assemblies and groups; it begins with the Communard's universalization of politics and property; it begins with the council's experiment in the democratic excess. Insurgent universality shows to what extent democracy and private property are compatible with each other—and to what extent they are incompatible.

What emerges in insurgent universality, when the temporality of the state is interrupted, is not a wasteland but, rather, a society rich in groupings and associations that are entrusted with forms of self-government, as appeared in the French Revolution, in the Paris Commune, in the Russian Revolution, and in the Zapatista communities, as well as in countless other times and places.

1793: THE NEGLECTED LEGACY OF INSURGENT UNIVERSALITY

> Paris between March 1793 and July 1794 was one of the supreme epochs of political history.
>
> —C. L. R. JAMES[1]

WHAT OF UNIVERSALITY?

Human rights, wrote Bruno Bauer, were "only discovered by the Christian world during the last century," and this idea "is not innate to man, but is rather achieved in struggle against the historical traditions."[2] Indeed, human rights are neither a gift by the state nor the consequence of the progressive development of right. The revolutionary statement of the first Declaration of 1789 ("men are born and remain free and equal in rights") or the assertion of the Declaration of 1793 ("all men are equal by nature and before the law"[3]) does not define a metahistorical content but, rather, a political and historical one. Affirming that men are equal by nature means reinventing *nature* in two different ways. On the one hand, ancient privileges cannot be justified by nature or birth; on the other hand, the declaration that men are equal by nature heralds a new kind of "human subject" that did not exist before the declaration of those rights.

There are two ways to consider the "man" of the Declarations. The rights of men can be assigned to subjects that are designated as "men" insofar as they are the addressees of those rights. By contrast, "man" can be understood not as the presupposed subject of the Declaration but as the common name for those who practice the self-assignment of rights. In the former case, the rights are considered from the perspective of the state; in the latter, they are the expression of a political praxis by individuals who act together. Indeed, as Ernst Bloch noticed, it is "not tenable to hold that man is free and equal from birth. There are no innate rights; they are all either acquired or must be acquired in battle. The upright path is inclined to be something that must be won; even the ostrich walks upright and yet sticks its head in the sand."[4] Walking upright is a historical conquest, as are human beings and human rights. On the one hand, equality, freedom, and human dignity reactivate the tradition of revolutionary natural rights; on the other hand, they transcend the political framework of the modern state and introduce political *universality* beyond juridical *universalism*. From the perspective of these two concepts—universality and universalism—it is possible to outline diverse legacies, which lead to different conceptions of universal human rights and politics.

Prima facie, it is important to note that the political content of the first French Declaration is polemically oriented against the Ancien Régime and its privileges,[5] whereas the second expresses the excess of political universality. Indeed, the tradition of the first Declaration shows how individuals strip themselves of their social characteristics in order to become "simple individuals," and therefore citizens of the state.[6] This is the origin of an ever-expanding universal suffrage for the subjects of right. With the Declaration, the old privileges of the aristocracy were abolished, but new privileges replaced them: the privilege of a subject that is male, white, and a property owner. Citizenship today represents the ultimate privilege of status as an instrument for exclusion and discrimination.[7] The second Declaration, instead, finds its own background in the insurgencies of women, the poor, and slaves, which questioned the presumed abstract character of the citizen. The Declaration of 1793 must be read together with the insurgencies that directly and indirectly took part in its drafting. These insurgencies, rather than asking for pure inclusion, challenged the social and political order and opened up the political form to change.

The two perspectives cannot be more dissimilar. On the one hand, the Declaration of 1789 constitutes the origin of the legacy of juridical universalism. This is the universalism from above that implies a juridical person who is either a passive subject or a victim who has to be protected. Insurgent universality, on the other hand, whose character distinguishes the second Declaration, does not presuppose any abstract bearer of rights. On the contrary, it refers to particular and concrete individuals—women, slaves, the poor— in their political and social agency. Paradoxically, the universality of these particular individuals acting in their specific situations is more universal than the juridical universalism of the abstract bearers of rights. In the former case, universality is a political practice based on local institutions as places of democratic experimentation; in the latter, universalism is a juridical assumption guaranteed by a coercive power. The distinction can be expressed in more dramatic terms: if universalism refers to a passive subject and a potential victim who must be protected and have his rights guaranteed, universality refers to the agency of individuals and groups that do not claim rights but, rather, practice rights and liberties.

Comparing the two declarations, we immediately notice important differences, which concern the liberty of opinion, religion, and assembly.

Declaration of 1789[8]	Declaration of 1793
Art. 10. No one should be disturbed for his opinions, even in religion, provided that their manifestation **does not trouble public order as established by law**.	Art. 7. **The right to express** one's thoughts and opinions by means of the press or in any other manner, the right to assemble peaceably, the free pursuit of religion, **cannot be forbidden**.
Art. 11. The free communication of thoughts and opinions is one of the most precious of the rights of man. Every citizen may therefore speak, write, and print freely, if he accepts his own responsibility for **any abuse of this liberty in the cases set by the law**.	Art. 32. **The right to present petitions** to the depositories of the public authority **cannot in any case be forbidden, suspended, nor limited**.

The first notable dissimilarity concerns the right to express one's thoughts and opinions, and the limitation on this right by the state. Indeed, in the Declaration of 1789, as in the following declarations of human rights,[9] the liberty to express one's own opinions and to profess religious belief always hits a limitation: Article 11 states the freedom of communication of opinions, but it adds that one should not "abuse" this liberty and the manifestation of this liberty should not trouble "public order" (Art. 10). In view of this dialectic of liberty and its limitation, a legitimate question arises: What is the line that distinguishes "use" from "abuse" and "public order" from "disorder?" Both sides of this question are related to the power of the state to decide whether or not to restrict liberty for reasons of public order. This is not an anomaly concerning the Declaration of 1789. A close relationship is put into place between the declaration of rights and the restriction—and even the suspension—of those rights in cases of emergency. We will see that this legacy affects contemporary theories of human rights.

If the Declaration of 1789 is crushed in the grip of rights and their potential limitation, the Declaration of 1793, on the contrary, does not express any limitation. The "right to express one's thoughts and opinions" and "the right to present petitions" are declared without limit. The Declaration of 1793 announces rights of another nature, or what I call *insurgent natural rights*. Instead of claiming protection by state or supranational powers, insurgent natural rights express the political agency of human beings beyond the state.

The contrast becomes even clearer in the following set of articles from the two declarations.

Declaration of 1789	Declaration of 1793
Art. 2. The purpose of all political association is the preservation of the natural and imprescriptible rights of man. These rights are liberty, property, security, and **resistance to oppression.**	Art. 33. **Resistance to oppression is the consequence of the other rights of man.**

Declaration of 1789	Declaration of 1793
Art. 7. No man may be indicted, arrested, or detained except in cases determined by the law and according to the forms which it has prescribed. Those who seek, expedite, execute, or cause to be executed arbitrary orders should be punished; but citizens summoned or seized by virtue of the law should obey instantly, and **render themselves guilty by resistance**.	Art. 34. **There is oppression against the social body when a single one of its members is oppressed**: there is oppression against each member **when the social body is oppressed**. Art. 35. When the government violates the rights of the people, **insurrection is for the people and for each portion of the people the most sacred of rights and the most indispensable of duties**.

The American Declaration of Independence (1776) contains the right to resist against tyranny as well, but it actually expresses a polemical principle against the king of Great Britain in order to justify the separation of the colonies as "Free and Independent States."[10] Its grammar is that of an independent state. In its opening, the American Declaration refers to the principle of equality, but it remains halfway trapped and, in the conclusion of the text, becomes equality among states. By contrast, the French Declaration was not a polemical statement against the colonial order. Its aim was not the birth of an independent nation. Rather, it was oriented against the statist order of the Ancien Régime and left equality free to disorder the existing relations of domination.[11]

Both French declarations contemplate the right to resist. But there is a difference. The fact that the article on resistance in the 1789 Declaration is listed as a second item does not mean that it is more important. On the contrary, the following articles mitigate its strength: "the law is the expression of the general will" (Art. 6), therefore "citizens summoned or seized by virtue of the law should obey instantly, and render themselves guilty by resistance" (Art. 7). The principle of representation, which is the core of the mechanism of the modern state, is deployed. As long as the law is the expression of the general will, citizens must obey and resistance is a crime. Moreover, the "general will" expresses the *unity* of the political body that cannot be disaggregated into conflicting parts. Rousseau's idea of "general will" encounters Hobbes's principle of representation: a "multitude of men are made one person when they are by one man, or one person, represented. . . . For it is the unity of the representor, not the unity of the represented, that maketh the person one."[12] In this way, the representative makes the invisible unity of people visible, giving existence to the "peuple" as nation and political subject. And since the nation is the embodiment of the people, "a partial, separate and unequal representation," states Sièyes, "would be a political monstrosity."[13]

The Declaration of 1793, in contrast, undermines the mechanism of the representation of the people as a unity and totality, which constitutes the theologico-political core of the modern state.[14] Article 4 states that the "law is the free and solemn expression of the general will" and continues by announcing that the law "can command only what is just and useful to society." These additions are not innocent. Law is not just the expression of the general will that is represented by the state. Moreover, it is the matter of a dispute between people and government: the "law ought to protect public and personal liberty against the oppression of those who govern" (Art. 9). Affirming this, the Declaration of 1793 expresses a gap between those who govern and those who are governed—that is, those who want to defend themselves from the oppression of the government and preserve their "natural and imprescriptible rights" (Art. 1).

This political discourse achieves its own climax in the last three articles of the 1793 Declaration, which constitute a declaration within the declaration. From the perspective of the state, they are scandalous articles or, paraphrasing Sièyes, they introduce the monstrous. Article 33 declares that the right to resist is the consequence of the rights of man—that is, the right to be free, equal, and not oppressed by the government. Individuals have not (yet) renounced the exercise of political power beyond and against the state. Indeed, if only "a single one of its members is oppressed" (Art. 34), the people and "each portion of the people (*chaque portion du peuple*)" have the right of insurrection (Art. 35). Had the Declaration stated that oppression occurs only when the social body is oppressed, then the decision about the social body's oppression would have been vague and eventually determined by the representatives of the state, which do not have any interest in upholding insurrection against themselves. On the contrary, the sequence of the last three articles leaves in the hands of the people the right to judge if and when there is oppression and provides to *each portion of the people* not only the right but also the *duty* of insurrection.

THE DECLARATION OF 1793 IN ITS HISTORICAL-POLITICAL CONTEXT

If the first French Declaration is polemically oriented against the Ancien Régime for the constitution of the modern nation-state, and frees individuals from old feudal bonds, the second Declaration, read in the historical context of the discussions within the Convention and the voices of the subaltern, shows the tendency to keep the constituent process open beyond nationality and the framework of the representative political system. Indeed, in the Declaration of 1793, resistance is not a right that the state has to guarantee. Instead, ongoing insurrections are everyday practices that keep the political system open. Article 28 of the 1793 Declaration stipulates: "A people has always the right to review, to reform, and to alter its constitution. One generation cannot subject to its law the future generations." This opening up of the system has to be understood both synchronically and diachronically. A "people" is constituted by political subjects who have agency before, against, and beyond the state; the constitution expresses only a temporary compromise between those who govern and those who are governed.

The Declaration of 1793 was a compromise not only between diverse political perspectives among the Conventionists but also between the Convention and the crowds. The insurrections of the slaves in Saint-Domingue during August 1791 imposed the new political agenda for the revolution in Paris; the insurrection of August 10, 1792, forced the Legislative Assembly to abolish the active–passive citizenship distinction; the insurrections of May and June 1793 reopened the question whether the deputies should speak in the name of France as a whole, or in accordance with the people's will as expressed in squares, assemblies, and societies.[15] In this political context, the Declaration and the Constitution, which were drafted and approved on June 24, were not just the results of a quarrel between individuals or groups within the Convention. Their authors were not only Condorcet, Hérault de Séchelle, or Robespierre but also included the sections, the Paris Commune, and the people who, formally, may not have had any part in drafting the Declaration. Their names, among many others, were Olympe de Gouges, who penned the Declaration of the Rights of Woman; the antislavery rebellion leader Toussaint Louverture; the naturalized French citizen Anacharsis Cloots, the "citoyen de l'humanité," who argued for a universal republic and the sovereignty of the human race; and the *Enragés* like Jean-François Varlet, who "thought that the essence of democracy lay not in formal constitutions but in the constant readiness of the people to assert their fundamental sovereignty by action."[16]

The first draft of the 1793 Declaration was presented to the Convention on February 15, and it was based on Condorcet's ideas.[17] In his plan, Condorcet included the right to resist, but he tried to legalize the "means of resisting oppression" (Art. 31), saying that "the mode of resistance . . . ought to be regulated by the constitution" (Art. 32).[18] And indeed his constitutional project included a Title VIII that developed a complex mechanism of "people's censure" on the acts of national representation by the primary assemblies. Read in its historical context, on the one hand, this procedure was certainly democratic and aimed to defend the right of the minority; on the other hand, it aimed to reduce the political weight of the most active portion of the citizens. Condorcet expected that, thanks to his constitutional mechanism, "the active portion of citizens will cease to appear as the entire people."[19] Girondins tried to restrict the right of insurrection so that an organized minority could not use it against the majority of the people. However, despite the differences between Jacobins and Girondins, they shared the idea that the unity of the nation had to be safeguarded, that sovereignty was indivisible, and thus that it belonged to the whole people and not just to primary assemblies.[20] Condorcet's conception of federalism did not undermine the unity of the nation-state.[21] Rather, it gave greater voice to the countryside, where the Jacobins were less strong. The conflict was mainly tactical.

The true antinomy, which remained alive throughout the French Revolution, was between the principle of the indivisible sovereignty of the nation, a principle which Girondins and Jacobins shared, and the sovereignty of the assemblies. There was the antinomy between the democratic excess of the sections and its constitutional anesthetization. It was only in the polemics with the Girondins that Robespierre adopted the language and slogans of the *Sans-culottes*, as when, in his speech on the new French Constitution on May 10, 1793, he talked of mandatories and not of representatives. Against Condorcet's attempt to enclose resistance within legal means (Arts. 31–32), Robespierre, in his draft for a Declaration of the Rights of Man presented on April 24 to the Convention, proposed a polemical Article 31: "subjecting resistance against oppression to legal forms is the ultimate refinement of tyranny."[22] Robespierre considered bizarre any attempt to determine by law when the law is oppressive. It is up to the people, he stated, to make such a decision, and one cannot regulate the mode of resistance by law.[23] Robespierre introduced, in this draft, even more radical ideas, which were generated by the pressure of sections, clubs, and assembles.

Draft Declaration of April 24, 1793[24]

Art. 14. The people is sovereign: the **government is its product and its property, public officials are its assistants.** The people may, if they wish, change their government **and revoke their mandatories.**

Art. 18. **Any law that violates the imprescriptible rights of man** is essentially unjust and tyrannical: **it is not a law.**

Art. 34. The people have the right to know all the operations of its **mandatories**; they must give to the people a **complete account** of their management and submit to their judgment with respect.

The language of the imperative mandate became part of the draft Declaration. At least two fundamental points were in question in the debates on insurrection: *What* is the kind of oppression that prompts people to resist? and *Who* can exercise the right of insurrection? Hérault-Séchelles, one of the redactors of the 1793 Constitution, stated that the character of the insurrections cannot be determined and thus the questions should be best left to the "genius of the people" and its justice.[25] The articles on resistance were much more a kind of compromise between the Convention and the crowds than the outcome of the quarrel between the Girondins and the Montagnards. The Girondins, as Brissot stated at the Convention, thought that it was time "to end the insurgency"[26] and pointed to the need to neutralize insurgencies through the constitutional mechanism, transforming the right of insurrection into the "right of censure." The Montagnards, by contrast, spoke the language of the insurrection and acted under the pressure of the many assemblies and societies of women, the poor, and the transnational revolution of slaves. However, they only spoke the language of the insurgency, which they "were able to encase in a parliamentary revolution with some of the features of the coup d'état."[27] The result of the June 2 insurrection was the elimination of the Girondins. As soon as the Montagnards had the power, they began to eradicate the insurgencies. The articles on the people's right to "revoke their mandatories" were no longer necessary and, therefore, were not included in the Declaration.[28] If the final version of the Declaration could not delete the articles on insurrection, this was because the popular insurgency was not quelled. The Terror would bring the course of the French Revolution within the levees of the modern state and national representation.

From the standpoint of the women, the poor, and servants, the Terror was nothing but the Jacobin anti-crowd policy that ended the revolution by arresting the *Enragés*,[29] closing the *Société des républicaines révolutionnaires*, and atomizing the crowd. The Terror, if one wants to give sense to this term, was the powerful state instrument of the production of political unity, which synchronized and neutralized the insurgent temporalities of the revolution. The Declaration of 1793, written under the pressure of insurgent universality, was not an expression of the Terror, but on the contrary, the first victim of the Terror.

The stages of the drama are well known. In June–August, the Declaration and the Constitution were approved and ratified by public referendum. On October 10, 1793, the Convention suspended and indefinitely postponed the application of the Constitution in the name of the revolutionary provisional government of France. On December 25, Robespierre stated that exceptional circumstances—that is, conspiracies, counterrevolution, and war—required, for the salvation of the people and the revolution, the derogation from constitutional principles.[30] Suspending the Constitution, the Jacobins experimented with the modern state of exception, the "sovereign dictatorship," and the practice of constituent power by the revolutionary government.[31] Robespierre himself emphasized the difference between a constitutional government, whose goal is "to preserve the republic," and the revolutionary government, whose goal was that of "founding the republic."[32] And Saint-Just stated: "What makes a Republic is the total destruction of all that is opposed to it."[33] In the name of the fusion of the Convention and the French people, all oppositions were eliminated, step by step. The script for the construction of the modern state was achieved by the Thermidorian Constitution of 1795, in which "*no part* of the citizen can assume the sovereignty" (Arts. 17-18). The sovereign subject had definitely become the totality and the unity of citizens—the singular collective, the *people*. There were, however, other revolutionary pathways within the revolution. They contain, in their legacies, possible futures that are still encapsulated in the past.

INSURGENT UNIVERSALITY

Insurgent universality has to be understood in the concrete situation of individuals who act in common and put into question the hierarchical organization of the social fabric. The matter of insurgent universality, whose echoes can be found in the Declaration of 1793, is structured around the gap between juridical citizenship and the practice of citizenship by women, mulattos, blacks, and the poor. These groups were not merely the excluded who demanded inclusion but also true citizens who questioned the political and social order beyond the formal recognition of legal citizenship. They were the parts that were not reducible to the *peuple* of the nation-state and, in their actions, even exceeded it. In other words, they expressed the excess of the "rights of man" over legal citizenship.

1. *Women*. During the French Revolution, women "acted as citizens despite the fact that they were formally denied the rights of citizenship";[34] as a result, they reconfigured both the relationship

between government and the governed and the distinction between the private and public spheres.[35] Comparing the Declaration of 1789 and the Declaration of the Rights of Woman written by Olympe de Gouges in 1791, we can see how the political form is opened up by the insurgent claims of women.

Declaration of 1789	Declaration of the Rights of Woman and the Female Citizen of 1791[36]
Art. 6. The law is (*est*) the expression of the general will.	Art. 6. The law should be (*doit être*) the expression of the general will.

Olympe de Gouges rewrote Article 6 and replaced the indicative present "is" with the "natural right" tense "should be." Pace Hobbes and Rousseau, the law *is not* the expression of the general will, but it is subjected to the judgment of the people. The expression "should be" opens the gap between the law and the general will. If the law is unjust, or if the government violates the rights of people, the collectivities of true citizens have the right to practice insurrection, which belongs to "each portion of the people." Instead of permitting the constituent process to end, egalitarian insurgencies continually open the political system to reform and change. The insurgent citizenship of those who have no part,[37] but act as true citizens, challenges the constitutional order and keeps open the constituent process, which cannot be reduced to the power of a constituent assembly. In her rewriting of the Declaration, de Gouges audaciously added one line to Article 16: "the constitution is null if the majority of individuals comprising the nation have not cooperated in drafting it." Since women, blacks, and the poor, who were now acting as citizens, were excluded in drafting the constitution, the existing constitution had to be considered null. That meant that those acting as citizens exceeded the terms of legal citizenship and the boundaries of the constituent power embodied in the National Assembly.

Women, indeed, were acting as citizens already, beyond the legal recognition of their citizenship. In 1792, Pauline Léon claimed a revolutionary citizenship for women that included the right to bear weapons. No wonder that, in March 1792, a deputy of the Legislative Assembly replied by saying that if the petition of Léon were honored, "the order of nature would be inverted."[38] The deputy understood what was at stake, even if he caught it from a very conservative point of view: "insurgent universality" refers to an order of natural rights that transcends the given order and its hierarchies, an order that the conservatives would like to freeze by calling it the "order of nature." Two concepts of nature confronted each other: on the one hand, nature was called upon to legitimize the existing order of relations and its immutability; on the other hand, revolutionary natural rights referred to the "right of man" to be human and concerned the dis-ordering of the unjust existing order. Women did not want to and could not become male patriarchs, just as black slaves did not want to and could not become privileged white slaveowners. Instead, both these insurgencies adopted the generic concept of the "homme" that was implied in both declarations and pushed it against legal citizenship and the mere politics of inclusion. The term "homme" thus became a political operator that exceeded the particular political, social, racial, or gender identity conferred by a specific belonging to or position in the existing social order.

2. *Slaves.* On a broader scale, the Haitian antislavery insurgencies interacted with the French Revolution and pushed the French revolutionaries to edit Article 18 of the Declaration of 1793, which stated: "Every man can contract his services and his time, but he cannot sell himself nor be sold: his person is not an alienable property. The law knows of no such thing as the status of servant." Indeed, the 1793 Declaration is the long-neglected document of abolition.[39] The Haitian Revolution was

not an appendix of the French Revolution. Instead, interacting with the French Revolution, the revolts of the slaves in Haiti pushed the revolution beyond its national borders.[40] The Haitian Revolution extended both freedom and citizenship transracially and transnationally, and did not lend "itself to political appropriation as a definition of national identity."[41] Making visible the universal idea of freedom, the Haitian Revolution revealed other possible pathways of modernization that were linked to traditions within and outside the West. Aimé Cesaire was right when he said, "to study Saint-Domingue is to study one of the origins, one of the sources of Western civilization."[42] Actually, he was doubly right: he was right because modern Western civilization is founded on colonies and their exploitation; and he was right because Saint-Domingue, as "one of the sources of Western civilization," shaped a constellation whose spatial-temporal boundaries exceeded nationality, built bridges with other excluded subjects, and introduced a new radical concept of universality, whose legacy branches into many trajectories of human emancipation.[43]

In 1790, on behalf of the Committee on Colonies, Antoine Barnave declared that "the National Assembly does not intend to make any innovations in any of the branches of commerce between France and the colonies, whether direct or indirect; it puts colonists and their property under the special safeguard of the nation."[44] In *theory*, the Girondist and president of the Société des amis des Noirs, Jean-Paul Brissot, in December 1791, believed that slaves were indeed worthy of freedom, but not yet ready for it.[45] In *practice*, it was the insurrection of the slaves in August 1791 that forced the National Assembly to recognize a new level of universality. The uprisings of slaves were philosophy in action, previews of theory that forced philosophy to envisage the new field of possibilities that were opened. In the daily practices of insubordination, of refusing to work and maroonage, slaves occupied public and political spaces and imposed, in August 1793, the abolition of slavery.

THE NEGLECTED LEGACY OF INSURGENT UNIVERSALITY | 45

Proclamation. In the Name of the Republic. August 29, 1793[46]	Declaration of the Rights of Man and Citizen. August 10, 1793	Decree of the National Convention. February 4, 1794[47]
Men are born and remain free and equal in rights. Art.1. The Declaration of the Rights of Man and Citizen will be printed, published and posted everywhere necessary by the municipal authorities in the towns and villages and by military commanders in the camps and posts. Art. 2. All Negroes and people of mixed blood currently enslaved **are declared free and will enjoy all rights pertaining to French citizenship.**	Art. 18. Every man can contract his services and his time, but he **cannot sell himself nor be sold: his person is not an alienable property.** The law knows of no such thing as the status of servant.	The National Convention declares that **the slavery of Negroes is abolished in all the colonies.** In consequence, it decrees that **all men, without distinction of color, domiciled in the colonies, are French citizens and will enjoy all rights guaranteed by the constitution.** This decree is referred to the Committee of Public Safety, which will report immediately on measures for its implementation.

Synchronous correspondence between events is only apparent because communications between Santo Domingo and Paris at that time took three months to reach their respective recipients. The Emancipation Proclamation of the slaves that

Léger-Félicité Sonthonax wrote in Santo Domingo on behalf of the French Republic did not fall from the sky nor drip with ink from Sonthonax's quill. Article 14 of the Peace Treaty (October 19–23, 1791) between whites and black men stated that terms like "citizens of color and the free black, free mulatto, free quadroon" were to be strictly prohibited in the future: "Henceforward, there will be used for all the colony's citizens only those terms used for the whites."[48] Starting from the Santo Domingo uprising in 1791, there took shape the self-establishment of a mass of slaves in the community who asserted their own culture and who differentiated themselves from the French colonists.[49]

As C. L. R. James noticed, slaves have always wanted to be free.[50] During the Haitian insurgencies, the universal idea of freedom encountered all the past attempts of liberation that the oppressed have always practiced. This deeper idea of freedom appeared in the French Revolution and galvanized an alternative pathway of universality beyond Europe and modern European universalism. Freedom could be neither octroyed nor protected by power in the name of passive subjects. The hero of the Haitian Revolution, Toussaint Louverture knew that when he wrote to Napoleon in 1799: "It is not a freedom of circumstance, conceded to us alone, that we wish; it is the absolute adoption of the principle that no man, born red, black or white can be the property of his fellow man. We are free now because we are the stronger. The Consul maintains slavery in Martinique and Bourbon; we will thus be slaves when he will be the stronger."[51] Freedom and equality are not historical stages in a gradual process characterized by juridical progress. Rather, they are historical conquests that must be constantly defended.

The idea of freedom that emerged in the Haitian Revolution built bridges between the Haitian revolts and the Paris insurgencies. The gradualists who considered slaves not yet ready for freedom could not see these bridges nor did they want to see them.[52] For the gradualists, there was a single concept of freedom that, however universal, remained trapped in the gap between latent universal and its actualization. Entire populations could be kept in the waiting room of history, ready for freedom. However, if it is necessary to relocate the Haitian Revolution to the Atlantic and transnational context, it is also necessary to follow the revolutionary trajectory of a different conception of freedom, which exceeds Toussaint's understanding of freedom. This conception of freedom is based on communal and spontaneous self-organization, as in the case of the Bossale community that functioned as an "egalitarian system without state."[53] From this perspective, posing the question of the Haitian Revolution only in terms of the abolition of slavery and anticolonialism would mean staying within the dominant conception of Western emancipation. The question must be rearticulated. Facing the landowners and the white colonialists there were the freed men and the Creoles, but there was also the majority made up of the slaves born in Africa, the Bossales. Each of these layers moved politically in the same space and chronological time, but with different temporalities: the white colonialists defended the colonial slave system, trying to separate, as was possible in America, social and political revolutions to preserve the slave system on the basis of racial discrimination. The Bossale communities put into practice nonindividualistic modes of self-regulation of the egalitarian peasant system in the absence of a state. Toussaint, in order to restore the normal functioning of the plantation economy, imposed on Haiti an accelerated course in modernization based on forced labor on large plantations and large-scale production for the world market and the state.[54] Indeed, as can also be seen from the Constitution of 1801, Toussaint tried to synchronize the nascent state of Haiti with the course of European statehood through an enormous concentration of power in government hands[55] and a defense of the modern proprietary system, as stated in Articles 13, 73, 75, and 76. The latter drew almost verbatim on Article 9 of the Thermidorian Declaration of Rights and Duties of Man and Citizen of 1795. Beginning in 1796, at least two different conceptions of freedom faced off: an individualistic one based on the nation-state and a system of production for the market and the other an egalitarian, communitarian one based on a subsistence economy.[56] From this perspective, during the Haitian Revolution, the Bossale communities, which experimented with a "stateless egalitarian system" able to regulate itself and limit the accumulation of both political power and property,[57] do not represent a premodern residue but, rather, a chronotone with respect to the dominant modernity and its synchronizing principle.

3. *Peasants.* In March 1793, the Vendéen insurrection exploded. This insurrection, since it was directed against the Jacobin revolutionary government, was viewed as a counterrevolutionary phenomenon organized by peasants, clergy, and aristocracy. In substance, however, these were the same peasants who had effectively abolished the feudal system even before destruction of feudal titles was decreed on August 4, 1789. A commander of the troops charged with suppressing the peasant revolts wrote that it was "a war declared against land owners and property."[58] These rebellions, largely supported by country priests, were often directed at urban bourgeois efforts to buy the commons, merge the farms, and impose practices of modern private property. Peasants' insurgency defended, instead, a very different property regime: "Goods should be common, there should be only a cellar, a granary from which anyone takes what they need."[59]

The rural communities were going along a revolutionary path on which equality and freedom were practiced differently from both the ancient feudal regime and the nascent nation-state. If, for the Jacobins in power, freedom corresponded to the individual rights of the members of a single superior community—that is, the nation— then the rural communities considered themselves the subjects of these freedoms.[60] For the rural communities, liberation from feudal bonds had created political expectations of self-government. These expectations were not, however, understood by the Jacobins in power.[61] This misunderstanding was structural: it derived from two incompatible revolutionary grammars. The revolution carried out by the rural communities did not so much speak the language of freedom and equality of individuals as the language of members of wider communities who viewed themselves equal with respect to the nobility. On the one hand, the Paris government presented itself as a centralized administration of a homogenous nation; on the other hand, the rural communities defended their autonomy and their communal, fiscal, administrative, and religious liberties—initially as a possible articulation of the French Revolution, and later against the central government that, in their view, presented itself as a new tyranny. While the decree of August 4 incorporated and formalized the content of the peasant revolts, it was on a collision course with the rural communities' expectations of local self-government. Article 30, wanted by Sieyès in 1789, concentrated power in an undivided national sovereignty and removed authority from rural communities, which were juridically pulverized into individuals and individual rights.[62] The trajectory of the construction of the nation-state and a new private-property regime immediately entered into tension with the revolutionary trajectory of the rural communities.

This tension continued to grow the more the two trajectories diverged, and it reached a climax when the rural communities, facing mass conscription (*levée en masse*), began to oppose the revolutionary government as a new tyranny. However, the position of these communities was not immediately reactionary. In March 1793, the assailants of Ancenís affirmed that "we do not demand the return of the seigneurial rents, we are not friends of the despots; we are very happy to see our lands and our people free from all servitude."[63] In this context, the peasant revolts, born as antifeudal revolts, indicated at least initially a third possible trajectory between that of the Ancien Régime and that of the centralized nation-state. It was a trajectory following a different political principle, based on local rural communities, self-government, and administrative autonomy, rather than on the centralized power of the nation as a single, superior community. The peasants did not defend the Ancien Régime, but envisioned another revolutionary trajectory that was more communitarian instead of that based on the centralized state and its monopoly of power.

4. *The poor and the foreigners*. Something of the transnational nature of freedom merged into the 1793 Constitution, whose Article 4 extended exercise of the rights of French citizens to every man born and living in France twenty-one years of age, and to "every alien, who has attained the age of twenty-one, and has been domiciled in France one year." In the reactivation of the ancient law that the inhabitants of medieval communities had practiced, citizenship was granted to foreign residents after a year. It is hard to imagine something like this in today's democracies, which are instead obsessed with national identity and fear of aliens.

The expansive dynamic of insurgent universality went even further. The poor began to challenge the census system that bound active citizenship to property, a system that merely substituted the feudal aristocracy with the new aristocracy of white, rich men. Here, however, something really interesting happened: demanding inclusion, the poor put into tension the universal revolutionary natural rights and the right of private property that had operated as the basis for justifying exclusion. The tension intensified and became a contradiction between the natural right to exist (*droit à l'existence*) and the unlimited economic liberty of property.[64] This contradiction was not a theoretical one but, rather, a practical one. It was based on the insurgencies of the poor and was expressed in the economic program of the *Sans-culottes* in September 1793: a *maximum* was imposed on the price of bread to prevent economic speculation, but a *maximum* was also demanded for individual property so as to limit it; this was because the unlimited economic liberty and the concentration of property in a few hands violated the right to exist and the freedom of the rest of the population.[65] In the petition presented by the *Sans-culottes*, an alternative institution for property was drafted: "the foundations of property lie in physical needs."[66] Actually, in his proposal for a Declaration presented on April 24, Robespierre included two articles (Arts. 7 and 8) that explicitly bounded the right of property ("Le droit de propriété est borne");[67] however, after June 2, when the Montagnards "were the masters and could make their ideals prevail,"[68] they did not insert into their Declaration any of the radical articles on property that

Robespierre had proposed. Once again, they used the language of the poor to appear more democratic than the Girondins and to woo the crowds.

The question of a *maximum* for both prices and property was, instead, debated in the everyday assemblies of the people, whose spokespersons were the *Enragés*. Théophile Leclerc stated: "All men have an equal right to food and to all the products of the land which are indispensably necessary to preserve their existence";[69] and Jacques Roux, in his address presented at the Convention, declared: "Freedom is nothing but a vain phantom when one class of men can starve another with impunity. Equality is nothing but a vain phantom when the rich, through monopoly, exercise the right of life or death over their like."[70] Their words revealed an insurgent universality that questioned the entire political order, the division of labor between those who govern and those who are governed, and the rules that regulated property relations. According to the *Enragés'* claim for a limit to the right of property, it was the natural right to life that established such a limit because the life of a human being was considered more sacred than the "property of villains," and freedom was nothing if economic liberty became the right to create a new "merchant aristocracy," which Roux defined as more terrible than the aristocracy of the noblesse.[71] Against the private ownership of land, the *Enragés* claimed another tradition, which was founded on "la grand communale de la Nature," in which ownership of the land could not be a right. Humans, wrote Pierre Dolivier, have only the right to use land, but not the right to own land.[72]

Even if Robespierre and the Montagnards put the French Revolution on track regarding the right to property, the insurgent legacy of the poor and the *Enragés* continued with the proto-communist Gracchus Babeuf, whose nickname recalled the ancient Roman reformer and whose praxis was linked to the principles of 1793, on the one hand, and to the revolutions of 1830 and 1848, on the other.[73] The question is not what history could have been if the Conspiracy of the Equals had not been defeated; nor whether this defeat was inevitable owing to the "undeveloped state of the proletariat," as Marx and Engels argued in the *Communist*

Manifesto.[74] We need neither counterfactual histories nor a philosophy of history. Actually, these views are two sides of the same coin, since they share a unilinear conception of historical time. What the 1793 interruption shows us, instead, is an alternative pathway toward modernization. Its legacy goes through modernity and extends beyond its heroes, deeds, and misdeeds. Many revolutionary temporalities interacted within the French Revolution. They show us, today, different political and social possibilities beyond the conservative Thermidor, the Napoleonic epilogue, and the rearrangement of the modern nation-state.

LOOKING FOR NEW INSTITUTIONS

In insurgent universality, concrete subjects—men and women—question the social and political order that confines them in the private sphere, in servitude and misery. They do not demand an abstract equality that would refrain from challenging the social order; they practice a dis-ordering of the order. Just as the natural rights of the second Declaration exceeded and questioned the law, so did the term "man" exceed the citizen and become the bearer of the most radical political question: the need for justice. Insurgent universality took upon itself precisely this question and the risk that it involved. As a result, this insurgency not only interrupted the continuum of a specific historical configuration of power[75] but also disclosed and anticipated new political pathways, which indicated alternative trajectories beyond political modernity. These pathways were fluid in the red-hot magma of many abandoned or repressed experiments. The experiment was the virtuous "skidding off course" (*dérapage*) of the revolution during which slaves, women, and the poor gained a voice and acted as if they were citizens.[76] This experiment and its legacy have to be understood as a constellation joining the *right of man, insurrection,* and *imperative mandate* in a new political framework.

The hidden focus of the entire debate on the right of insurrection was whether the insurgent movements should be brought to an end,[77] and even more important, whether they could be allowed to challenge the unity of the nation as represented by the Assembly. The question arose at the beginning of the French Revolution, when, in 1789, twelve assemblies were convened in the sixty electoral districts in which Paris had been divided in view of the convening of the Estates General. The districts, however, also immediately began to deal with administrative and government tasks, claiming their political autonomy. In order to stem this autonomy, the central government, in May–June 1790, redefined the districts' functions and reduced their number. At this point, a political tension between two principles came into view. On the one hand, there was the National Assembly, which represented the unity of the French nation; on the other hand, there were numerous sections that, in order to maintain their autonomy and political power, decided to exercise control over their representatives, subordinating them to the primary and communal assemblies. In other words, as in the beginning of the revolution, the unity of power was challenged by an "innumerable amount of elective administrations" that placed "in the constitution, next to the throne, the excess of democracy."[78] The clash was not simply between the Ancien Régime and the nascent representative state. When, on May 10, 1791, the Constituent Assembly tried to limit the sovereignty of groups in the name of individual rights, the Fraternal Society of the Two Sexes protested that the attempt to restrict debates in the communal assemblies "deprives the communes, that is to say, the sovereign people, from exercising their basic public right, that is to deprive them of the right to exist."[79] In this political context, the *Enragés* aspired to replace the representative parliamentary system with one in which the representatives would be mandatories of the primary assemblies, thereby restoring the ancient imperative mandate (*mandat impératif*) in a new form.[80] The imperative mandate, which was suppressed in the name of the new sense of identity and unity of the French nation in the initial stages of the revolution,[81] was recalled to life by the *Enragés*. The discussion on the imperative mandate was entangled with the meaning of the term "insurrection," which was neither an abstract concept nor the extreme use of violence in cases of exception. "Insurrectionary" referred instead to the practices of the sectional societies and the new type of popular organization established by the *Sans-culottes*.[82]

The *Enragé* Jean Varlet, in his Proposal for a Special and Imperative Mandate, contended that an important article should be added to the Declaration: "the sovereignty of the people is the natural right possessed by the assembled citizens to elect every public official directly; to discuss their own interests, to draft mandates for the deputies..., to reserve themselves the capacity of recalling and punishing those of their agents who transcend their power."[83] Through mandates, stated Varlet, people could exercise their own sovereignty in the primary assemblies and establish their "guarantee against legislative tyranny."[84] Finally, Varlet argued that the inclusion of this natural right in the Declaration would require revision of all the articles of the constitution that stood in opposition to the sovereignty of the assemblies.

Imperative mandate was not an abstract concept; it was a dimension of the insurgent practices of the sectional democracy. In this conjuncture, Hérault-Séchelles stated that the primary assemblies should retain the right to judge or, as Robespierre proposed, even to revoke the deputies.[85] On the opposite side, the Girondins and other Jacobins upheld the general will against the particular wills of the sections and the assemblies.[86] For instance, the Jacobin François-Agnès Montgilbert affirmed that the right to resist belonged only to the *peuple* and not to the particular will of some citizens. Indeed, he said, putting the latter in place of the former would mean that there is "no longer a government and the social contract has been broken."[87] Robespierre's position was ambiguous. On the one hand, with the *Sans-culottes*, he defended the right to revoke the mandatories; on the other, he saw in the continuous convocation of the primary assemblies the expression of an "excess of democracy (*excès de démocratie*), which overturns national sovereignty."[88] It was not so much the alternative between direct and representative democracy that was at stake but, rather, the unity of national sovereignty represented by the Convention, on the one hand, and the democratic excess of the plurality of powers exercised by the assemblies and districts, on the other. From the point of view of the state, this democratic excess had to be contained so as not to undermine the autonomy of the national representatives and the unity of the nation they represented. The debate on the right to insurrection took the same path. The prohibition of insurrection was the corollary of the principle of national representation, since insurrection could only express the will of a part of the people against the people's representatives. However, this was only the voice of the representatives. The subalterns voiced a different demand.

The new political experiment of nonrepresentative democracy did not have the time to name its own concept; rather, it borrowed the premodern concept of "imperative mandate," on the one hand, and articulated itself with the term of "insurrection," on the other. The imperative mandate—this anachronistic term—was premodern only insofar as it was not modern; it expressed an alternative trajectory of political modernity that was not based on the idea of political unity.[89] When the subaltern demanded the imperative mandate, this demand was closely related to insurrectionary practices, understood as the natural right of the assembled citizens. Indeed, the everyday political practice of the Commune of Paris, the forty-eight sections, the sectional societies, and even more, the practice of the imperative mandate, which undermined the sovereign unity of the people and the representative principle of democracy, were insurrectionary.

The modern state knows only the "free mandate" in which each deputy, regardless of the specific locality from which he is elected, represents "the people" as a whole; each speaks in the name of the people and not for a part of the people.[90] For this reason, each law approved by the majority of representatives is considered to be the expression of the people's will, which each citizen must obey. Free mandate is thus the consequence of the concept of the unity of the people's sovereignty and its political representation. Imperative mandate binds deputies to the instructions and directions of a particular assembly, which has the right to revoke them: it shatters the dogma of the unity of the people's sovereignty and goes beyond the framework of representative democracy.

In other words, the imperative mandate is incompatible with the logic of national sovereignty and its representation.[91] This is also evident from the French tradition that "normalizes" the exception of 1792–93.

French Constitution 1791[92]	1792. Proposal for a Special and Imperative Mandate[93]	French Constitution 1795
Title III, Art. 1. Sovereignty is one, indivisible, inalienable, and imprescriptible. It belongs to the nation; no section of the people nor any individual can attribute to himself the exercise thereof. Sec. III, Art. 7. The representatives elected in the departments **shall not be the representatives of one particular department, but of the entire nation, and no mandate may be given them.**	"You will add this important article to the Declaration of the Rights of Man: the sovereign of the people is the natural right possessed by the assembled citizens to elect every public official directly; to discuss their own interests, **to draft mandates for the deputies they have chosen as legislators, to reserve for themselves the capacity of recalling and punishing those of their mandatories who transcend their power or betray their interests.**"	Art. 1. The French Republic is one and indivisible. Art. 2. The totality of French citizens is the sovereign. Art. 52. The members of the Legislative Body are not the representatives of the department which has selected them, but of the entire nation. **No mandate can be given to them.** Art. 360. Corporations and associations contrary to the public order cannot be formed.

French Constitution 1791[92]	1792. Proposal for a Special and Imperative Mandate[93]	French Constitution 1795
	"If **the people** knew what they are, if, **through mandates**, they **had used their right to exercise their own sovereignty in the primary assemblies**, then the laws would be what they must be by their essence: acts of the sovereign imposed upon its delegates, and not acts of the agents imposed upon their principals. **This is how Republics operate**."	Art. 361. No assembly of citizens can style itself a popular society (*société populaire*). Art. 364. All citizens are free to address petitions to the public authorities, but they must be as individuals; no association can present them collectively, except the constituted authorities.

The friction between the tradition of the nation-state and the legacy of insurgent universality is evident here. The Constitution of 1793 is ambiguous with respect to the imperative mandate. It drops the ban otherwise expressed in the Constitution of 1791.[94] The terminology used is also ambiguous. If Article 29 of the 1793 Constitution refers to the deputies and the nation—"Every deputy belongs to the whole nation"—Articles 29 and 31 of the 1793 Declaration speak instead about the "mandatories." The Constitution of 1795 normalizes the anomaly and expressly reintroduces the ban on the mandate.

Saying that "sovereignty has come back to its source,"[95] Varlet located that source in the primary assemblies and sections in which the people were really assembled and where they discussed, controlled, and tabulated orders to the mandatories. The assemblies were practicing a different conception of sovereignty. Varlet continued: "In drafting our mandate, we did not worry about whether this procedure was followed by all the sections of free France. It was enough for us to know that we had the right to do it."[96] The right that Varlet was asserting was, indeed, already realized in the practice of sections and primary assemblies. What is notable in that statement is the reconfiguration of the concept of people's sovereignty. In the insurgent conception, each single section and assembly could practice that right of drafting mandates, whether the same procedure was followed by all sections of France or not. This principle undermines the existence of the nation-state and its sovereignty, which is split in the plurality of assemblies. From the standpoint of the state, that principle is untenable. So it was for both Jacobins and Girondins, whose opposition vanishes when the stakes are the inviolability of the deputies and the unity of the nation. The conception of the imperative mandate pointed out an alternative political modernity, which cracked the crystal of sovereignty in the hands of the singular-collective "peuple." Indeed, in the context of the imperative mandate, the concept of "people" expresses neither the collective singular "peuple" nor a multitude of individuals. People are the real articulation of districts and primary assemblies, clubs, and political meetings.

If the insurgents were experimenting with an alternative trajectory of political modernity, at the beginning of the revolution, Le Chapelier had already tried to hinder this possibility by affirming that there was no place for associations and clubs—that is, the so-called "associative life of democracy," which replicated the corporations of the past era and were going to rival "the assembly in what must be its monopoly: to represent the people as a unified entity."[97] The revolution attempted to impose on the preexisting system of corporations, which had constituted the institutional basis of the social and productive fabric since the Middle Ages, a new social structure based on individualism, formal freedom, and private property.[98] In a session of the National Assembly, Le

Chapelier clearly outlined his plan of attack for imposing the new system: "There are no longer corporations in the state, there is no longer anything but the particular interest of each individual, and the general interest. It is permitted to no one to inspire an intermediary interest in citizens, to separate them from the public interest by a spirit of corporation."[99] In substance, the tripartite structure of society, composed not only of individuals and state but also of other bodies and intermediate interests holding authority, had to be destroyed. The opportunity to accelerate the attack on the corporations was provided by the grievances of the carpenters who, in May 1791, asked for government intervention to regulate their employment contracts. Le Chapelier introduced a bill, which passed in the National Assembly in a vote on June 14, of which Article 1 declared the "abolition of any kind of citizen's guild in the same trade or of the same profession. . . . [I]t is forbidden to reestablish them under any pretext or in any form whatsoever." Article 4 went on to state that, "It is contrary to the principles of liberty and the Constitution for citizens with the same professions, arts, or trades to deliberate or make agreements among themselves designed to set prices for their industry or their labor. If such deliberations and agreements are concluded, whether accompanied by oath or not, they will be declared unconstitutional, prejudicial to liberty and the Declaration of the Rights of Man, and will be null and void."[100] Two opposing conceptions of freedom collide here. On the one hand, in the name of an individualistic conception of freedom and the rights of man in the tradition of 1789, Le Chapelier attacked the collective forms of craft guilds as a remainder of the Ancien Régime, and he specifically forbade their restoration.[101] On the other hand, there was the corporate system of guilds that the workers had reactivated in an innovative way from prerevolutionary traditions. The stakes went beyond the workers' attempt to establish agreements and collective bargaining. It concerned a different way of understanding sovereignty and freedom. Once again it was Le Chapelier, on February 28, 1791, on behalf of the Comité de Constitution, who stated as the first constitutional principle: "The entire nation has only the sovereignty that it exercises through its representatives, and that cannot be alienated or divided; no department, no district, no commune, no section of the people participate in this sovereignty, and any citizen without exception is subject to it."[102] It outlined a conflict between the concept of a single, indivisible national sovereignty expressed through representative power, and the sovereignty of the popular assemblies that took seriously the inalienable sovereignty of the people in the forms of the imperative mandate and the right of recall of representatives.[103] This position, initially held also by some Jacobins, was opposed by the Girondins.

For the Girondins, and for Condorcet, it was necessary to solve the paradox of a sovereignty that risked being at the same time indivisible and made up of sovereign parts. Condorcet tried to channel statehood into the flow of modern national sovereignty, bringing the whole matter to the issue of constituent power. For him, the problem was not, and could not be, the revocation of the mandatories by the sections, which would have led to the destruction of the unity of will and action of the nation, but, rather, it was only the right to "disapprove a constitution" through referendum.[104] The insurrectionary dynamics of the sovereign assemblies had to be defused in the name of the constituent power of the people; sovereignty could be articulated territorially, but not through a return to the social bodies that, as Le Chapelier constantly reiterated, belonged to the archaic Ancien Régime. That which was not possible for Condorcet and the Girondins—that is, the elimination of the sovereign assemblies of the *Sans-culottes*—was possible for the Terror and Robespierre. The alternative to modern sovereignty of the nation-state was not in the theories of the Girondins but, rather, in the practices of the coarsest *Sans-culottes* and *Enragés*.

Later, the Jacobins in power synchronized the different insurgent temporalities of the revolution in the name of national unity of the French people, which they created and made visible by representing it. The decree of October 10, 1793, put into place a strong centralizing push of national power and, at the same time, a war against the *Enragés* and clubs, including those of women. On February 5, 1794, Robespierre stated: "Democracy is not a state in which people, continually assembled, regulates by itself all public affairs; even less is it a state in which one hundred thousand fractions of the people . . . would decide the fate of the whole society."[105] The internal war against the plurality of powers was over, having first crushed the autonomy of the self-government of the peasant communities, then the political practice of the assemblies of the *Sans-culottes*. The Jacobins crushed the democratic experiment and their assemblies, and built political unity and identity by focusing the polemical strength of exclusion against internal and external strangers, who became the "enemies of humanity."[106] With their concepts of unity and representation, they were sympathetic to the Girondins and to Sieyès's obsession with the "totality of the Nation against the vagaries of a few electors."[107] The virtuous *dérapage* was crushed in the name of the unity of the general will, and the dominant pathway of the representative state was restored.

Despite the violence of the state that tried to synchronize the institutions of the country with the new model of national sovereignty, the corporate community system survived as an "underground tradition of working-class 'philanthropic' or 'associationist' ideas" and was the basis for the socialist experiment of 1848, when workers reactivated the assemblies and corporate traditions in the form of their associations.[108] The tradition of the corporate system was reactivated by the workers, not against artisans and proprietors but, rather, against the new capitalist configuration of proprietary and competitive individualism. It is important to pay attention to this aspect because, again in the Commune of 1871, craftsmen, small-business owners, and workers were not opposed to one another. The conflict was not polarized between two classes—bourgeois and proletarian—but, rather, involved different layers of the population and different forms of life. On the one hand, there was the nascent proprietary individualism, formal freedom, and the right to private property; on the other, there were communities and associative structures that practiced their freedom in relation to their specific sphere of authority. This community fabric not only limited the power of the state expressed in the General Assembly but also looked for a new articulation of powers and property relations that limited the right, otherwise limitless, to private property.

TWO LEGACIES

The two proto-declarations of the Rights of Man and the Citizen inaugurated two different legacies. In each case, the "rights of man" were brought together with the "rights of the citizen"; however, the "and" that links these two syntagms can be understood either as a conjunction or as a disjunction. Diverse political consequences follow.

We have seen the dialectic that traverses Articles 10 and 11 of the Declaration of 1789, whereby liberty was subjected to limitation by the power of the state for the protection of public order as soon as it is proclaimed. This dialectic is articulated in the relationships between rights, the subject of rights, and the power that protects them. A similar dialectic is present in the catalogue of liberties born by the revolution of 1848, in which each liberty is proclaimed to be an unconditional right of the citizen while, at the same time, it is limited by laws, which are supposed to mediate the liberties of different persons with each other and with "the public safety" in harmony.[109] Reading the Constitution in the historical-political context of the rise of Louis Bonaparte in France, Marx made the point that both those who were demanding freedom and those who were denying freedom appealed to the Constitution, whose legal boundaries were not able to hinder the dictatorship of Napoleon III.[110]

If one wants to follow the juridical legacy of human rights, the dialectic between the simultaneous declaration and limitation of the liberties is echoed in the European Convention for the Protection of Human Rights and Fundamental Freedoms, drafted in 1950. The European Convention denies systematically in the second paragraph of each article what is declared in the first. For instance, Article 9 declares, in the first paragraph, the "freedom of thought, conscience and religion," adding, in a second paragraph, the exception—that is, the "freedom to manifest one's religion or beliefs shall be subject only to such limitations as are prescribed by law and are necessary in a democratic society in the interests of public safety, for the protection of public order, health or morals." A similar antinomy marks Article 8 on "private and family life," Article 10 on "freedom of expression," and Article 11 on "freedom of assembly and association." The climax is achieved in Article 15, in which the "protection of the public order" allows the sovereign state, "in time of emergency," to derogate from those rights. The same dialectic also resonates in the 1948 Universal Declaration of Human Rights. Article 29 of the Declaration states, in the second paragraph, that the exercise of human rights is subject to the limitations "of meeting the just requirements of morality, public order and the general welfare in a democratic society," as determined by law.

In each case, public power has to establish the boundary between use and abuse in order to prevent the use of liberty from becoming abuse against the equal rights of others or against public order. It is up to the state to define what "abuse" and "public order" are. How is it, then, that the individual can also be protected by the abuse of state power? Stated differently, fundamental rights exist to limit the power of the state in order to protect the private sphere of the individual; however, it is the same state that, nevertheless, has the power to decide whether and when these rights should themselves be limited. Indeed, as the Declaration of 1789 specified, the "safeguard of the rights of man and the citizen requires public power."[111] And here is the contradiction: public power can always displace or even abolish the limits it imposes on itself, especially in the name of a true or presumed emergency. This aporia can be displaced to the international register, but it cannot be suppressed.

Furthermore, this current conception of universal human rights is problematic because it is based on a construction of the political subject as completely passive. This is a subject whose human dignity has to be protected against the possible violation of its rights, against humiliation and degradation.[112] This is all well and good. Nevertheless, this subject always appears to be a potential or actual victim, on the one hand; the "man" of the rights declarations, on the other hand, can easily be considered abstract. Many conservative thinkers have pursued this critique. As long as the subject of human rights is not the individual who belongs to a political and social context, the "man" of the declarations seems to be the human being without any further specification. According to Arendt, for instance, "the Latin word *homo*, the equivalent of 'man,' signified originally somebody who was nothing but a man, a rightless person, therefore, and a slave" or "certainly a politically irrelevant being."[113] For this reason, her idea of the "right to have rights" corresponds to the right to belong to a political community as *bios politikos* in contrast to the human as bare life—that is, the "abstract nakedness of being human and nothing but human," which is the result of not being part of the political institution of community.[114] According to Arendt, the loss of "home and political status becomes identical with expulsion from humanity altogether,"[115] and the loss of belonging to a political community corresponds to the loss of rights and protections. Arendt thus contemplates the human outside the political community as a deprived form of life; she does not see, or she is not interested in seeing, the "human" whose political agency exceeds and dis-orders the political order. Arendt's position has been reframed by Agamben, who assumes that the concept of man is subsumed in the concept of citizen. According to Agamben, since the essence of the *homme* lies in the legal belonging to the nation-state, the latter can declare the state of exception and through the radical dejuridification of individuals can reduce them to the status of *homo sacer*.[116] From this perspective one can develop the theory of a generalized "state of exception," but one cannot develop any idea of emancipation. In 1793, Pierre Guyomar, member of the Convention and author of "Le partisan de l'égalité politique entre les individus ou problème très important de l'égalité en droits et de l'inégalité en fait," offered the counterpoint to those who would condemn the concept of man for being abstract. Indeed, during the discussions for a new constitution, he evoked the Latin etymology of the word *homme*: "*homo* [in ancient Rome] expressed by itself these two words consecrated by usage, man, woman.... Let us liberate ourselves rather from the prejudice of sex, just as we have freed ourselves from the prejudice against the colour of Negros."[117] For Guyomar, the term *homo*, or *l'homme*, referred neither to "a political irrelevant being," nor to a citizenship that had to be demanded as a "right to have rights," nor even to a white, rich, male subject of rights. On the contrary, it referred to the universality of being human, or a universal human republic in which individuals, whether they were formally included or excluded, would *act as citizens* in their political assemblies. In such a rendition, the generic term "homo" exceeded the horizon of citizenship and separated "the rights of man" from "the rights of citizen."[118]

It is the divergence of the two terms that leads us to the legacy of insurgent universality. The women, the slaves, and the poor practiced universality beyond the nation, performed political citizenship beyond legal citizenship, and accused even the most radical Jacobins of being "insufficiently universalist."[119] These insurgents did not simply dispute their status in the order, demanding inclusion in the formal equality of an unjust political order.[120] Even if they can be designated as "the part of those who have no part,"[121] this should not be construed to imply that their demand was to become a part of the existing juridical order. Instead, they intensified the gap between *homo* and citizen, urging us to think of universality beyond the constitutional shell of the state. In insurgent universality, the human is the subject who, by acting *as a citizen* beyond one's legal status and the putative boundaries of citizenship, puts both the political *and* the social orders into question. One can say that performing the universality of the human in the "rights of man" is not only the questioning of right but, furthermore, the questioning of society itself.[122] Furthermore, this kind of universality is everything but abstract; it has to be understood in the historical conjuncture in which assemblies and societies were experimenting with politics beyond the framework of representative democracy.

This is not about producing types of universality.[123] It is by digging into the historical material that the concept of universalism presents different stratifications that orient its meaning. Insurgent universality does not correspond to Balibar's idea of universality as symbolic or ideal universality. The latter is still grounded in equality and liberty as the rights of individuals that "unite and join forces against oppression."[124] Balibar's definition of this universality is still polemic because it establishes something common starting from an opposition. As in the revolution of 1789, it starts from a resistance and ends in the actual exercise of a constituent power that forces the horizon of democracy to expand to include new subjectivities and, eventually, to become a state itself, a new constituted power. If the question of equality and liberty is infinite, as Balibar says,[125] it is a bad infinity that remains blocked by the binary tension between constituent and constituted power. Balibar's notion of "egalitarian sovereignty" exposes a permanent tension between the politics of rights and their irreducibility to institutions, which even if it leads to the democratization of democracy as an open process from below, nonetheless remains constricted by the polarity between constituent and constituted power. As a result, Balibar's discourse oscillates between the moment of the auto-constitution of the people and the "representation of the sovereign in its deputies, inasmuch the sovereign is the people."[126] In other words, his discourse reduces the excess of the rights of man to the institutional, public inscription of freedom and equality. The juridical framework of the state is not in question, nor is the juridical understanding of universalism. His point of reference is still the 1789 Declaration.

Insurgent universality, instead, begins with equal access to politics in the form of assemblies and groups; it begins with local self-government and control over mandatories; it begins with the plurality of powers and the democratic excess; it begins with the excess of *homo* when it calls into question the national character of formal equality; it begins with denouncing the illusory character of liberty, equality, and republic condemned in the Manifesto of the Enragés of 1793. Insurgent universality is about this third institutional dimension beyond the binary opposition of constituent and constituted power.

There are two legacies: the 1789 Declaration questions the feudal order, introduces individuals into the nation-state, defines their private and political rights, and opens up an expansive dynamic for the production of civil rights; the 1793 Declaration questions the political and social order, and individuals act as members of groups and assemblies—hence, as citizens beyond legal citizenship. They practice their freedoms without the limits imposed by state and eventually question the reasons of obedience or disobedience.[127] Universalism is related to the abstraction of individuals in relation to the power that has to protect them; universality, on the contrary, concerns the agency of concrete individuals who belong to groups that enact the democratic excess beyond the nation and the horizon of state representation.

From the perspective of insurgent universality, whose forgotten legacy I want to reactivate as an alternative pathway toward political universality, only one right of man really exists: the human right to be human. As the basis of this right, there is no essentialist definition of the human being. Rather, it reverses the structure of law, whose function is to individualize the human individual, which in fact does not preexist law but, rather, follows from it. The *homo*, to which Guyomar refers, is instead the *common term* that from time to time takes shape in a political practice. It is not applied to single individuals to be integrated later into the legal sphere, but instead is practiced politically by women, slaves, and the poor who, in their practice, modify both the social and the institutional fabric, as well as themselves. This practice of insurgent universality is local and refers to certain subjects. The term *homme* in the Declaration does not only exceed the divisions of the political and social orders, but also transcends the provincialism of space. Not because the rights of man aim toward a world democracy, but because they exceed the boundaries of any legal citizenship. Indeed, understanding the antislavery rebellions as one of the revolutions within the French Revolution allows us to indicate that the political space in which that insurgency takes place is not the nation but, rather, the Atlantic world. And it allows us to understand surprising bridges between their insurgency and that of the *Sans-culottes* of Paris.

The wrong to which the subaltern are subjected occurs not only because they are excluded from the representation of the sovereign people. It comes about also because the dominant construction of citizen as the autonomous, free, and rational subject is built as its antithesis—the construction of its "heteronomous," "irrational," "emotional," and "immature," nonwhite, non-male, non-Western subject. The struggling, oppressed classes, therefore, did not simply demand inclusion. They also challenged the very construction of the "man" and the citizen together with the social order. By doing so, they questioned the social partitions that the juridical universalism of 1789 had pushed into the private sphere. In fact, the questions of women, slaves, and the poor are political and social at the same time. Challenging both the political and the social fabric allowed them to open new emancipatory pathways according to which the emancipation of the slaves exceeded the nation; women's emancipation questioned the gendered division of labor; and the poor questioned property and plenty. The matter of the dispute did not concern the privilege of being included as citizens in an unjust order. Insurgent universality exceeded legal citizenship and questioned race, gender, and poverty—that is, the aristocracy of the white, male property owner as the citizen of the new configuration of exclusion, hierarchies, and inequalities within the paradigm of the legal equality of the nation-state. History shows us how the layers of exclusion are continuously reconfigured in response to the emancipatory claims of human beings.

Insurgent universality dis-orders the social and political order and, by doing so, challenges the distinctions between political and social, public and private. When the women left the "privacy" of their homes and dared to act as public citizens, they reconfigured the public sphere, and the so-called private sphere as well.[128] In the feminist project of Olympe de Gouges to make women political subjects, emancipation questioned the distinctions between the public and the private, the active and passive, and "the attempt to achieve this project involved an act of self-creation, in which a woman defining herself as woman enacted the public/political role usually performed by men."[129] From this perspective, the transformation of external circumstances was strictly related to the self-transformation of the human and required the reconfiguration of modern binary distinctions between the social and the political, the private and the public. In the Pétition à la Municipalité (May 1792), Olympe de Gouges wrote that she "made herself a man for the country."[130] This assertion does not mean that she questioned her sex. On the basis of the excess expressed by the term *homme*, she questioned the specific form of individuation, division of labor, and social and political roles founded on gender. Refusing the existing opposition of the public and the private, productive and reproductive, political and domestic, rational and sexual, she rejected the division of labor on which both Sieyès and the Jacobins based their notion of representation.

Since what is being challenged is an entire social and political order by the insurgencies of women, slaves, and the poor, the process is not limited to them. Anyone can take part in their rebellion, since what they question is not only their particular social position but also the position of everyone else within the existing, unjust order. This is not a gesture of abstract solidarity from a privileged position. Real solidarity is a kind of bond that concerns questioning our own position in all existing relationships. For example, the order based on slavery cannot be challenged merely by putting into discussion the social position of the slave, but, even more so by questioning each person's position in the existing order. It is the practice of dis-belonging that shapes insurgent universality. And this practice refers primarily to ourselves insofar as it is the expression of the excess of the human (rights of man) in relation to legal citizenship (rights of citizen). But this dis-belonging is not just the denial of belonging or resistance to power. It is above all a practice of belonging to a different order articulated in institutions, assemblies, districts, and political groups that reconfigures the meaning of politics, citizenship, and property relations. It is from this legacy of 1793 that Théodore Dézamy takes inspiration for his Code de la Communauté in 1842. Dézamy writes that the legacy of 1793 is constituted not by the violent measures of the government but by the communism of the *ateliers communs*[131] and the assemblies organized everywhere by the population.

1871: THE INSTITUTIONS OF INSURGENT UNIVERSALITY

> The Commune felt itself to be, in all respects, the heir of 1793.
>
> —WALTER BENJAMIN[1]

THROUGH THE PRISM OF THE COMMUNE

On the centenary of the Paris Commune, Pierre Sorlin published an article in the journal *Études* in which he itemized the new tasks for the historiography of the Commune.[2] Sorlin invited historians to stick to its essential importance. And the essential importance was that the proletarians "practiced their political and social responsibility and the ruling class, resolute in not wanting to relinquish any of its privileges, preferred massacre instead of negotiation."[3] The massacre has been widely investigated. But who and what were massacred with so much violence? What had frightened the ruling classes so much as to provoke such a reaction? What "natural order" had been violated in such a way as to justify that massacre? And, principally, what social and political forms violated that order, while contemporaneously showing alternatives to it? We know that the banking and business worlds were pushing Thiers to end things with Paris.[4] We know that the repression was fierce. Sorlin wrote that the Communards were killed mechanically, almost industrially, as if to remind people that there were no alternatives to the time and space of capital.⁵ As soon as it had finished dealing with Paris, the Versailles government could concentrate its troops against another insurgency, which was taking place in Algeria. Indeed, the "uprising of the Paris Communards was closely linked with the revolutionary events in Algeria of 1870–71, and coincided with the big national liberation uprising of 1871."⁶ Surprisingly, the vast literature on the Paris Commune has often disregarded the link between the events in Paris and those in Algeria.

The Arab and Berber insurgency headed by Mohammed el-Mokrani, the ruler of the Kabyle region of Medjana, began on March 14, 1871. In April, the insurgency spread to peasants and nomads united in the religious brotherhood of Rahmaniya. At the same time, the Republican Association of Algeria claimed that "power in Algeria should be vested in the elective municipalities-communes, and that Algeria should be a federation of such municipalities-communes."⁷ When the news of the institution of the Commune in Paris arrived in Algeria, the Republican Association of Algeria sent delegates to France and published the declaration of La Commune de l'Algérie:

> Algeria's delegates declare on behalf of their mandatories that they completely adhere to the Paris Commune. The whole of Algeria claims communal freedoms.
>
> Oppressed for forty years by the double concentration of the army and the administration, the colony has understood that the complete emancipation of the Commune is the only way to achieve freedom and prosperity.⁸

The document, dated March 28, bears the signatures of Lucien Rabuel, Louis Calvinhac, and Alexandre Lambert, who went to Paris as delegates of the Algerian Commune and joined the Paris Commune. But if Alexandre Lambert expressed enthusiasm for the Paris Commune, his position toward the popular uprisings in Algeria was certainly different. Lambert publicly distanced himself from popular local uprisings.⁹ While he was ready to challenge the domestic political order along with the Communards, Lambert was not ready to question the colonial order. Like other Communards, Lambert was not free from orientalist prejudices of the time: "Although the members of the Republican Association admitted Arabs to their ranks, however, at best they remained indifferent to the native population's struggle for national liberation."[10] Despite the inability of the Algerian radicals and the *mouvement communaliste* to find common political ground with the national liberation uprising of 1871,[11] these events were united by a tragic destiny: as soon as Adolphe Thiers had suppressed the Paris Commune in blood, he dispatched troops to Algeria, where they "burnt villages, drove away the cattle, destroyed wells and murdered women and children. The guerillas of Kabylia, however, courageously continued the unequal fight for another six months."[12] Six French military columns were mobilized against the insurgents, and the sinister connection was drawn: "The Versaillists cynically stated that they had dealt with the Algerian insurgents in the 'Parisian manner.'"[13] The methods of colonial violence and those of repressive violence of the state against the working class overlapped. In different forms, the Commune and the peasants and nomads of the uprising had questioned a trajectory of modernity. The dominant one. And for this, they were repressed. Those who were not massacred were imprisoned and sent, together with the Communards of Paris, to New Caledonia.

In New Caledonia, there was Louise Michel, among the few to pay attention to the spread of communal forms in the French colony, who cited the Declaration of the Algerian Commune in her memoirs.[14] And Michel would be among the few to support the 1878 revolt against French colonization by the indigenous Kanak population in New Caledonia, where she had been deported. Other former Communards deported to New Caledonia sided with France against the insurgents. If the Commune did not have time to test its new institutions, it had even less time to give rise to a new subjectivity, freed not only from the forms of external dominion but also and especially from the internal ones formed by prejudices of the time. The Commune was an experiment of this kind. Far from being a legal-political model to be realized, the

Commune was a political practice that sought to define a new institutional fabric and a new subjectivity. Or better yet, a new subjectivity that could only be born in the practice of the new institutions and forms of life.

> I am not the only person caught up by situations from which the poetry of the unknown emerges. I remember a student. . . . He had a volume of Baudelaire in his pocket, and we read a few pages with great pleasure when we had time to read. What fate held for him I don't know, but we tested our luck together. It was interesting. We drank some coffee in the teeth of death, choosing the same spot where three of our people, one after another, had been killed. Our comrades, anxious about seeing us there at what seemed to be a deadly place, made us withdraw. Just after we left a shell fell, breaking the empty cups. Above all else, our action was simply one of a poet's nature, not bravery on either his part or mine.[15]

This episode recounted by Louise Michel shows the poetic nature of the actions of the Communards. It is not the reading of Baudelaire itself which renders that moment poetic, but the pleasure of reading it together with an unknown young man and putting the moment of this human relationship above the fear of death. Michel's poetry is not the aesthetics of death but, rather, of a life that rises above the fear of death. Modern theories of the state cannot disregard the anthropological assumption of the fear of violent death. It is from this premise that Thomas Hobbes shows the need of the state to ensure individual security. And that is why the state, to legitimize itself, must constantly play with security and insecurity.

The Commune, as the "political form at last discovered,"[16] created something new. But this novelty needs to be clarified. The politics of the Communards defied the state in the sense that it challenged the dogma of the indivisibility of national sovereignty and the monopoly of state power. Obviously, questioning the monopoly of state power also meant giving up the pivotal functions of modern sovereignty: security and neutralization of conflict. This was not for the sake of chaos but, rather, because the Commune was dismantling the grammar of *Leviathan* that, starting from the Hobbesian anthropological assumption of the fear of violent death, demonstrates the need to renounce the use of force in favor of the state. The Communards were not afraid to die. They courageously faced the brutal executions carried out by the army of Versailles. The repression was extremely fierce not only for its spirit of revenge but also because they dared to place justice higher than the preservation of life. Without this reversal of the anthropological paradigm of modern politics they would not have been able to experience the democratic excess, in which conflict is a dimension of politics and not something to be neutralized. The Communards were not only experimenting with new institutions but, as it were, also experimenting with themselves. Just as they were dismantling the state, so too were they dismantling their own subjectivity by testing a different political anthropology—a more mature one because it could handle the anxiety that comes from the instability of politics. In practice, they were somehow responding to Kant's question on the Enlightenment, and with their actions they were showing the way out of the condition of self-incurred immaturity, including the immaturity of not being able to cope with the anxiety of the conflict that accompanies politics. Political maturity is also the ability to face the instability of an experiment with democracy. This is the difficult task: the combination of the political and social change of external circumstances with self-transformation.

The Communards instead experimented with politics beyond the state, which does not mean against the state but, instead, beyond the binary opposition of state power and counterpower, or constituent power.[17] In order to practice politics beyond the state, the Communards created new institutions.[18] I assume here the definition of "institution" provided by the Italian jurist Santi Romano: "A revolutionary society or a criminal association does not constitute law from the viewpoint of the State that they try to subvert, or whose laws they violate, just as a schismatic sect is considered antilegalistic by the Church; but this does not imply that in the above case there are not institutions, organizations, and orders which, taken per se and intrinsically considered, are legal."[19] Through their new institutions, the Communards experimented new forms of life and subjectivity. That is where their poetry of the unknown begins.

"THE POETRY OF THE UNKNOWN"

What is the Commune in light of a history of the present? The Commune challenges us to think politics beyond the state. It challenges us to think society beyond private-property relations. In other words, it challenges us to question two "unquestionable" assumptions of our time: parliamentary politics and private property. The crisis of representative democracy creates a vacuum of political participation that today is occupied by populism. This, in substance, expresses a sense of dissatisfaction with the present that can be oriented in either an emancipatory or an authoritarian direction.

The insurgency of the Communards showed the field of possibilities that opened up beyond dissatisfaction with the state. The Communards put into practice new institutional forms *not* based on the representative state and relations of private property. In the trajectory that they were able to travel in the short time available to them we can find traces of a legacy that allows us to respond more effectively to the questions of our present. In fact, many of the alternatives to today's crisis do not have to be invented from scratch; it can be reactivated from the countless futures that have remained caught in the past.

If today we are witnessing authoritarian changes that do not need either revolutions or coups, the rule of law shows itself powerless when it comes to restraining the concentration of power in the name of real or perceived emergencies. Like us, the Communards lost confidence in the rule of law. They had seen the Constitution of 1848 overturned in the plebiscitary dictatorship of Napoleon III.[20] The Constitution of 1848, written after the revolution of June 1848 had been crushed, canceled the social measures provided for by the National Assembly and, as had happened with the Constitution of 1795, reaffirmed the principle of singular and indivisible national sovereignty over particular societies and assemblies. Those constitutions were a celebration of the unity of the nation. A unity that had to be stronger, the greater the class divisions.

French Constitution of the Year III. 1795[21] *Declaration of Rights and Duties of Man and Citizen.*	*French Constitution. 1848*[22]
Art. 17. Sovereignty resides essentially in the **totality of the citizens.**	Art. 1. **Sovereignty** resides in the entirety of French citizens. **It is inalienable and imprescriptible.** No individual nor any part of the people can claim for themselves the exercise thereof.
Art. 18. No individual nor assembly of part of the citizens can assume sovereignty.	
	Art. 34. The members of the National Assembly are the representatives not of the department which nominates them, but of the **whole of France.**

These constitutional texts are not neutral. No constitution is. They are acts of war against the particular societies and their authority. Citizens are individualized, meaning they are produced as private individuals, and are placed in front of the monopoly of state power exercised in the name of the French people. From the dualism between individuals and state power follows the typically dichotomous structure of constitutional articles that promise "freedom by destroying it."[23] Indeed, the power that guarantees rights is the same power that can suspend them in case of emergency. Thus proceeds the Constitution of 1848.

French Constitution. 1848

Chapter II: Rights of the Citizens Guaranteed by the Constitution.

Art. 2. No one can be arrested or held in custody **except according to the provisions of the law.**

Art. 3. The residence of every person living on French territory is inviolable: it **can be entered only according to the forms and in the cases provided by law.**

Art. 8. Citizens have the right to form associations, to assemble peaceably and without arms, to petition, and to express their opinions by means of the press or otherwise. **The exercise of these rights can only be limited** by the equal rights of others, or **for the public safety.**

All Louis Napoleon had to do was multiply the exceptions in the name of "public safety." If that was not enough, the law of August 9, 1849, by means of a "state of siege," gave the military the power to bring political offenders before a court-martial. Resorting to "public safety" accelerated the process of de-politicization of the social, accomplished by means of decrees that subjected the clubs and associations to a mass of police regulations. The exception had become the rule and the concept of national sovereignty was made manifest through its primordial function: security. From 1848 to today, these authoritarian twists of the state have not diminished and were often able to be made without breaking the framework of the constitution.

The Communards grasped that, in order to avoid the authoritarian trajectory of the modern state, what was needed was not a rule of law but, rather, a different articulation of the relationship between the political and the social. Certainly not their separation. In this way, the Commune reconfigured the entire system of political and legal relations, taking seriously the asymmetries in social relations, reactivating the intermediate authorities, and integrating individual rights with those of groups and associations. In doing so, the Communards showed that a stateless society does not mean falling back into the state of nature dominated by a war of all against all. On the contrary, it is the state that, by destroying the intermediate bodies, produces individual atomization. The Communards were not trying to create a new ideal political order out of nothing. They were changing the present by reactivating temporalities, institutions, and traditions, which they recombined in a new order.

Today, the Commune prompts us to think about politics beyond the horizon of the representative democracy and the principle of private property. The Communards dared to do it, giving themselves, in the Déclaration au Peuple Française, a dual task: the "universalization of politics and property."[24] They showed a new field of possibilities for politics. It could be said that the Commune acted as a kind of collective mind. To this effect, the documents of the Commune, its declarations and its newspaper articles, are considered here as the complete works of this collective mind, to whom only seventy-two days of life were granted to create its own work. On the title page of this work there is no name of an author. Indeed, the Commune was anonymous and the Communards were aware and even proud of that: "One of the biggest reasons of anger against us is the obscurity of our names."[25] There are no leaders and "this flaw is its merit."[26]

One of the characteristics of insurgent universality is the lack of what Hegel called world-historical heroes who play pivotal roles in the progress of world history.[27] When the people are really the protagonists and they act politically, not through representatives and leaders but in their own assemblies, clubs, and councils, then the people don't need big personalities. It is the political insignificance, the people becoming little, that generates the mechanism of compensation that gives rise to the great personalities. Where they emerge and take up the scene with their own name, it is there the innovative strength of the insurgent universality fails or is diminished. This is why I analyzed 1793 without the figure of Robespierre casting a shadow over the others. And for the same reason I will analyze the insurgency of 1917 leaving Lenin in the background.

The Commune was a collective experience, a generous experiment in the field of politics. But the Communards had no time to develop a political theory of their institutions. "Time," observed Marx, "was not allowed to the Commune."[28] This is true. But the Commune produced a new experience of time in which everyday life was interrupted and the people of Paris were reinventing new forms of life and togetherness.[29] And so the Commune found itself at a crossroads similar to that of 1793. Either the decision-making time had to be accelerated and power centralized in order to deal with the situation of siege or, as the clubs urged, the rhythm of politics had to be requalified: "Do not be too hasty to judge and make decisions in the name of the people and instead of them."[30] At the club Saint-Nicolas-des-Champs, there was "a speaker calling on the Commune to 'act like in '93 and grant two hours a day to hearing petitions.'"[31] There emerged two different, incommensurable temporalities. On the one hand, the urgent need to make decisions leads to an increasing concentration of power in the hands of the government against the slow pace of democratic procedures.[32] On the other, the temporality of the Commune does not correspond to the simple slowing down of the accelerating temporality of the state; it is a qualitatively different rhythm, which favors democratic practice over procedural efficiency. A rhythm that lets democratic creativity run its course. In this sense, the Commune is comparable to a *fête*.[33]

Even the experience of work took several forms. In the reinvention of artisan craftsmanship, art and production were recombined, as they were in ancient *poiesis*. The shoemaker Gaillard, by questioning the familiar distinction between the useful and the beautiful, elaborated a philosophy of the shoe that claimed to bring the work of the artist shoemaker "back to the anatomical principles of the foot."[34] This was not romanticism. Gaillard's attempt to redefine the work of the artisan according to the "anatomical principles of the foot" expressed an attempt to mobilize different temporalities in order to find an alternative to the alienating, repetitive, and impersonal work of nascent industrial production. The Commune, as a collective artisan, was experiencing new forms of division of labor beyond the separation between production and art, manual and intellectual labor, production and reproduction.

It is not the division of labor in itself that denotes the capitalist mode of production as such. The division of labor also exists in noncapitalist societies, but in a different way. Individuals are different, have different aptitudes and abilities. The problem exists when a society is structured around a division of labor whose purpose is not the common good but, rather, the maximum production of profit, and therefore inequalities—Marx would have said, when the goal is no longer use value but, instead, exchange value. And this reversal is articulated through its own specific division of labor. This is what the Communards were questioning, along with the spatial separation put into practice by Haussmann in the 1860s, between a bourgeois center and proletarian suburbs.

In the Commune, the rupture in the state machinery came about not with the seizure of power but through new political institutions that reclaimed and reactivated other traditions of politics, channeling them into a new trajectory of modernity. A new institutional and productive texture was taking shape in the daily life of the Commune. Its temporality was innovative because day by day it changed the forms and modes of social togetherness. It is this different experience of time that still makes it so attractive. Arthur Arnould wrote that with the Commune, the tradition of the state was broken and "something new had happened in the world."[35] It was those bifurcations, which according to Blanqui characterized every second, showing the crossroads between "the road taken and road that could have been taken."[36] The Communards showed us the way toward the roads not taken. And for this they were severely repressed. Our task, regarding them, as well as all those who have ventured along those roads, is to think of the philosophical content of their actions in light of the present.

As we said, the roads were not opened from nothing. The myth of the creation of a political form *ex nihilo* is a totally modern presumption: Cartesian and Hobbesian. That's a presumption the Communards did not share. Those roads had different temporalities, indicated by alternative traditions to be reactivated in new forms. In Paris, the clash between temporalities opened an unprecedented field of possibilities for social and political experimentation. Decentralization, as a practice for the dismantling of the nation-state, was both internal (administrative and political) and external—that is to say, oriented toward the union of the different provincial Communes, from that of Marseille to the Commune of Algeria. Indeed, the Universal Republic evoked by the Communards was not a slogan but a concrete articulation of communal institutions beyond the nation-state. Nothing could be further from the modern cosmopolitanism that yearns for a global democratic state. The universality of the Universal Republic was not about scale. It expressed political citizenship beyond national identity. Being "French" in Paris during March–May 1871 was not a matter of national belonging but, rather, a political and social practice. The adjective "universal" in reference to the Republic conveys the completion of the twofold task of universalizing power and property. It was around these vectors that the Commune's plans were articulated.

UNIVERSALIZING POLITICS, OR *LIBERTÉ*

"We must aim to build up socialist institutions (*établissements socialistes*) everywhere,"[37] stated Édouard Vaillant during a debate on the control of theaters. We now have to investigate the nature of the institutions of the Commune. Opposing each other were two conceptions of politics, one based on centralization and unity (*l'unité*), the other wanting "to break centralization" and substitute it with the union (*l'union*) of differences and the autonomy of the groups.[38] The former, explained Arnould, was an expression of an identity like the barracks—it was military and national; whereas the union expressed the spirit of the association, "an essentially moral thing, where everyone sees his rights and autonomy respected."[39] In our terms, opposing each other were two political trajectories of modernity: that of the nation-state and the primitive accumulation of capital and political power, on the one hand; and the communal associations, the disaccumulation of capital, and the pluralism of powers, on the other.

What makes the experiment of the Communards so interesting is that their "poetry of the unknown"[40] was an intense laboratory of practices and institutions. On the evening of May 13, in one of the many clubs that used to meet in churches, the *clubistes* wrote and approved a document in which they demanded that a new articulation of powers be drawn up in accordance with the "new institutions and the aspirations of the people" (Art. 1).[41] In the same declaration, they also stated that working enterprises had to be placed under the authority of laborers' corporations (Art. 6).[42] The new configuration of the political would take place through new institutions and new property relations. Through new institutions, the Communards were experimenting with new ways of access to politics, redefining the role of the state without taking its place. This is the democratic excess, which configures itself as democratic self-government when it exceeds the constitutional form and keeps open the political form to transformation by creating new institutions that provide universal access to politics. One of the differences with respect to the framework of the modern state is that access to politics is organized through groups and associations, and not in terms of individuals called upon to vote every few years. The difference with respect to anti-statist politics is that the tension between democratic political practice and the unity represented by the government is fulfilled by a third political dimension—that is, insurgent institutions. The clubs of the Communards should be viewed as segments of political reality, institutions that imposed internal rules and therefore also a legal order that redefined the political reality in a pluralistic sense. The political experiment implemented by the Communards did not suppress the state but, rather, reshaped it by distributing power on different levels, which were sometimes even in conflict with each other.

The Communards did not want state power to be handed over. However, merely the will to break up the state machinery was not enough. It was necessary to articulate political reality in new institutions. Their practice was guided by communal traditions that came from medieval times to the present through the workers' associations of the nineteenth century. The old communal liberties crisscrossed with the clubs and workers' corporations of 1848 in a new historical configuration. The Club Républicain des Travailleurs-Libres published an appeal in 1848, which declared that "the clubs are the living barricades of Democracy" and they claimed their right to act as a "second National Assembly," which had the task of shaping a "new social order."[43] In a similar way, the clubs of the Communards were practicing a new articulation of the powers that surpassed the modern paradigm of the monopoly of power in the hands of the state. In other words, the clubs were dis-ordering the legal and political order through the pluralistic articulation of institutions that kept open the democratic process. Universalizing these institutions meant universalizing a kind of political practice that spread into the neighborhoods where daily meetings and clubs took their time to discuss the decisions of the Commune.[44]

The conflict between different trajectories of modernity that had been left unfinished in 1793 was resumed. Indeed, the so-called Le Chapelier law, which had been decreed on June 14, 1791, stated in the first article that the "abolition of any kind of citizen's corporations in the same trade of the same profession is one of the fundamental bases of the French Constitution." Furthermore, Article 4 said that corporative deliberations and agreements for setting prices for their labor "will be declared unconstitutional, prejudicial to liberty and the Declaration of the Rights of Man, and will be null and void."[45] The law aimed to speed up the destruction of corporations, which were defined as residual institutions of the Ancien Régime. However, the law was broadly directed against both workers' associations and popular societies, which had acquired, during the revolution, a kind of political existence that, according to Le Chapelier, they should not have had.[46] In other words, the law meant to destroy any kind of intermediary body and establish the modern political and constitutional framework characterized by the binary relationship between individuals and the nation-state. The dominant trajectory of the French Revolution, from the Le Chapelier law to Napoleon's Code Civil, crushed the social fabric constituted by co-operative societies. In its place the revolution produced a new social fabric founded on individualism. In this way, the contrast between two opposing legacies was outlined: that of "solidarity and ordered trade community," on the one hand; and "the powerful individualistic tendencies of contemporary society," on the other.[47] This conflict reemerged when the *Sans-culottes* rearmed their assemblies and clubs with their insurgent natural rights, and the Communards reactivated that legacy in their associations. The French Revolution, which apparently had broken continuity with the Ancien Régime, had actually accelerated the process of the concentration of state power against the authorities of intermediate bodies. The result was that the revolution had given birth to a power that was "more extensive, more minute, and more absolute" than the power that previous kings had ever exercised.[48]

The French aristocracy opposed this process when it saw itself progressively deprived of its political authority. But if we abandon the historicist representation of this conflict that sees the progressive temporality of the modern state on one side and the regressive temporality of the aristocracy's privileges on the other, we can grasp, in the tension between different temporalities, a field of possibilities in which modernity could and can be oriented beyond that binary opposition. Binary oppositions are the traps of modern conceptuality. Nevertheless, *tertium semper datur*. It is the field opened up by insurgent universality. The outcome of the dissolution of the feudal order was not prescribed in any teleology of the state and its centralization of power. The social and legal material of the Middle Ages could have been combined according to nonstate trajectories. And these are not pure theoretical hypotheses. The legacy that we are following is punctuated by the emergence of these alternative possibilities. Different conceptions of freedom and politics are at stake. Indeed, it is a conflict between two conceptions of freedom that Le Chapelier implicitly showed by declaring corporate freedoms "prejudicial to liberty and the Declaration of the Rights of Man." Individual freedom was consecrated in the Declaration of 1789: "Liberty consists in the freedom to do everything which injures no one else." A conception that at the same time absolutized individual freedom while creating tension between it and the state, which guarantees the freedom, but also determines and limits it. Differently, the Commune reactivated the nonmodern tradition of "communal liberties" as the basis of new "republican institutions."[49] Explicitly, the Manifeste des Vingt Arrondissements declared that it is the "communal idea, pursued since the 12th Century . . . , which has now triumphed on March 18, 1871."[50] The Communards were moving in historical material, not the way one moves along the railroad tracks of progress but as in a huge building where some rooms of what-has-been contain different not-yets that have remained encapsulated and can be freed now. If the French Revolution had produced the Declaration of the Rights of Man and of the Citizen, the Commune, recombining the old communal freedoms in a new configuration of the present, proclaimed "La Déclaration des Droits du Group."[51] By doing so, the Commune changed the course of political modernity by trying to complete the experiment on sectional democracy that was interrupted in 1793: it put groups and associations, rather than single individuals, at the foundation of politics. The French Revolution, with its Declaration of the Rights of Man, wrote the newspaper Le Père Duchêne, had "consecrated the interests of the isolated man, but had not affirmed the rights of the group, the rights of men who live in the same place, who have the same customs, are taken by the same desires, and suffer from the same needs."[52] It is the "Declaration of the Rights of Man transposed to the city."[53] And being part of a group, concluded *Le Père Duchêne*, meant taking on duties toward the group and toward the Commune.

With this, they wanted to affirm that free men and women are such not because they are isolated monads, individual legal subjects, but because they live in a political and social context of freedom. Precisely, the freedom to exercise political power in order to change the existing order. If the dominant trajectory of modernity had tried to universalize individual rights, the Commune instead pursued a universalization of power through the reactivation of local and trans-local institutions. Universality was not a premise from which to start to include someone in the legal sphere, but it was the practice of political citizenship beyond legal citizenship, the practice of power beyond national sovereignty. The politics practiced by the Communards could never be reduced to a matter of inclusion and recognition; instead, it questioned the binary logic that defined inclusion/exclusion together with the separation between public and private, political and social, and the multiple forms of dominion that demarcated the functions of class and gender. They did this because they believed that people could not become citizens without changing the relations of dominion underlying those demarcations. For instance, the women of the Commune usually bypassed the goal of civil and political rights, and focused instead on political, economic, and social relations and their transformation.[54] They acted as though they were political citizens already, with no need to claim recognition by the state. Communard women were not interested in obtaining formal civil rights but, rather, in changing the social forms of dominion that confined women to a subordinate position. Their political agency, which "placed them outside the liberal tradition,"[55] showed that universality is not simply a matter of inclusion; rather, it has to do with a way of accessing politics that dis-orders the multiple relations of dominion of the social and the dichotomic grammar that separates public and private, the political from the social, male from female, rational from irrational. A grammar that often not even the revolutionaries dared to alter.

It is not surprising that many pro-Commune texts usually ignored insurgent women, and anti-Commune literature depicted them as unnatural, wild, evil, or insane.[56] This fate befell Louise Michel when, in 1890, she was arrested again and hospital doctors declared her insane and threatened to have her committed to an asylum.[57] For having "violated" many of the lines of political demarcation of dominion relations, Louise Michel was pushed to the margins of those dichotomies, and both her sexuality and rationality were impugned. Similarly, the Communards, after being slaughtered, were downgraded to inferior, pathologically criminal human beings.[58] Nothing is worse than when a social order, raised to a natural order, is questioned by subjects who are not authorized to act. These subjects change the political grammar so that their language becomes incomprehensible, "irrational."

It is not the request for recognition or inclusion that provokes scandal, because that request is part of the binary code of the political, trying at best to make itself more inclusive and dynamic. What is deemed foolish, as Hobbes had put it, is considering it rational and just to break covenant.[59] It is foolish because, according to the modern political theory of social contract, the breakdown of the state machine means falling back into the state of nature, in which individuals conflict with each other in a war of everyone against everyone. But the Communards, like the *Sans-culottes* before them and the Russian workers and peasants later, had shown that beyond the state there is no necessary war of all against all but, rather, a rich articulation of rearranged institutions building on the enormous material of alternative traditions of modernity. This network of local authorities often conflicts with the state.

The mistake, very often made by the Left, is to consider the state a progressive element and the local authorities as regressive. Both of these assumptions are wrong. And not because of the fact that the state can pursue authoritarian politics that the local authorities try to resist, as is the case of sanctuary cities in the United States. Those assumptions are wrong because they are missing the main point, which is that the tension between these two elements is what is of importance. This tension can take various forms, but it is from the tension that the possibility of democratic politics opens up. In this sense, Machiavelli wrote that "the multitude is wiser and more constant than is a prince."[60] In fact, the desire of the latter is to dominate others and the private good; the desire of the multitude is "not to be dominated; and, in consequence, a greater will to live free."[61] This does not mean that the multitude cannot be cruel. It certainly can be. But that is not the point. The issue is that politics has to do with risk. Machiavelli's point of view is all the more interesting because it comes at a historical moment when the modern state was yet to be born, and for that to happen, Machiavelli freed the forces of politics. He tried to revitalize the communal forms of free government without extinguishing the tension between the power of government and that of the multitude. This tension is reopened every time the state exposes its crisis. It resurfaced in 1871. And it is resurfacing now, in the crisis of the nation-state. Machiavelli returns to speak to us as a theorist of the elements of politics before they configured themselves in the form of the state—that is, while they were still open to different outcomes from that of the modern representative state.

UNIVERSALIZING POLITICS, OR THE IMPERATIVE MANDATE

"The aims of the Club Communal are the following: . . . To recall our mandatories, . . . to uphold the sovereign of the people, who must never renounce their right to supervise the actions of their mandatories. People, govern yourself directly, through political meetings, through your press."[62] Communards did not usually designate those they elected as either *deputies* or *representatives*. Those terms, which are still in use today, denote the representative system; they were utilized in the Empire and in 1848. The Commune broke with the representative system both in theory and in practice. In the language of the Communards, the elected were called *mandatories* (*mandataires*) and the link between them and the people was the *imperative mandate* (*mandat impératif*).⁶³

Eugène Varlin, who supervised the relations between the Commune and the workers' associations, had repeatedly emphasized that a republic, to be such, must take the people's sovereignty seriously. And taking the people's sovereignty seriously meant that "the right to revoke leaders or mandatories is an absolute right, in the republic, for electors . . . , the Assembly declares its intent to claim the absolute right to appoint its chiefs and revoke those who have lost the trust of those who elected them."⁶⁴ Varlin's is not a lone voice. Arthur Arnould defined himself a "partisan of the imperative mandate," and saw in the mandate the principle of "subordination of power to collectivity the principle of the transformation of the state."⁶⁵ If these were some of the voices of the Communal Council, from below the clubs pressed for the implementation of that principle. "The aims of the Club Communal are as follows: . . . To recall our mandatories. . . . [T]o uphold the sovereignty of the people, who must never renounce their right to supervise the action of their mandatories."⁶⁶ For the *clubistes*, democracy in action was exercised "through political meetings" and the press.⁶⁷ As Gustave Lefrançais, member of the Communal Council for the 4th *arrondissement*, observed, "true democracy" implies a responsibility that is greater for the elector than for the elected. In fact, it is the elector who is sovereign over the mandatory, and is therefore responsible to his fellow citizens for the quality of the administration and institutions.⁶⁸ True democracy brings about a relationship between the governed and those who govern that is different in nature from that of a representative democracy. In the latter, the representative has free mandate, since what he is required to represent is the nation's undivided totality. Democracy here means the power of the *demos*, which is the nation in its unity. True democracy is something different. It redefined the relationship between the governed and those who govern through the mediation of assemblies that elected their mandatories and had the responsibility of monitoring their actions and, if necessary, recalling them.[69] In this way, responsibility opened out horizontally and vertically. The mandatories were no less responsible to the assemblies of the *arrondisssements* than the assemblies were accountable to other citizens gathered together in clubs and associations. Indeed, among the inalienable rights of the "sovereignty of the electors" there was the right to "demonstrate and freely exchange ideas through speeches and writings, as well as the right to form groups in order to achieve the realization of what seems to them more favorable for the public good."[70] The public good took shape at the bottom and was then translated into legal language by those who were in government. The bond between them was made up of the imperative mandate, through which insurgent institutions controlled the actions of the government.

The Communards were dismantling the pillars of the modern representative state, one by one. They considered "that the Republic is more important than majority rule and therefore does not recognize the right of majorities to deny the principle of popular sovereignty either directly, by plebiscite, or indirectly, through an assembly representing these majorities."[71] Communards were suspicious of both the representative system and the rule of majority, which had not prevented Louis Napoleon from transforming the Republic into a dictatorship, and today does not prevent the election of an authoritarian or racist leader. For the Communards, neither were the representatives released from the mandate and control of the assemblies, nor was universal suffrage to be understood as a panacea against tyranny. In a document of March 16, *l'Ouvrier de l'avenir*, it was expressly stated that "universal suffrage is nothing but a universal absurdity."[72] Four-fifths of the votes, continues the document, only express an opinion, and nothing guarantees that this opinion is even right. It was not the extension of suffrage that was questioned but, rather, its political depletion. By political depletion I mean its becoming mere procedure, as if the procedures were a guarantee against authoritarian degeneration of power. This point of view proves inadequate today from at least two perspectives. Many authoritarian populist movements have risen to power through normal electoral procedures. And while respecting those procedures, which provide for a state of emergency, they carry out actions that sometimes culminate in a forced change of the constitution. And further, not only is the constitutional armor inadequate to preserve the formal democracy from authoritarian abuses.; it also brings about the neutralization of democratic excess that instead could give rise to a real democratic praxis, in which individuals never act alone, but in groups and associations. This is the same democratic excess that the Terror of the French Revolution suppressed in the name of national sovereignty. When power is not monopolized by the state but, instead, is distributed in a plurality of municipalities and assemblies with specific political authority, new institutions arise, alternative to those of the nation-state. Such is the case of the imperative mandate.

In the Western tradition, the imperative mandate is usually rejected on the basis of two arguments. One is technical, the other is logical: (a) the decision-making time of the imperative mandate is considered too long, while the state tends to accelerate decision-making, even at the cost of a loss of democracy; (b) in the era of the nation-state, it is the nation as a whole that must be represented, and no single sovereign entity. If the parliament is the deliberative assembly of one whole nation, the representation of the unity of the nation is not compatible with the imperative mandate, which is instead the expression of local sovereign assemblies and districts. Indeed, according to Schmitt, the imperative mandate "contradicts the idea of political unity as well as the fundamental presupposition of democracy." The "deputy's dependence on the instructions and directions of the voters would, indeed, eliminate the representative character of the popular assembly" with the additional

THE INSTITUTIONS OF INSURGENT UNIVERSALITY | 93

necessary consequence of the "introduction of a special procedure of continuous voting in every electoral district, . . . but not by the people as unity."[73] If in fact sovereignty resides in the people, who exercise it through their representatives, then the will of the people (collective singular) can only emerge from the deliberations of deputies pursuant to legislative procedures defined by the constitution. In order for the state law to be issued in the name of the sovereign people, and therefore oblige every individual to obey, it is necessary to replace imperative mandate with free mandate, so that each deputy represents the entire nation and the majority decision expresses the will of the nation.

The tradition of the imperative mandate follows a different trajectory.

French Constitution November 4, 1848	*Declaration to the French People, April 19, 1871*[74]	*Manifesto of the 20 Arrondissements, 1871*	*French Constitution, 1958*
Chap. II: The French Republic is democratic, one and indivisible. Chap. I, Art. 1. **Sovereignty resides in the totality of the French citizens**. It is inalienable and imprescriptible.	"Unity such as has been imposed on us up to this day by the Empire, the monarchy and parliamentarianism, is nothing but despotic, arbitrary and onerous centralization."	"**The accountability of the mandatories**, and therefore the **perpetual possibility to recall them**." "**The imperative mandate**, namely specifying and limiting the power and mandate of mandatories."[75]	Art. 1. France shall be an indivisible, secular, democratic and social Republic. Art 3. **National sovereignty shall vest in the people**, who shall exercise it through their representatives and by means of referendum.

French Constitution November 4, 1848	Declaration to the French People, April 19, 1871[74]	Manifesto of the 20 Arrondissements, 1871	French Constitution, 1958
No individual nor any part of the people can claim for themselves the exercise thereof.	"The choice by election or competition, with the responsibility and the permanent right of control and removal, of the communal magistrates and functionaries of all sorts."		
Art. 34. The members of the National Assembly do not represent the departments, which elect them, but **the whole of France.** Art. 35. They cannot receive **imperative mandate.**	"The **permanent participation of citizens in communal affairs** by the free expression of their ideas and the free defense of their interests"		No section of the people, nor any individual, may arrogate to itself, or to himself, the exercise thereof. Art. 27. **No Member shall be elected with any imperative mandate.**

THE INSTITUTIONS OF INSURGENT UNIVERSALITY | 95

French Constitution November 4, 1848	Declaration to the French People, April 19, 1871[74]	Manifesto of the 20 Arrondissements, 1871	French Constitution, 1958
Art. 36. The persons of the representatives of the people are inviolable. They cannot be questioned, accused nor condemned, at any time, for opinions that they have expressed win the National Assembly.	"The communal Revolution, begun by the popular initiative on March 18, inaugurates a new political era, experimental, positive, and scientific."		

The Declaration to the French People (April 19) emphasizes the spirit of the mandate: "The choice by election or competition, with the responsibility and the permanent right of control and revocation, of magistrates and communal functionaries of all orders."[76] This control had to be exercised through the "permanent intervention of the citizens in communal affairs," not as single individuals but as groups, clubs, associations, and cooperatives. The Commune's program announced, indeed, the autonomy of the cities and federations against centralization and the imperative mandate against the representation of the nation. This legacy related to and reactivated the chances missed in 1792–93.

We must not imagine that this new institutional structure was created by a stroke of lightning on March 18. Indeed, the imperative mandate is not an invention of the Communards, but it had already been evoked during the French Revolution and would be reactivated in the Russian Revolution. The phrase began to circulate already in the Red clubs during the siege of Paris.[77] The imperative mandate harked back to traditions that, since the fourteenth century, had seen guilds and municipalities oppose the process of concentration of power that gave rise to the absolute monarchy and finally to the modern representative state. The Communards were aware of this when they referred to the "communal idea of the 12th Century" to reactivate the "legacy of the ancient communes and the French Revolution."[78] In this way they took inspiration from a tradition dating back to the insurgency of Étienne Marcel in 1355–1358 and the potentialities left untapped in the revolutionary trajectory from 1789 to 1793. The provost of the Parisian merchants, Étienne Marcel, opposed royal power with self-government of the people and a "confederation of good cities."[79] In the medieval practice of imperative mandate, the instructed delegate acted as a local agent and not as a representative of the nation as a whole;[80] in Althusius, the imperative mandate and the right of resistance were designed in relation to associations and orders, the ephors, who exercised the *jus gladii*, the "right of the sword."[81] This means, historically, that the process of accumulation of political power in the hands of the state or a monarch had not yet neutralized the particular authority of guilds and corporations, as was the case in subsequent European history.

We can see the birth of two separate and contrasting traditions: on the one hand, there is an individualistic conception of society and the nation; on the other, a symbiotic conception according to which members of the city are groups—that is, "diverse associations of families and collegia," not individuals.[82] In the latter perspective, the "right of the sword" exercised by the ephors is the result of a different political conception, according to which the people have an already constituted reality, in their assemblies and associations, before those who govern. The right of resistance is neither an individual right nor the right of the people as an abstract entity, but the right of the ephors "to resist and impede the tyranny of a supreme magistrate who abuses the rights of sovereignty, and violates or wishes to take away the authority of the body of the commonwealth."[83] In early modernity, Althusius wanted to preserve the plurality of political communities constituting the universal commonwealth against the rise of territorial absolutism of the modern state.[84] To speak of imperative mandate in this perspective is to speak of control and the right of resistance of the governed against those who govern. In reality, it is precisely the dualism between the governed and those who govern that is being questioned by the reactivation of the imperative mandate tradition. The political structure goes from dual to tripartite, or plural. This means that the politics of the governed rearticulates the government *of* the governed in both senses of the genitive: objective and subjective. It is government exercised over the governed but also, at the same time, government exercised by the governed, through their assemblies and associations, over those who govern.

Today, it is clear that the protest of the governed can at most exert some pressure on the government, but it does not change the dualistic structure that underlies the representative state. Communard politics instead shows a third way, which is articulated around the double meaning of the genitive of government of the governed. The political theory of the Commune can be retraced from the associations and clubs that rearticulated the power of the Communal Assembly in a structure that was at least tripartite: (1) the Communal Council at the Hôtel de ville, which represented the central power; (2) the *arrondisssements* in which the people's sovereignty was actively in force; and (3) clubs, associations, popular organizations, squares, meeting halls—in other words, all the forms in which the people gave themselves organization and voice.[85] The clubs were connected to the vigilance committees, which were connected to the administration of Paris.[86] Power flowed in both directions, from top to bottom and from bottom to top, in the political practice of everyday life. Sovereignty was distributed on all three levels. And in this practice, the democratic excess is articulated as an unstable and often confrontational balance between the parties.

It was not enough to say that no particular group could or should become universal. This happened constantly. After all, even the Communal Council often made this claim, but it was blocked by the tension with the plurality of clubs and associations. For instance, the twentieth *arrondissement* tended not only to influence the Government of National Defense but also to replace it.[87] This dynamic between powers that reciprocally limit each other does not correspond to the modern constitutional division of powers. In the latter case, national sovereignty remains undivided and only constitutionally articulated according to different functions of the state: the executive, legislative, and judicial. Here the principle of unity of the nation is taken as a principle of the state. In the case of the Commune, there is a plurality of powers, and unity ceases to be political dogma. What the Communards share is a political space, and not an abstract national belonging. This belonging always needs the identity/exclusion duo, whereas the Communards were experimenting with new ways of universal access to politics—ways not based on that binary opposition.

From excerpts of documents that we have examined, it becomes clear how the imperative mandate constituted, using the words of Arnould, a principle of the "transformation of the state," a principle that does not put to sleep the democratic excess.

UNIVERSALIZING PROPERTY, OR *ÉGALITÉ*

The universalization of power would have been interrupted halfway without the universalization of property. During the French Revolution there took place, on a linguistic, legal, and institutional level, a huge effort to eliminate the exercise of *dominium* over men by authorities who were not those of the sovereign nation. It should be remembered that, from a historical point of view, concepts such as "a subject with individual rights" and "private property" did not exist in the medieval legal structure, which instead was articulated in an order of cooperatives and guilds, so that which in modern language we call the right to property (*dominium*) was instead associated with an authoritative sphere, be it a guild or a house.[88] It would be improper to project modern and postrevolutionary concepts such as "private" and "public" into the context of the Ancien Régime, in which the concept of *dominium* included both "private" ownership and "public" power. There were, in fact, in the feudal order multiple strata of lords who exercised authority, regulatory powers, and police functions over their tenants. This system survived in Prussia and elsewhere until the early nineteenth century and even later.[89] The revolution worked a two-pronged process that can be conceptually exemplified as the "great demarcation" of the concept of *dominium*.[90] The starting point was the attack on the feudal order celebrated in the decree of the night of August 4, 1789.[91] Through the abolition of private ownership of public power, a removal of power from the sphere of property was also carried out. Property progressively became private property in the hands of private individuals: they were private because they were deprived of all authority. The other prong of *dominium*, power, was in fact taken out of the hands of the *corps* and concentrated in undivided, national sovereignty. The New Regime had to avoid the accommodation of *corps* of any sort since, as Mirabeau posited, "individuals are the only elements of any society whatsoever."[92] The birth of the modern concept of private property took place together with the process of singularization and concentration of political power in the nation-state. From this process there emerged the modern demarcations between the political and the social, state and society, sovereignty and ownership, the public and private. It was through the elimination of "privately" owned public power that the modern citizen was built, "an individual rather than a collective entity."[93] To reactivate the political nature and authority of the groups and assemblies in the spirit of the communal republicanism of insurgent universality, it was necessary to deconstruct the demarcation and then address the issue of private property. It was clear that the republican political form and modern relations of private property were two intertwined aspects. What was less clear was how to reconfigure that link. Once again, this is an issue that has been left open since 1793.

In *Les Éléments du républicanisme*, Jacques-Nicolas Billaud-Varenne had pointed out the question of the division of property: "Since property is the fulcrum upon which civil society turns, not only must the system of government guarantee each person the peaceful enjoyment of what is his, but this system must be set up in such way as to establish, as far as possible, a division of property which, if not absolutely equal, is, at the very least, one that revolves around a common mean."[94] Indeed, he continued, the right to property "is not sacrosanct, and cannot be considered to be sacrosanct, when viewed from the perspective of the common good which is being undermined by a handful of individuals."[95] For Billaud-Varenne, the common good was to be considered greater than the right to property and a serious agrarian reform should have accompanied true republican politics. Similarly, John Oswald maintained that "the land must be cultivated in common" or equally divided among the members of the nation.[96] Billaud-Varenne and Oswald, expressing the common feeling of the *Sans-culottes*, sought a different solution to the destruction of feudal relations and the birth of modern private-property relations—a solution that did not impose absolute individual private ownership on land and the depoliticization of the social. Their attempt, interrupted by the Terror and then by the Napoleonic course of the state trajectory, was taken up by the Communards.

Billaud-Varenne was mainly interested in the agrarian question and the distribution of land against the accumulation of land ownership. The Communards also pointed a finger at the link between property relations and relations of dominion in the productive and reproductive spheres. It was clear to them that the relations of personal dominion had not been reset in the social sphere. It was clear that the legal relationship, which put the seller and the buyer of labor power on the same level, concealed the asymmetries of power, which the Communards instead questioned in their daily practice. But the Communards went much further. When they questioned the centralization of state power, they did not merely oppose a general decentralization of power in the different administrative spheres. The Communards arrived at the root of the "great demarcation." They questioned the individualistic foundation of rights and freedom, exercising the rights of groups; they questioned national sovereignty, exercising power in their assemblies and clubs; they questioned the principle of political representation, exercising the imperative mandate. To disassemble the great demarcation, the Communards looked to traditional forms of communal freedom and ownership, not to bring them back to life as if for display in a museum but, rather, to recombine them in the present as alternatives to it.

"The social revolution," wrote Arnould, "must have a collective character, that is to say it must proceed with the restitution of the soil and all the instruments of labor, capital or otherwise into the hands of the collective."[97] The term "restitution," used by Arnould, is important. The same term was used in relation to sovereignty, finally returned to the hands of the people.[98] Now, in relation to property, the issue is the organization of a new property regime, and not the expropriation of property in favor of the state or the corporations. Putting property into the hands of the co-operatives does not solve the question of private property; it only changes the owner. Restitution to the collective means doing the opposite of accumulation. In this sense, the Commune intended "to universalize property."

There is the dominant trajectory of Western modernity characterized by the centuries-old war against communities, collective possession, corporations, and particular authorities. Marx told this story in his chapter on original accumulation. Its declaration of victory is the Code Civil of 1804, which in Article 544 formalized the new relations of private property and the new anthropology of a possessive individual: "Ownership is the right to enjoy and dispose of things in the most absolute manner." Immediately after the Coup of 18 Brumaire, Napoleon promised: "We will have a republic founded on liberty, equality, property, and the sacred principles of national representation."[99] Fraternity was replaced by property, and the conception of national representation was raised to the rank of sacred principle. But the trajectory of individual private property continued to conflict with that of collective possession. Louis Napoleon, who through dictatorial power imposed a crash course in urban, financial, and agricultural synchronization-modernization on France, in his address to the people for the election of the president of the French Republic under the Constitution of 1848 stated:

> I pledge beforehand my co-operation with any strong and honest government which shall re-establish order in principles as well as in things; which shall efficiently protect religion, our families, and our properties—the eternal basis of every social community.
>
> To protect property is to maintain the inviolability of the fruits of every man's labours; it is to guarantee the independence and the security of possession, an indispensable foundation for all civil liberties.[100]

Two elements are worth noting here. First, private property is elevated to "the eternal basis of every social community." Similarly, Adolphe Thiers, in 1848, had published a pamphlet on *The Right of Property*, in the third chapter of which, entitled "On the Universality of Property," he intended to show that "property is a permanent fact, universal in all times and in all countries."[101] Property was presented as a "general and universal fact," a metahistorical and geographically universal. We can see at work here an episode of the ideological war against common possessions. This ideology is rooted in the tendency of modern universal history to subsume every historical-concrete instance displacing the differences in the historical temporal axis of the trajectory of Western modernity, and turning them into backward or residual forms, which are therefore worthy of being wiped out.

There is a second noteworthy element of Louis Napoleon's speech that deserves to be highlighted. It consists of the link between property and "civil liberties"—a link already established by the Code Civil: "Property belongs to the citizen, empire to the sovereign."[102] This is the overall sense of the code, according to the words of the greatest of its architects, Jean-Étienne-Marie Portalis. And this is the sense of the dual process of accumulation: the concentration of power in the hands of the state destroyed the remaining authorities of civil society by depoliticizing the social and individualizing individuals. Citizens were subsumed in the category of owner and their lives were governed by civil law. Modern property relations could assert themselves only by destroying customs that had real authority over the regulation of land use. With the revolution, the great enterprise of private ownership was brought to completion by destroying the existing traditions, such as compulsory rotation, which prevented the "owners from varying at will the products and the cultivation of their lands."[103] It was the Constituent Assembly, on June 5, 1791, that gave the individual owners the freedom to use and abuse property.

The tradition to which the Communards instead referred transcended the binary code of the individual/state and, in general, the great demarcation. The question concerned the change in direction with respect to the trajectory of the dual accumulation of power and capital. The Communards did not contest the capacity of ownership but, rather, the absoluteness of the right to property. In legal terms, they did not contest the *ius utendi* but, instead, the *ius abutendi*. In 1840, in his famous text *What Is Property?* Proudhon took inspiration from Article 544 of the Code Napoléon to attack a conception of property that recognizes in "the proprietor an absolute right over things."[104] According to Proudhon, this tradition dates back to Roman law, which "defined property as the right to use and abuse a thing within the limits of the law—*jus utendi et abutendi re sua, quatenus juris ratio patitur*."[105]

Proudhon stresses that this limit only works for the defense of property rights, in order to prevent the domain of one proprietor from interfering with that of another proprietor. While accepting the interpretation of that time, which projected the modern right of property in Roman law, Proudhon has the correct intuition. It must, however, be stressed that the Latin expression *jus utendi et abutendi* does not exist in Roman law. It is a modern invention that Jean-Etienne-Marie Portalis, the author of Article 544 of the Civil Code, took from a work of 1772 by Robert Joseph Pothier,[106] and which clearly shows the entirely ideological tendency to project the modern individualistic conception of the right of ownership in Roman law, which instead contemplated a rich and stratified limitation on the right of ownership.[107] It is an ideology that, on the one hand, legitimizes the absolute right of property by inscribing it in the long term, and on the other hand, works polemically against the medieval structure in which ownership is vertically split between different personalities, neither of which has the full right of disposal.[108]

Proudhon goes back in history in search of a different genealogy. He contrasts the dominant understanding with a different interpretation of what Cicero has to say about property when he compares the earth to a great theater: "though the theatre is a common place (*commune*), yet it is correct to say that the particular seat a man has taken (*occuparit*) belongs to him."[109] In this way, Proudhon accepts the right of possession, but limits it to use and need. It makes no sense that someone, in a theater, appropriates "at the same time one place in the pit, another in the boxes, and a third in the gallery."[110] In this way, the occupant, for Proudhon, is a "possessor or usufructuary, a condition that excludes proprietorship."[111] The right of usufruct is regulated by use and need, which varies over time and according to the number of occupants.

Proudhon did not invent a tradition of possession as usufruct, but referred to it to indicate an alternative to modern property relations. So did the Communards. In this way, the question of ownership was not defined either in terms of expropriation—that is, of a change in hands of ownership from one owner to another—nor in terms of a simple limitation of *jus abutendi*. In general, one could say that "the Commune explicitly refused measures of expropriation."[112] This did not mean in any way that the Commune had not "contested the general rights of property,"[113] because by reconfiguring the right as a right of groups, rather than of the mere individual, the Communards were experiencing new property relations, and not simply handing over ownership. The new property relations were being defined parallel to the principle of autonomy of the associations practiced in politics. The Artists' Federation claimed to apply to the theaters the regime of cooperative associations: "It is a duty of the present theater administration to transform the system of private ownership and privilege into a system of co-operative associations to be run entirely by the performers themselves."[114] The Communards insisted on the use, which at the same time configured rights and the delimitation of the right of property. And that meant at least two things: for instance, if there had been the requisition of empty apartments and closed-down workshops, this had happened not by virtue of the logic of expropriation but because property was not conceived as an absolute right—that is, as the right to abuse, or leave entirely unused, the goods of the collective. The owners could continue to have ownership, but their right to property was delimited by levels of use by the collective. In the case of theaters, the owners could continue to be the owners, but this gave them neither the absolute right to decide what to put on stage nor, all the more so, the right to exploit the actors. The Communards' democracy in action redefines property relations, superimposing on the unidimensional world of modern individual law, in which the single owner's will is in relation to the thing, a pluridimensional and vertical division of ownership, in which the single levels correspond to the different uses of the thing and to different legal relationships that, in relation to the thing itself, mutually limit each other.

To state the importance of this reconfiguration of property relations, reference was made to the fundamental issue of land.

"We want land, which is not the product of any human labor, but only the raw material given freely to everyone by nature, to not be the property of any individuals, but to become the inalienable dominion of humanity."[115] The Communards thus broke the appropriative link based on labor and glorified by John Locke. By making land an inalienable dominion of humanity, they limited its use by any one person, who was merely a usufructuary; and at the same time, they redefined it based on a multiplicity of layers of use. If the expropriation discourse is still inside the logic of modern property law, and all it does is change the owner, the restitution of property into the hands of the collective is grounded on a different practice of freedom, law, and politics. Just as with the reactivation of the imperative mandate, the Communards did not entirely invent new institutions but, rather, took them from the same traditions as the *Sans-culottes* had. Indeed, the *Sans-culottes'* view on property, according to which they considered merchants, farmers, and shopkeepers "trustees of their lands and goods, rather than absolute proprietors,"[116] had more affinity with the communal-regulated property of the Ancien Régime than with the private individual property of the Declaration of the Rights of Man and Citizen. In fact, during the revolution, it was the *Sans-culottes* and the peasantry who tried to curb the birth of modern property relations.

Following the Communards, we need to reimagine a different relationship with property, which reactivates in a completely new configuration the "archaic" conception of *dominium utile*.[117] The reference to *utilitas* meant a limit and a content to the property relation that could be not understood as an abstract relation between mere juridical subjects. "Archaic" forms, rather than being destroyed and subsumed in the conceptual framework of individual property rights, were reconfigured, starting from the conflict with dominant modernity. These were forms that have continued to exist for many centuries and that have defined not only the common use of land but also the ways in which the owner could and should use the land. Land, because it is considered a common good, was also subject to strict regulations by the community and corporations. These customs had to be respected unless you wanted to end up with peasant revolts that were difficult to manage in the absence of a monopoly on state force. Two different conceptions of rights and possession were at war with each other: individual rights against collective rights; the use of land according to traditions that preserved it in view of future generations against the right to make the most of it. In other words, the conflict was between the forms of collective ownership by the "incessant concatenation of generations," on the one hand, and the nascent conception of property for the exclusive use of individuals, who use it according to their own will, on the other.[118] The establishment of this second juridical framework signals a real reversal: from a *rei-centric* relationship, in which primacy is given to the thing (*res*), to the primacy of the individual exercising an unlimited and illimitable right over nature. It is a new anthropological and political model that gives rise to possessive individualism.[119] The destruction of community bonds that freed individuals from the ancient hierarchical ties and made them formally free subjects is not the result of a linear development that can be reconstructed by placing theological and political conceptions in historical succession. It is, rather, the result of centuries of struggle by subordinates against feudal hierarchies. But these struggles did not have as their objective either private property, or the state, or the transformation of the servants into formally free workers. Rather, the state, as a process of concentration of political power, was the way in which the ruling classes reorganized the social and political fabric, and neutralized the demands for freedom and equality of the oppressed by channeling them into the form of a legal person of the modern state. In this way, two temporal layers were differentiated: one characterized by egalitarian instances and the communal freedom of the oppressed classes; the other by the subsumption of these instances in the modern juridical machine, which individualized people, transforming them into formally free, equal, and proprietary subjects. These two layers have continued to flow atop each other, generating conflicts that reach us today. Marc Bloch reports a case that happened in 1864: "Dupin found in *Coutume de Nivernais* by Gui Coquille some words that shook him deeply.... [T]he old jurist of the Renaissance had written: 'Before the ownership of things was distinct, everything was public and common.... Therefore one can say that the lord of a hay field was not its lord in full ownership, but only to use it in the forms according to which habit gave him right and license.' Similar ideas, comments Dupin, 'would seem a bit socialist if isolated from other doctrines of this author, which are essentially conservative.'"[120] Bloch's comment is that this is a "misleading antithesis."[121] In fact, the antithesis between socialist and conservative makes sense only in a unilinear view of historical time. What is at stake is the modern reconfiguration of the common-possession tradition as an alternative to modern private-property relations. In a certain way, Dupin was right in saying that, in that description of proto-modern relations of property, there echoes a socialist conception, but only in the sense that their not being entirely modern leaves open a different political trajectory of modernity.

The Communards had not had time to develop a theory and practice of the new property relations. Its positions were diverse: the Club de la Révolution hoped that the Commune would deliver the factories to working cooperatives;[122] a reader of the newspaper *Le Cri du Peuple* reassured owners that the workers would defend the goods of their class enemies;[123] meanwhile, the artists, who defined theatre as a means of popular education, asked "to transform the system of private ownership and privilege into a system of co-operative associations wholly in the hands of the performers."[124] The common good had returned to being greater than the right to property, which ceased to be absolute. Today, this tradition deserves our attention. The concentration of wealth in a few hands requires us to rethink a limit on property.[125] The destruction of natural resources and the environment requires us to consider a different relationship between the use of goods and property relations. Faced with the urgency of contemporary problems, there resurfaces the contemporaneity of the *Sans-culottes*' and the Communards' attempts to practice different property relations with respect to those imposed in European modernity and that the Napoleonic Civil Code had formalized in Article 544. In light of those attempts, which harked back to traditional forms of collective ownership, often considered archaic or residual, it is the modern concept of private property that is obsolete. The legacy reactivated by the Communards shows us a way to rearticulate property without putting it into the hands of the state. Limiting property abuse is not a matter of state legislation but, rather, a democratic articulation of the pluralism of powers.

For the Communards, discussing property relations meant discussing the relations of dominion in the sphere of production and reproduction. It meant calling into question the role of women in society and workers in production. During a meeting in the women's club of the Trinité, the president, a Polish woman by the name of Lodoiska, read the point that was on the agenda: "How is society to be reformed?"[126] And the women's answer was that "the social disease that must be cured first is exploitation by the employers" since there are "bosses who treat the worker as a producing machine."[127] The question was echoed in a public statement of the Central Committee of the Women's Union for the Defence of Paris and the Aid to the Wounded, the famous organization set up by Elisabeth Dmitrieff, which asked for:

a. The diversification of work within each trade to counter the harmful effects on body and mind of continually repeating the same manual operation;
b. A reduction of working hours to prevent physical exhaustion leading to loss of mental faculties;
c. The abolition of all competition between men and women.

The remedy presented by the Communards was in line with the principle of the Commune to universalize power and property: "Let the workers form co-operative associations, let them organize their labour collectively and they will live happily."[128] It is evident that the cooperative associations of workers, in making decisions on the organization of work, limited the power of the owner over the means of production. Indeed, Article 1 of the regulation submitted to the Paris Commune by the workers of the Louvre workshop, an armament factory cooperative, stated: "The manager will be elected by all the workers and will be liable to be revoked if found guilty of failing in his duty. His mandate consists in hearing the reports of the shop foreman, the charge-hand and the workers, and in submitting them to the Director of Artillery Supplies."[129] Again, property was not taken out of the hands of the owners, but they had no right to dispose of it according to their will or to exploit workers. Factories were considered common goods, and it was up to the community, organized into cooperatives and associations, to regulate their use. The decree of April 16 entitled workers "to take over any abandoned workshops to form co-operative associations to start production up again."[130] The decree, however, in accordance with the labor-movement tradition, "was a co-operative measure, not one of nationalization."[131] The factories were not expropriated. Abandoned factories were taken under the control of associated workers; likewise, abandoned houses.

The Communards posed a question, as timely today as then, regarding the limits of the compatibility between democracy and the absolute right of property. It is a limit that is not up to the state to establish. The Communards wanted to leave the state out of the relations between social parts. For them, weakening the monopoly of state violence, and decentralizing its functions and reorganizing sovereignty on an associative basis, meant accepting the possibility of conflict. For example, during the debate on bakers' night work, Billiory stated that he was "opposed to all these rules and regulations you [Vermorel] seem to want to institute.... Let the workers themselves defend their interests in relation to the owners; today they are powerful enough to act as they wish."[132] Many Communards opposed a decree banishing night work because they rejected state intervention and believed that the use of centralized power would have hindered the independent people from taking action. Arthur Arnould, who was a member of the Communal Council, wrote against the decree on night work stating, "it is up to the bakery workers to find an agreement and to refuse that work."[133] There exist power relationships, and therefore also different perspectives on what is right with respect to those relationships; hence, the conflict is a dimension of politics. It is important to point out that the Commune was not a transparent social form in itself, in which the people lived harmoniously without conflict. Conflict can take different forms, but it cannot be eliminated. As long as human beings continue to question what is right and wrong, the possibility of disagreement and conflict will always arise.

THE UNIVERSAL REPUBLIC, OR *FRATERNITÉ*

1. "*France is dead, long live humanity!*" This is how Jules Nostag, pseudonym for Gaston Buffier, ended his article in the journal *La Révolution Politique et Sociale*.[134] But do not misunderstand. The way the Communards intended the word *humanity* is not abstract. Neither is the Universal Republic. It is not a matter of contrasting the universal of the nation with another universal—that is, humanity. What is at stake is a different conception of universality that is not grounded in polemical, existential opposition. There is a conception of the universal that overcomes local differences and produces identity pursuant to its juxtaposition to another universal. In this way, a nation, a religion, or even a class operates as a universal concept, contrasting itself with another nation, religion, or class. The same fate falls to the concept of humanity when it is translated into a political concept: it generates counterconcepts that allow the dehumanization of the enemy and justify a war without mercy against it. This was the spirit of the revolutionary wars against the internal and external enemies of France. In 1794, Barère proclaimed to the Convention that "Humanity involves

exterminating its enemies."[135] Universal concepts were attracted to the gravitational field of the nation-state and became instruments for legitimizing absolute forms of war and exclusion. This deadly trajectory would take place in the twentieth century.

In their approach, the Communards began to dismantle this logic. "What does it matter if a man is born in one place or another?" asked *Le Père Duchêne* in one of its anonymous articles.[136] The fortuity of birth cannot define citizenship, just as skin color or gender cannot define position in the social hierarchy. The Commune was experimenting with the dis-ordering of a social and political order, questioning its relations of dominion. If the French Revolution constitutionalized the principle of modern popular sovereignty by channeling it into the ideas of nation and representation, the legacy of insurgent universality has repeatedly experimented with nonnational paths for exercising sovereignty.

2. *"France is dead."* And with it died the nationalism that was imposed on peoples and individuals. The term *fraternité* that the French Revolution had reactivated from previous traditions had taken on different colorings.[137] *Fraternité* had painted itself with the tricolor to become synonymous with national belonging, unity, and the principle of exclusion. Or it could take the color of the "Sociétés fraternelles des deux sexes," in which men and women gathered, the petty bourgeoisie and the poorest layers of the population. The Communards took inspiration from the second legacy. Along the other path, however, *fraternité* had become synonymous with the nation, and the Universal Republic had degenerated into the Empire. Napoleon was the name that represented this trajectory. And his name was the symbol that was blocking the Communards from jumping toward the other past to be reactivated. For this reason, by destroying the Vendôme column, the Communards could get rid of the symbol that prevented the change of course, as the column represented, in the words of Félix Pyat, "a perpetual insult to one of the three great principles of the French Republic, Fraternity."[138] Similarly, Louise Michel wrote in her memoirs of the Commune that the column was "the symbol of

brute force, the declaration of imperial despotism, in other words a monument that undermined peoples' brotherhood."[139] After the demolition of the column, the Place Vendôme was renamed "Place Internationale."[140] The term was not entirely rhetorical.

3. *"Long live humanity!"* Place Internationale indicated the new symbolic place where the alternative legacy of *fraternité* could be reactivated. With it, the Communards meant to refer to neither an abstract notion of humanity nor the fortuity and naturalness of birth, which "changes our nationality and turns us into friends and enemies."[141] If the dominant political grammar produces identity and national groupings based on the binary opposition of friend/enemy, included/excluded, the grammar of *fraternité* opens up different political possibilities.

The transformation of society that the Communards were experiencing saw the different classes mix and merge: "Aristocracy, bourgeoisie and proletarians, these three fragments of the great human family, have the tendency to reunify. Youth especially does not care for the old barriers and the old days. They pick friends, girlfriends, in all ranks, and are happy."[142] This was also the practice of *fraternité*: a transformation of social and political relations so as to live like brothers. The Communards, while not fearing class conflict, were not at war with the other classes. On March 18, 1871, the proletariat, which had been driven toward the suburbs by Haussmann's urban plan, poured into the center of Paris, took possession of it, and the classes mixed again. Everyday life was interrupted and the people of Paris were reinventing new forms of life and togetherness.

Fraternité, as a politics of fraternization, also redefined the deep sense of the concept of citizenship. In this regard, the Commune had gone beyond both the concept of *jus soli* and that of *jus sanguinis*: citizenship was neither determined by place of birth nor by having one or both parents who were citizens of the state. If nationality, as a result of birth, was defined as an evil to be destroyed,[143] the Commune's plan also provided for the withdrawal of passports and *laissez-passers*[144] in order to actually implement a "universal federation"¹⁴⁵ in which the random circumstance of birth could eventually become insignificant.

The Communards' idea of federalism referred to the tradition of the Universal Republic, whose flag, raised by Anacharsis Cloots, was let fall to the ground in 1793. The Prussian-born Cloots, for his participation in the revolution, was a naturalized Frenchman in 1792 and was elected member of the National Convention in September of the same year. Cloots took the Declaration seriously, and with a focal point of the importance of man with respect to the citizen, he developed a draft of a universal constitution, whose first article reads: "There is only one sovereign: the human kind."¹⁴⁶ The idea, however naïve, was to bring together in departments ("réunir départementalement") all peoples in a federal France.¹⁴⁷ Cloots actually thought that the word "French" should be abandoned in favor of the term "Universal Republic."¹⁴⁸ In this spirit, Cloots advocated overcoming nationality, and on April 26, 1793, he read his proposal to the Convention, which was discussing the new French Constitution. But his emphasis on the unity of human kind, rather than on the nation, went in the opposite direction of the Jacobin plan. His ideas were accused of federalism, and Cloots was arrested and accused by Robespierre of being a foreign agent. He was executed on March 24, 1794. The Universal Republic, together with the 1793 Declaration, was another victim of the Terror.

What is interesting, albeit in Cloots's confused proposal, is that he caught a contradiction between the Declaration of the Rights of Man and the national frame of the state, and he tried to resolve the contradiction by projecting it into a Universal Republic of the rights of man. To him, this move apparently seemed possible by accepting the modern principle of representation which, just as it had made present and visible the unity of the nation, would have had to make present and visible humanity. In doing so, Cloots, replaced one abstract universalism with another—namely, the nation with humanity, implicitly showing, but against his intentions, a common core logic between nationalism and cosmopolitanism. This common dogma became manifest when the revolutionary wars were justified in the name of humanity, temporarily represented by France, against the European monarchies that were criminalized and downgraded to the status of enemies of humanity.[149]

But there is one aspect of Cloots's utopia that could have been developed in a different direction. And it is into the segment of this other tradition that the Communards inserted themselves. The emphasis on the excess of humanity with respect to national citizenship that Cloots had caught in the Declaration of the Rights of Man made him question the nation-state. For Cloots, the term "foreigner" was nothing more than an expression of barbarism, to be abandoned in favor of the "Universal Republic."[150] The Communards, by referring to Cloots and the Universal Republic, did not call attention to his idea of representation extended to all humanity. Indeed, the Communards were suspicious of political representation. What they referenced was the criticism of the nation-state and legal citizenship pursuant to the excess of humanity contained in the Declaration. But the question that was left pending was the orientation to be given to that excess.

Another text from 1793 allows us to look at the Universal Republic from a different perspective. John Oswald, a former lieutenant in the British army who joined the revolution and became an Anglo-French citizen in 1792, wrote a pamphlet in which he proposed an articulated system of self-government of the people. He titled his project: *Le gouvernement du peuple, ou Plan de constitution pour la République universelle*.[151] Oswald, who also organized an army of *Sans-culottes*, firmly believed that each district had the right to an autonomous army and to directly participate in the common affairs of the republic. He esteemed representation as a "magic lantern" that deceives people and steals their sovereignty.[152] He advocated instead an alternative system in which issues previously discussed in the primary assemblies had to be presented by the national assembly to the sections of people assembled in the districts, which had the power to approve or reject laws.[153] In that way, the national assembly would no longer have been the place of representative power, and sovereignty would have been split among the sections of people. Oswald called his project "Universal Republic," without making reference to the state of humankind. This Republic was to be called "Universal" because its citizens were not represented by any national assembly, but they carried out their universal political citizenship in the sections in which they participated despite their nationality, gender, or status. This is the legacy gathered from the Commune, a legacy in which citizenship takes shape by the level of active political participation.[154] The Universal Republic does not extend sovereignty to a world state. The Universal Republic splits sovereignty and breaks the link between national belonging and citizenship. The Commune had abolished the nation, not by decree but in the everyday political practice of a different conception of citizenship: "the title of member of the Commune implicitly means that of citizen."[155] And one was a member of the Commune insofar as one was a member of its associations. To find what is universal in the insurgent practice of the Communards, one does not need to scale up to the global level. One must, instead, look at the institutional forms that took shape in everyday life.

The Commune did not extend the privilege of citizenship, intended as the individual right to have rights, but it changed the logic of it. The logic of political citizenship of insurgent universality is inverted compared to that of citizenship of the modern state: citizens are neither members of the nation nor members of humanity but, rather, members of the Commune, who have rights seeing as they have duties, and have duties because they are part of groups, associations, and clubs. This different foundation of one's rights gives rise to a different way of thinking about politics, which would have facilitated the dialogue on human rights with non-European conceptions, in which *human* does not refer to the single legal person but, rather, to human interaction.[156] It is a different political grammar from the liberal grammar based on the individual and his rights.

For the Communards, making the republic universal was the way of practicing politics from the very particularity of clubs, associations, and cooperatives, which transformed politics into a daily reality for the people. *Universal* means access to politics, and not the abstraction of a political form comprising all of humanity. The important matter was that universal access to politics was not bound to some world citizenship but, instead, to local institutions in which citizenship was practiced politically, not as a request for inclusion or recognition but by questioning the existing relations of dominion. "The Revolution is the liberty and the responsibility of every human being, limited only by the rights of all, without privilege of race or of sex," affirmed André Léo.[157] The destruction of these privileges was not the result of a formal universalism built on some conception of the human being; the privileges of race and sex, along with those of nationality, were called into question starting from a universality that took place in the concrete practice of concrete subjects. The alternative of insurgent universality meant citizenship beginning from the concrete political capacity of individuals, foreign or native, who exercise it in their assemblies and councils. On the contrary, in the modern concept of the nation-state, the exclusion of certain categories of subjects is assumed as a prerequisite. The degree of exclusion is variable and depends on the state and its willingness or need to strengthen the nation's unity and identity. The modern concept of national citizenship is entirely based on exclusion: not only does the national identity of the citizen presuppose the exclusion of other nationalities, but the citizen is also devised as male and as a proprietary subject, and the modern concept of property is absolute and exclusive. Three years after the repression of the Commune, Léon Gambetta expressed this connection in an exemplary way: "Every property that is created is a citizen who is formed."[158] The formation of new national citizens, which for Gambetta was a moral formation, was, therefore, also the formation of a new subjectivity. On the one hand, it required the destruction of proprietary relations based on common usage, both in France and in the colonies. The repression of the Kabyle insurgency of 1871–72 cost the Muslims of eastern Algeria the loss of 574,000 hectares of land, taken from common and traditional uses and subordinated to the modern regime of individual private property. On the other hand, the construction of the modern national citizen required a new attitude, which was cultivated in the various institutions of the state. What the property-owning citizen expected from the state was not the common good but, rather, the security of his property. The revolutionary slogan "Liberté, Égalité, Fraternité" was replaced by *liberté* of enterprise, formal *égalité* of whoever was a French citizen, and *sécurité* guaranteed by the state. *Fraternité*, which Napoleon replaced with property, was dropped and would constitute one of the missed possibilities for universality.

Fraternity, as a politics of fraternization, is not the abstract brotherly love that matters despite the circumstances but, rather, the stimulus to change the circumstances in order to live as brothers. For this reason, *fraternité* is neither a fact nor an irenic ideal but, instead, a political practice that requires a transformation of what exists and of itself. It's a practice that does not exclude the possibility of conflict. In fact, even brothers can be in conflict. But they must learn to live together without invoking the intervention of a third party and without defining boundaries that delimit friends from enemies. The difference with the concept of friendship, often taken as a political paradigm since it is founded on the activity of choice, is that brothers and sisters are not chosen, but they cohabit the same political space. With them, one must learn to coexist. It is the opposite of a passive commonality. It is political practice oriented toward external circumstances, which must be changed in order to live together as brothers and sisters. Humanity is exemplified not in friendship but in fraternity,[159] since fraternity is not sentimental; it makes political demands about the world that we share, without having chosen either our brothers, sisters, or the country in which we live—or the world. What human beings can choose are the political and social conditions in which to live, to change them in the name of what is right and human in human relations. And in doing so, they can cast off the cloak of possessive individualism with which they have been covered. If this cloak has become their habit or, using a Hegelian term, their second nature, the Commune stands before us as a sign indicating a path toward a third possible nature.

4

1918: AN INSURGENT CONSTITUTION

> We must cast off the last traces of slavery in our psychological outlook.... We must become better, purer, more sincere, so that no one should dare say that our insurgency is bringing forth hatred and evil."
>
> —MARIA SPIRIDINOVA, *November 15, 1918, at the All Russian Central Executive Committee of Soviets*[1]

POLITICS BEYOND THE STATE: SOVIET ANOMALIES

The Soviet Constitution was like a path marker, indicating a direction leading out of the French experiments carried out in 1793 and 1871. The Declaration of the Rights of the Toiling and Exploited People was drafted in January 1918, and would become an integral part of the Russian Constitution. The references to both the Paris Commune and to 1793 were constant during discussions on this new constitution.

> The Jacobin constitution of 1793 was the most democratic constitution until today. It was the first to raise its hand against "sacred" bourgeois property; it proclaimed universal suffrage ... and recognized some of the rights of the toilers.... This constitution was never put in effect; the bourgeoisie ... killed it. Nevertheless, it remained as a flag around which all democratic classes rallied,

and when the working classes came forth with revolutionary protests against the shameful domination of the bourgeoisie they shouted for "bread and the constitution of '93." If our constitution were to meet a similar fate . . . the workers of the world would still regard it as their own.[2]

Philosophy has dealt with the French Revolution many times, the Russian Revolution less. Hegel justified the Terror in terms of a philosophy of history, writing that it was "not despotism but tyranny, pure frightening domination. Yet it is necessary and just, insofar as it constitutes and sustains the state as this actual individual."[3] According to Hegel, the Terror was a "necessary and just" domination, and was only overturned when it was no longer needed—that is, when it had fulfilled its historic task: the construction of the modern state. The revolution instead showed a nonstate path of political life.

In these pages I examine the Russian Revolution, not judging it from its outcome, as if the revolutionary trajectory had been teleologically predetermined, but from the possibilities enclosed in its origin. The Soviet experiment is often read through a reverse teleology. The authoritarian outcome is projected onto the origin, so that the missed opportunities of the Russian Revolution, after being blocked a first time by the process of centralizing state power, are cut short a second time by historiography which, proving to be a totalitarian tragedy never to be repeated, cancels the countless possibilities opened up by the revolution. The historiographical intent of this chapter moves in a completely different direction. It is to show the roads not taken, which are scattered throughout what I have called "insurgent universality."

Kant and Hegel reflected on the French Revolution philosophically, and this in turn retroacted on their philosophy. The Russian Revolution, except for rare exceptions, has not been considered philosophically. Ernst Bloch, rightly defined as "the German philosopher of the October Revolution," drew a parallel between Robespierre's Terror and the Moscow trials: "There is a parallel between the shock of then and the shock of today—between the shock regarding the Revolutionary Tribunal and the shock regarding the Moscow trials. . . . The similarity lies in the hurried and almost totally unheralded desertion at the very moment the Revolutionary Tribunal put enthusiasm to the test—to the test of a concept rooted in the concrete."[4] Just as for Kant, the Terror did not extinguish enthusiasm; so for Bloch, the Moscow trials did not suppress enthusiasm for a concept "rooted in the concrete." For Kant, it was the enthusiasm aroused by the idea of freedom: the right of a people to give themselves the most worthwhile constitution. The Russian Revolution showed the right of the masses to change property relations into a democratic practice articulated in the institutions of the soviets. To do this, the Russian Revolution experimented with roads that were different from those taken by the nation-state. Just as Kant defended the principle of the French Revolution, even in the face of the Terror, Bloch defended the principle of the Russian Revolution, even in the face of Stalinist trials. Bloch could perhaps justify his gesture in light of political possibilities that, wrongly, still seemed viable in the 1930s. From the point of view of insurgent universality, the possibilities that had opened up in 1917 closed when the direction taken by the revolution was violently channeled into the dominant modernity characterized by the nation-state and the originary accumulation of capital.

The process of instituting a concentration of power in Russia can be described as "a war against time,"[5] which I have called "synchronization." For the Bolsheviks, the backwardness of Russia imposed "the need to accelerate the pace, the need to skip stages, to use state power abundantly as a key factor in this catching up."[6] According to the unilinear conception of historical time, if compared to the course of Western modernization, the Russian disparity was viewed as a developmental delay to be caught up with in as short a time as possible. In 1931, in his speech to the industrial managers, Stalin stated that, "we are fifty or a hundred years behind the advanced countries. We must make good this distance in ten years. Either we do it, or we shall be crushed."[7] The economic, political, and social structures formed through local self-government were to be dismantled and synchronized in rapid decisions made by the central government. In this way, the state monopolized not only political and economic power but also power over the future and time. Forced collectivization was justified with the need to politically and economically synchronize Russia both internally, destroying the backward rural communes, and externally, aligning Russia with the capitalist course of Western nations.

The space temporalized in the gap between the advanced city and the backward countryside was occupied by equally temporalized social strata: the industrial workers, who accelerated the race for accumulation, and the peasants, who slowed it down. The result of this clash was devastating: the peasants were subjected to a violent depeasantization, aimed at destroying their traditional mentality and their social forms; the workers had to follow a similar course of industrial rationalization. By April 1918, Lenin was pushing for the Taylorist system to be introduced in Russia in order to increase labor productivity as a way to make up for their backwardness: "To raise the productivity of labor it is necessary first of all to safeguard the material bases of large-scale industry. . . . The other condition for increasing the productivity of labor . . . is the raising of workers' discipline, the ability to work, to hustle. It is necessary to introduce into Russia the study and teaching of the Taylor system."[8] At the same time, numerous factories were nationalized and removed from the control of local Soviets. The obsession with rushing ahead in order to accelerate the socialist outcome transformed the state into an extremely centralized apparatus, and shaped industry into a Taylor-disciplined laboratory.

In the second half of 1918, the Bolsheviks attempted to replace millions of small peasant holdings with large-scale collective farms, controlled by the government and integrated into a system of national economy. This violent transformation of the social fabric, along with food-requisitioning campaigns, led to an open war between peasants and Bolsheviks.⁹ The city, where the Bolsheviks were stronger, accelerated the race toward capital accumulation, increasing the tension with the backward temporality of the peasants. The latter resisted, not because of hatred toward the revolution but because of the Red Army, which seemed to them an army of occupation, destroying traditional forms of self-government in order to impose new, centralized forms that were alien to the peasant culture. The clash between temporalities and the war for their synchronization would lead to Lenin's introduction of War Communism and the interlude of the New Economic Policy (NEP), and then to Stalin's own terror.

The war against time extended to the backward-looking cultures, which were to be destroyed in order to inculcate the "new man" with the new discipline of labor time. Local ethnicities and cultures were temporalized within the transition scheme from a "pre-class" to a class society. Where there was no clear class differentiation, that difference was created in the name of progress toward socialism by destroying existing social forms and redefining new hierarchies—even on an ethnic basis. So, Anatolii Skachko took up Stalin's speech to the industrial managers of 1931 and extended it to the small peoples of the north: "if the whole of the USSR . . . needs ten years to run the course of development that took Western Europe fifty to a hundred years, then the small peoples of the north, in order to catch up with the advanced nations of the USSR, must, during the same ten years, cover the road of development that took the Russian people one thousand years to cover, for even one thousand years ago the cultural level of Kievan Rus' was higher than that of the present-day small peoples of the north."[10]

A multiplicity of temporalities was synchronized in order to catch up with the European capitalist countries. In this competition, in the name of socialism, the various temporalities of the Russian mosaic were aligned with the dominant temporality of the state and the capital. As Hegel affirmed for the French Terror, which was dissolved when no longer needed, the same can be said for the red flag raised on the Kremlin: it was lowered when the accumulation of capital and political power reached a sufficient level so as to allow development of capitalist economic relations, and the enormous state apparatus that had put it into operation became superfluous, even an obstacle.

But between 1917 and 1918, alternative ways of modernity were also opened, which would have allowed (a) a different practice of democracy, (b) a different way of understanding citizenship, and (c) a different articulation of property relations. Each of these aspects deserves to be reconsidered today: first, in light of the crisis of representative democracy and the traditional forms of representation and participation that give rise to populism; second, in light of migratory movements that show the inadequacy of the nation-state and the obsessive defense of its borders; and third, in light of an ecological crisis produced by a way of considering the whole planet as material to be endlessly exploited. We must now analyze these aspects, not as isolated issues, but in their mutual implication.

The Constitution of the Russian Socialist Federated Republic of 1918, if compared with any modern Western constitution, presents so many striking anomalies as to make it difficult to use the word *state* for the Soviet experiment. In this respect, it has been claimed that the socialist experiment in Russia did not fail but, rather, that it never happened, because in places where the elements of capitalist society were destroyed, they were replaced with feudal conditions.[11] This way of seeing things, even before taking a political-ideological position, is typical of a historicist way of reading history in linear and progressive terms, whereby that which does not correspond to the normative model of Western European representative democracy can present itself only in terms of a reconfiguration of premodern (feudal) and pre-capitalist elements.

But if we abandon this philosophy of history, then what we see are not residual and premodern elements that prevail, but legal and political anomalies pointing toward another direction of modernity. The German jurist Otto Kirchheimer emphasized some of these anomalies when he observed that Soviet elections are public and denote "a total break with the traditions of parliamentary, individualistic, and liberal concepts."[12] Kirchheimer also pointed out how the Soviet Republic was redefining the concept of sovereignty: no longer was it tied to the idea of a homogenous nation but instead was linked to a class—a political form not limited by nation-state borders but instead was basically universal.[13]

There is another element of interest in Kirchheimer's writings that deserves to be highlighted. For Kirchheimer, the study of the Soviet Republic is interesting in light of the crisis of the rule of law, which was in his time, as well as today, essentially reduced to "legal mechanisms." In substance, Kirchheimer shares Carl Schmitt's criticisms of the rule of law, its depoliticization and transformation into a "mere shell of the state";[14] however, unlike the Nazi jurist, he would see an alternative to the nation-state crisis in the Soviet anomalies.

Kirchheimer gives us the right starting point from which to address the possible Soviet trajectory indicated by the Declaration of the Rights of the Working and Exploited People and by the Constitution of 1918—a trajectory to reconsider and reactivate in light of the current crisis of representative democracy. For Western constitutionalism, power must be checked and constitutionally limited by legal enactment; in the Soviet Republic, power was not limited by the constitution but, rather, by the pluralism of powers exercised by the soviets. In this difference there lie the many *anomalies* of the Soviet Constitution. These are anomalies in the etymological sense of the term: deviations from the rule and from that which is homogeneous.

There are two different conceptions of power at stake: on the one hand, the sovereignty of the people-nation, whose unity is made visible through the mechanism of political representation;[15] and on the other, the powers exercised by classes and strata of the population through their organizations and soviets. The latter frame expresses a kind of democratic excess, which democratic constitutionalism seeks to tame and put to sleep within the political form. The Soviet experiment shows how, in the Russian historical-political situation, the trajectory of modernity could have taken a different direction that was not based on private property and the nation-state; these were established historically through an enormous concentration of power that dismantled intermediate bodies and corporations to give rise to a society of individual, depoliticized atoms. The Soviet experiment, as with those in France in 1793 and 1871, latches onto a different tradition, made up of groups, associations, and councils that practice a plurality of powers. This is the legacy of insurgent universality that resurfaces in the revolutionary ruptures, when the political surface cracks and allows a new dimension of possibilities to be glimpsed between the fissures.

The anomalies of the 1918 Soviet Constitution are not the product of abstract ideological conceptions; they an approximate formalization of the institutional reality brought into being by the soviets. In fact, the soviets were not mere places of public discussion; they were institutions that exercised political power and rearticulated political and social relations, forms of citizenship, and property relations.

The first period of the Russian Revolution was characterized by the rise of new soviets. In 1918, there were about 12,000. There were so many, in fact, that according to a report by the commissariat of the interior, "the whole of Soviet Russia was crumbled across a number of republics . . . almost independent of each other."[16] Labor communes were born, businesses were socialized, taxation was organized locally. One of the first executives of the Commissariat of the Interior wrote that many efforts had to be made, "sometimes with repressive measures, to subordinate to the general Soviet will and to direct in the riverbed of vigorous unitary work the activity of all these Soviet workers and peasants, dispersed in the endless Russian plain."[17] This outlines the alternative that

I want to emphasize: on the one hand, "vigorous unitary work" aimed at building a unified general Soviet will and at centralizing and reorganizing state power; on the other hand, experimentation on a territorial basis, with forms of self-government, soviets, direct democracy, and control and socialization of production. The first constitution (1918) of the Russian Soviet Federative Socialist Republic (RSFSR) was born into the tension between these two principles. Amid this tension, the constitutional anomalies of insurgent universality took shape.

FIRST ANOMALY: WHO ARE THE PEOPLE?

On January 18, 1918, Sverdlov presented to the Constituent Assembly the Declaration of the Rights of the Working and Exploited People: "Just as in the days of the French bourgeois revolution . . . there was proclaimed a Declaration of the Rights of Man and the Citizen . . . so today our Russian Socialist Revolution should likewise make its own declaration. . . . It is the hope of the Central Executive Committee that the Constituent Assembly . . . will also accept the declaration which I have the honor to read."[18] The Assembly voted against the Declaration, not because the majority of members did not share its spirit but, rather, for the way in which the Bolsheviks tried to impose not just that Declaration but also, through it, their party's hegemony. However, after having decreed the dissolution of the Constituent Assembly, the Bolsheviks included the Declaration in the 1918 Constitution.

The Declaration of Working and Exploited People, even starting with its title, shows a double anomaly with respect to the modern Western tradition of declarations. First, it does not speak about citizens but about people; and second, the people are not a political subject in the traditional sense of the term. What emerges is a new quality of political subject. This is not a national or ethnic identity but, rather, a social relation: the working and exploited people. One is exploited not in the abstract but only within relations of exploitation. The exploited people are not at war with the exploiters, as in Schmittian terms, because they do not establish their own political identity starting from an exclusion or from a friend/enemy opposition. Rather, the exploited people are a subject who calls into question the relations of exploitation because they are unjust. They are a subject who intends to modify the social and political relations in order to "abolish the exploitation of man by man" (Art. 3).[19] In other words, they are a subject who does not intend to assert his own identity but, rather, to cease being what it is: a subjugated subject. Of course, we are dealing with controversial political categories, but unlike what happens in the nation-state, oppositions here are not hypostatized in existential or essentialist terms. What defines the oppressor is not birth or religion but, rather, a social relationship that can be changed by the oppressor himself, who has the freedom to cease being such by ceasing to exploit others' work.

There is another reason the exploited people are not identical with a homogeneous nation. They are stratified into workers, soldiers, and peasants; the soviets distinctly represent each of these strata (Art. 1). This articulation of social strata also corresponds to just as many political powers exercised by the soviets. As with other anomalies, this articulation of powers according to social strata disappears in the Constitution of 1936, which would instead express things in terms of "Soviets of toilers' deputies" (Arts. 2, 3). The transition is from a plurality of social subjects exercising political powers to a homogeneous subject and, therefore, to a single, unified power.

The anomaly of 1917–18 was gradually bent toward the traditional categories of the nation-state. The normalization was brought to fulfillment in the Stalinist Constitution of 1936, which replaced the class language of the 1918 Constitution with that of realized socialism, or the national harmony and the "moral-political unity of Soviet society."[20] Stalin affirmed that the "kulak class in the sphere of agriculture has ceased to exist" and the working class and peasantry are emancipated from exploitation.[21] Workers and peasants are two classes, "whose interests—far from being mutually hostile—are, on the contrary, friendly."[22] The 1936 Constitution was aligning itself with modern Western constitutional history. Presented as the constitution of a whole people, it had a twofold effect: while it spoke the language of class neutrality,[23] at the same time, and not by chance, it also permitted the intensification of internal violence toward the enemies of the people and disruptors of state unity and public order. That is, the purges and the Stalinist terror were deployed in the name of unity of the people and national security. Insofar as the civil war had reached extremes of violence in the 1920s, a constitution that adopted the style of European nation-state was needed in order to deploy the terror of the sovereign dictatorship that is typical of the modern state.

The term "exploited people" indicated both the priority of the relationship and the trend toward a supranational dimension. Indeed, the working and exploited people are the holders of sovereignty, but they do not belong to a defined nation. This, in addition to presenting a clear-cut anomaly with respect to the dominant trajectory of modern Western statehood, has immediate legal and political repercussions. What does abandoning the national perspective of state politics mean? The first political consequence, the most visible, is set forth in Article 4 of the Declaration, which affirms "fraternization among the workers and peasants of the belligerent armies" (Art. 4). This was not an abstract or only a propagandistic article, but a practice that led whole regiments of Italian and German armies to fraternize with the "enemy." The second political implication is expressed in terms of "a complete break with the barbarous politics of bourgeois civilization which built the prosperity of the exploiters in a few chosen nations" (Art. 5). This is another consequence of the anomaly of a plural political subject in the Declaration—a subject, as we have seen, that is not a subject but, rather, a social relationship. Starting from this innovative element, the relationship of exploitation is questioned both in domestic politics (Art. 3) and in foreign politics (Art. 5). The first emancipation cannot be brought to completion without the second; otherwise, the liberation of the oppressed people in Russia would be based on the oppression of other peoples, and would therefore fall back into the dynamics of colonialism and nation-states.

The supranational dynamic is already enclosed in the supranational nature of the Declaration of the Rights of the Working and Exploited People. To draw a counterpart with the French Revolution, one could say that if the equality of human rights reverberated across the Atlantic and returned to France as an antislavery declaration in 1793, then Article 5 of the 1918 Declaration set the basis for *nonnational* anticolonialism. This experiment would be tried during the Congress of the People of the East, held in Baku in September 1920.

SECOND ANOMALY: INDIVIDUALS OR GROUPS?

The Declaration of 1918 does not guarantee individual subject rights, but does give freedom to groups. The first part of the Constitution incorporates freedoms whose structure diverges from that of the Declaration of the Rights of Man. In a completely anomalous way with respect to the latter tradition, the Declaration of 1918 lists the "real freedom of conscience" (Art. 13), "real freedom of expression" (Art. 14), "real freedom of assembly" (Art. 15), "real freedom of association" (Art. 16), and "real access to knowledge" (Art. 17). It is not about rights guaranteed by the state, and thus is subject to the specific antinomy of articles in modern Western declarations that claim a right in the first clause and then limit it in the second clause for reasons of public order and national security. These criteria of limitation are arbitrarily determined by the state and are always used in a declared state of emergency.

The Constitution of 1918 was written using a different grammar based on the freedoms practiced daily by the soviets and guaranteed not by the state but by the authority of the soviets themselves. This is why, as in the Declaration of 1793, and as different from the Declaration of 1789, the limit on freedom of association or assembly is missing. Soviet political procedure replaced individual rights with those of groups: the soviets. It's a move that reclaims the legacy of the Paris Commune, which declared a desire to move from the Declaration of the Rights of Man and of the Citizen to the "Déclaration des Droits du Group."[24] Similarly, in the Constitution of 1918, the holder of freedoms is not the individual but, rather, social groupings and associations of working people. The state is not called upon to guarantee those freedoms but, instead, to facilitate their implementation. Each article begins by stating, "In order to ensure for the workers real freedom," and goes on to list the technical material necessary to carry out those rights. Thus, Article 14, on the freedom of expression, specifies the means necessary for the realization of that freedom: the Russian Socialist Federated Soviet Republic must provide the "technical and material resources necessary for the publication of newspapers, pamphlets, books, and all other printed matter, and guarantee their free circulation throughout the country" (Art. 14). Or, Article 15, on the freedom of association, specifies that the Republic must provide for the fulfillment of that freedom with "furnishing, lighting, and heating" (Art. 15).

No other welfare system would push that far. And that is because in the 1918 Constitution, at least two inversions with respect to the modern state structure took place: on the one hand, the state is in a subordinate position with respect to the freedoms practiced at the soviet level; on the other hand, the language used is not that of the rights guaranteed by the state but, instead, of the freedoms that are exercised and guaranteed by the concrete authority of the soviets. The destruction of those liberties would have been possible only by removing authority from the soviets and concentrating power in the hands of the state—which is what actually happened through emergency decrees used to justify ways for dealing with a crisis situation.

From an institutional point of view, beginning in the first months of the revolution, tension was building between the Sovnarkom (Council of People's Commissars)—that is, the government—and the All-Russian Central Executive Committee of the Soviets (CEC), the body elected by the Congress of Soviets. On numerous occasions, the Left Socialist Revolutionaries (Left SRs) denounced the concentration of power in the hands of the Sovnarkom, which produced decree after decree "without any sanction by the CEC."[25] The concentration of power in the hands of the Sovnarkom went hand in hand with limitations on the freedom of opposition groups. At the November 4, 1917, meeting, Lenin's press decree, which by law prohibited publication of numerous opposition newspapers, was challenged. The Left SRs reacted to the government's repressive measures by stating that "one cannot emancipate society . . . by taking repressive measures against newspapers."[26] What the Left SRs defended was not the liberal concept of individual freedom of expression but, rather, a dual principle: the way out of a state of subordinacy cannot pass through someone else's dominion; and revolution should be understood as a process of self-education of the population grown enough to distinguish between good and bad information.

For the Left SRs, the revolution did not break the master–slave dialectic by overturning it in favor of a vanguard; rather, it stopped it by introducing new forms of life and socialist relations. As Malkin stated during discussions on freedom of the press, "we firmly repudiate the notion that socialism can be introduced by armed force. In our view socialism is a struggle not merely for material advantages but for supreme human moral value."[27] For the same reason, the Left SRs were opposed to the death penalty and they supported alternative forms of imprisonment. The Bolshevik's repressive politics not only undermined the liberties of the opposition but also concentrated power at the expense of the powers and autonomies of the soviets.

It is that concentration of power in the hands of the Bolshevik Party that placed Russia on track toward becoming a nation-state in the modern European tradition. In the 1940s, Procurator General Andrey Y. Vyshinsky wrote in the Russian standard textbook on public law: "From top to bottom the Soviet social order is penetrated by the single general spirit of the oneness of the authority of the toilers."[28] In this trajectory, the Schmittian friend/enemy categories become central to producing the unity and homogeneity of a nation. And, as is well known, the enemy can be either external, as in another nation, or internal—or a combination of both. In any case, the political equation is as follows: the controversial intensity of the opposition is directly proportional to the national unity to be produced. This political logic shows, especially in crisis situations, that the transition from a liberal-democratic state to an authoritarian one can take place seamlessly.

Regarding the 1918 Constitution, the comparison with the Constitution of 1936 is once again significant. The freedoms of expression, press, assembly, meetings, and demonstrations are reiterated in Chapter 10 of the 1936 Constitution, but in a new framework that sees the transition from the grammar of freedom (*svobóda*) to that of citizens' rights (*prava grazhdan*). Article 126 stipulates that the "citizens of the USSR shall be ensured the right to unite in social organizations." This article is no different from that found in a liberal-democratic constitution. The freedom to unite in social organizations becomes a right, guaranteed by the state to the individual citizens of the USSR.

THIRD ANOMALY: WHO IS A CITIZEN?

Sympathizers of the French Revolution, be they French or not, participated in the assemblies, and they received the title of citizen for their contribution to the revolution.

1793. The French Republic Constitution	1918. The Russian Constitution
Art. 4. Every man born and living in France fully twenty-one years of age, and every foreigner, who has attained the age of twenty-one, and has been domiciled in France **one year**, and lives there by his own labor; or acquires property; or marries a French woman; or adopts a child; or supports an aged man; and finally every foreigner who shall be thought by the Legislative Body to have deserved well of humanity, **is admitted to the exercise of the rights of French citizenship.**	Chap. 5, Art. 20. Acting on the principle of the solidarity of the toilers of all nations, the Russian Socialist Federated Soviet Republic shall grant **all political rights enjoyed by Russian citizens to foreigners resident within the territory of the Russian Republic** for purpose of employment and belonging to the working class or to the peasantry not employing hired labor. **Local Soviets shall be authorized to confer upon such foreigners, without any troublesome formalities, the rights of Russian citizenship.**

The Paris Commune raised the flag of the Universal Republic and overcame the random nature of birth with regard to privileges of both class and nationality. The soviets tapped into this tradition. Workers, soldiers, and peasants were part of the soviets; they were not Russians belonging to a nation. For this reason, it was not the Italians or the Germans to be excluded but, rather, the proprietors living off the labor of others. This is a thick and thin exclusion at the same time. It is thick because it left out part of the population; it is thin because it was extremely flexible, enough for the excluded to stop living off the labor of others so as to change their legal and political condition.

The Constitution of 1918 stated, "the non-working citizen is equated to a foreigner," a principle that would violate the legal principles of the modern state.[29] However, if we do not assume the modern state as a normative principle, we can see which democratic practice is at stake in the Soviet conception of citizenship. Looking at things without the liberal lens of individual rights, we see that the inclusion–exclusion relationship was not so much defined as the status of worker, peasant, or soldier as, rather, that of belonging to soviets, which were precisely the workers', soldiers', and peasants' soviets. The Mensheviks already considered the political citizenship practiced by the soviets as nondemocratic, since that excluded part of the population (specifically, the nonworkers). The Constitution, from this point of view, incorporated the ordinary manner of participation in the political life of the soviets, which were then taken as the basis for class franchise of the Soviet Constitution.[30] Political citizenship was not defined by the right to put a ballot into a ballot box once every few years but, instead, by participation in the political life of the soviets.

That seems like an aberration from a liberal standpoint today, according to which rights are thought of as universal for the abstract individual and not for an association or group. Moreover, the idea that local soviets could confer citizenship and political rights is in contradiction to the principle of national citizenship. Hence, it appears that Soviet citizenship was far more inclusive than exclusive, except that the manner of inclusion was not based on belonging to a nation. Article 20 of the Constitution states: "Local Soviets shall be authorized to confer upon such foreigners, without any troublesome formalities, the rights of Russian citizenship." No modern state would be able to tolerate such an extension of citizenship, which in substance would lead to its dissolution. Today especially, in light of the debates on citizenship and its becoming more and more strict in the face of widespread migration, this article talks about a state that is not a state. Political citizenship, says Article 20, is granted by any local soviet, "without any troublesome formalities." To draw a parallel with the contemporary world, it would be as if sanctuary cities, or even sanctuary neighborhoods, granted citizenship and political rights. It goes without saying that this is unthinkable in any modern state.

Article 20 does not fall out of the sky as an affirmation of a doctrinaire principle. Nor is it the manifestation of abstract solidarity between workers. The soviets, during the Russian Revolution, like what had happened in the sections in the French Revolution, already had a supranational nature. Article 20 expresses the political rights of those who, by enacting an insurgent citizenship, had already forced the limits of their national belonging toward a new supranational configuration of political citizenship. State sovereignty is replaced by that of class, and "this new sovereignty is not limited to any state frontiers; it tends to be universal."[31] As Kirchheimer pointed out, this universalism "raises the question whether Soviet Russia is still a state."[32] This universality is not juridical, but it is effective in the real practice of oppressed people in the soviets—of course, with an ambiguity that can, and in fact did happen, turn into a new imperialism. If, on the one hand, political citizenship applies to every member of the working class, it thus gives the opportunity to intervene in internal issues of the Soviet Republic; on the other hand, this principle can be read as new lines demarcating the friend/enemy opposition, so that Russia would acquire the right to intervene, in name of the defense of the oppressed, in the internal affairs of other states.

This last step could be taken by Stalin when Russia's domestic politics ceased to be the subject of discussion at the Communist International, and instead became an instrument in the hands of the Bolshevik Party. Symbolically, this turnabout can be dated to February 22, 1926, when at the Plenum of the Executive Committee of the Communist International, Amadeo Bordiga asked Stalin if he still believed that Russian politics and party problems were linked to the politics and developments of the international movement. In other words, Bordiga disputed Stalin's position and claimed the superiority of the Communist International over the Bolshevik Party. Stalin replied, "This question has never been directed to me. I would never have believed that a Communist could ask me that. God forgive you for doing so."[33] After that, Bordiga considered the Comintern to be virtually dead and went on to denounce "the sport of terror" in force in Russia.

With the Constitution of 1936, Russia aligned itself with the principles of Western states. The Constitution of 1936 established (in Chap. 10) a package of rights and duties for citizens of the USSR, distinguishing in Chapter 11, Article 14v, between "laws on Union citizenship" and "laws on the rights of foreigners." Belonging and citizenship were now defined in national terms; exclusion, which in the 1918 Constitution referred to those who took advantage of the work of others, now was based on national belonging.

The Soviet anomaly of citizenship can be explained by starting from the fact that its political reality was never founded on the rights of the individual but, rather, on the freedom and political authority of the soviets, social groupings, and workers' associations. "The delegates of the Soviets are not elected by all the voters, but by individual collective groups: factories, trade unions, authorities, units of the army and so on."[34] This is not so much an illiberal principle as one that broke away from assumptions of liberalism, individualism, and freedom based on the individual. The 1918 Constitution opened a road toward another political modernity, a road that the Constitution of 1936 would then close. If we want to find the principles of Russia's modern state constitutionalism, we must look to the Stalinist Constitution.

1918 Constitution	1936 Constitution
Art. 64. **The right to elect and be elected to the Soviets** shall belong...to the following citizens of the Russian Socialist Federated Soviet Republic, **of both sexes, who have reached the age of eighteen on election day**: a. All those earning their livelihood by productive and socially useful work....	Art. 135. Elections of deputies shall be **universal: all citizens of the USSR**... shall have the right to participate in the election of the deputies and to be elected. Art. 136. Elections of deputies shall be equal: **every citizen shall have one vote**. Art. 137. **Women shall have the right to elect and be elected on equal terms with men.**

1918 Constitution	1936 Constitution
Note 1: **Local Soviets may . . . lower the age limit** established by the present article.	Art. 139. **Election of the deputies shall be direct.**
Note 2: **Of foreign residents**, those mentioned in Article 20 . . . **shall also enjoy active and passive electoral rights.**	Art. 140. **Voting at elections of deputies shall be secret.**
Art. 65. **The right to vote or to be elected shall be denied to the following . . . categories:**	
a. Persons employing hired labor for profit;	
b. Persons living on unearned income, such as interest on capital, revenue from enterprises, income from property, etc.	

The extension of the right to elect and to be elected to the soviets was introduced in 1918 as a formalization of the political practice of the soviets, which included men, women, and foreign residents. But it is not in this universalism of the right to vote that the soviet anomaly plays out; other states had introduced women's right to vote. The anomaly lie, rather, in the powers left to the soviets, which included the ability to "lower the age limit established" by Article 64 and to extend active and passive electoral rights to foreign residents (Art. 64, Note 2). The 1936 Constitution speaks instead of a universal, direct, and secret vote. The soviets survived, but as appendages of the party. In 1918, the local soviets were the nervous system of the Soviet Republic, the real centers of power. Hence, there was considerable difference between the indirect voting system of the 1918 Constitution (Art. 70) and the direct one of 1936 (Art. 134). Unlike the 1936 Constitution, which redefined the binary opposition of citizens and foreigners, giving political rights to the former on the basis of nationality and denying them to the latter, the Constitution of 1918 expressed a different articulation of powers. So, if the exclusion from the active and passive electorate were those who take advantage of the work of others, and this was seen as an illiberal and antidemocratic principle, everything depended on what is meant by democracy. In fact, in the Constitution of 1918, both active and passive political rights were enjoyed by foreign workers residing in Russia. Western constitutionalism has often denounced the antidemocratic nature of this concept of citizenship. Rather, one might ask, as the Communards did in 1871, how democratic it is to anchor citizenship to the randomness of *jus soli* or *sanguinis*.

FOURTH ANOMALY: THE PLURALISM OF POWERS

One of the features of the representative institutions of the Soviet Republic is the imperative mandate, which revived the traditions of 1793 and 1871. The imperative mandate, for reasons inherent to the very logic of the modern representative state, is explicitly forbidden in many Western constitutions, and is considered "generally awkward to Western democracies."[35] This is because in modern representative democracies, the political subject that is represented is the sovereign people in its unity and totality. From this assumption there derives the free mandate of the representatives, who represent the universal interests of the people, and not the particular interests of a small body of voters. The imperative mandate, instead, requires a plurality of particular authorities and bodies, rather than a homogeneous political subject—the nation—which exists through the theological-political artifice of representation.

AN INSURGENT CONSTITUTION | 141

At stake are two conceptions of democracy: on the one hand, we have the democratic excess of the plurality of powers that holds open the political form to transformation; on the other, we find the constitutional democracy that seeks to tame the excess and reduce the plurality into unity—the unity of a sovereign nation.

Article 78 of the 1918 Constitution established that "electors shall have the right to recall at any time the deputy they have sent to the Soviet and to hold new elections in accordance with the general statute." The imperative mandate was common practice in the ordinary politics of the soviets and had real political meaning while the soviets continued to exercise political power alongside, and sometimes in opposition to, the central power. As mentioned, the political and institutional fabric that the Constitution, in part, formalized was made up of a plurality of local, urban, and rural soviets, which constituted the permanent source of power. And their power included determining election procedures, which Lenin initially wanted to make as fluid as possible.[36]

With the progressive construction of the centralized state, which occurred parallel to draining the soviets of any real political authority, the imperative mandate also lost meaning and the Russian state machine aligned itself with the modern state trajectory. Thus, as far as the Constitution of 1936 still mentions the possibility of recalling the deputies of the soviets (Art. 142), the structure of that relationship between the central party and the soviets had completely changed, and recall now functioned as a control mechanism. The articulation of the soviets of workers, soldiers, and peasants was dissolved, and in its place came the supposed homogenous people of toilers, who then were the only subjects worthy of representation. In this context, the voting system in 1936 became direct, so that the soviets ceased to be intermediate authorities supervising the practice of the representatives. This centralization of power took form through direct individual voting.

The dualism of centralization and decentralization, sometimes used to describe trends in the Soviet Republic, is misleading. That dualism, in fact, really implies the existence of a single power that can either be centralized in the hands of the government or a party, as happened beginning in the 1920s, or be organized in federal terms. But this definition is too broad and does not always call into question the unity of the sovereign subject: the people-nation. The Russian political and constitutional reality at the time of the revolution can, instead, be represented in terms of a pluralism of social strata, which corresponds to a plurality of powers exercised by the soviets.

Viewing the Soviet Constitution of 1918 from the perspective of dualism, therefore, confuses things rather than clarifies them. This is why a good piece of work on the history of the soviets, like the one written by Oskar Anweiler, seems contradictory when it comes to claiming that anti-centralist tendencies had no place in the Bolshevik Constitution of 1918, while at the same time presenting that constitution as the institutionalization of the council movement and as a first legal definition of new political forms developed from below.[37] What similarly risks being misleading is the dualism in the constitutional separation of powers, typical of the rule of law in liberal democracies in the Western tradition, and the lack of separation of powers in the soviets, even before the country became the Soviet Republic. Once again, the Soviet constitutional form tries to translate into formal language the reality of the soviet institutions, which exercised functions of legislative and executive power, as well as judiciary power. In other words, the separation of powers was abolished not by decree but in the political practice of soviet institutions, which is why the Mensheviks accused them of not being democratic.

The soviets acted like administrative bodies and governments with authority. Sometimes they insisted the central government not meddle in their affairs. It could be said that the denial of a constitutional separation of powers was replaced by a pluralism of powers from below. The principle of a separation of powers, which in James Madison's model should be checked and balanced, presupposes a *single* power to be constitutionally articulated in the legislative, executive, and judiciary branches. The power of the sovereign people remains the only source of this articulation of powers. Thus, this allows one of the branches to prevail over the others by calling upon the will of the nation and, if need be, declaring an emergency situation. We are witnessing this phenomenon in an ever-increasing number of states that, without formally breaking their democratic constitutional shell, transform their structure into authoritarianism.

To understand the soviet anomaly, we should also call into question the formula for the dualism of powers presented by Lenin and as elevated to a paradigm of the revolutions by Trotsky.[38] The discussion on dual power began as far back as March 1917 in numerous newspapers such as *Novoe Vremia, Den'*, and *Izvestiia*, which tried to depict the relationship between the soviets and central power. If the first two newspapers sought to outline the function of the soviet as an "organ of supervision over the Government" in order to keep the dual power from deciding on the hegemony of one power over the other,[39] *Izvestiia*, which arose as the newspaper of the Petrograd soviet, expressed a different point of view: supervision over the groups that are in power by the people, which "remain the highest source of any power and . . . , represented by their elected bodies, are endowed with the right to control any government."[40] The "real democracy," stated Yuri Mikhailovich Steklov at the All-Russian Conference of Soviets held on April 4, 1917, "is only influencing the bourgeois government in order to force it to take the demands of the revolutionary people into account."[41]

This was the nature of the dual power: control over government by another power, which puts pressure on the holders of power by "invading the jurisdiction of the Provisional Government," questioning its orders, and "independently publishing its own orders."[42] It was not the seizure of power that was at stake, nor the solution of the dualism problem to the benefit of one over the others. Of course, this was the way Lenin regarded the dualism: not as the way toward pluralism of powers but as a decision to be made between "the undivided power of the bourgeoisie" and the "undivided power of the Soviets."[43] Conversely, dual power could be understood not as a diarchy of sovereign powers to be resolved in favor of "the class which is called to realize the new social system,"[44] but, rather, as a dynamic pluralism of powers. In fact, in the first months of the revolution, popular assemblies and soviets controlled the actions of the provisional government, questioning its orders and enacting their own laws.

FIFTH ANOMALY: A DIFFERENT KIND OF FEDERALISM

The Soviet Republic was born as the Russian Socialist Federated Soviet Republic and would become the Union of Soviet Socialist Republics in 1922—the name it would hold until its end in 1991. The federal spirit of the republic was expressed in Article 2 of the Constitution of 1918, which established the Russian Soviet Republic "on the basis of a free union of free nations, as a federation of Soviet national republics." Soviet federalism contained a double anomaly: the territorial extension of the Soviet Republic was indefinite; and the right of secession of each national entity was fully recognized. This meant that the republic could expand by virtue of the internationalist program of the revolution and the nonnational nature of the political subject placed at the foundation of the Constitution; at the same time, the territorial entity of the republic could shrink "on the basis of the free self-determination of nations" (Art. 4), a principle that, as mentioned, included secession. In other words, the Soviet Republic leaves it "to the workers and peasants of each nation to decide independently at their own plenipotentiary Soviet congress whether, and on what conditions, they wish to take part in the federal government and in other federal Soviet institutions" (Art. 8).

In this constitutional framework, it emerges that the soviet federation was to be understood as founded neither on a territorial basis nor on the principle of national identity. It is, in fact "the workers and peasants of each nation" who decide, in their soviet congresses, the degree of their participation in the federal government—or secession, which was nothing more than the direct implication of a different notion of sovereignty, which was not national but, rather, distributed at the local level of soviets and organizations.[45]

The Soviet conception of federalism has often generated confusion, because it was not comparable to any other type of federal state tested in the modern Western tradition.[46] It has been written that it was not a federation but, rather, a confederation of republics (*Staatenbund*). This is only true in a first approximation. Each republic could, in fact, be understood as a confederation of soviets that, in some cases, actually went so far as to proclaim its independence.[47] Only slowly, and at the cost of many conflicts, would sovereignty be taken from them—until in 1923, they arrived at a "decentralized unitary state."[48] To put it differently, the Federated Soviet Republic was not an articulation of member states endowed with "potential sovereignty"[49] but, rather, of powers that sustained the tension between units and unity, between the soviets and the government. A contemporary commentator noticed that the first half of 1918 was "a time of very noticeable friction between the central institutions of the state."[50]

Underlying this anomalous conception of federalism is always the pluralism of powers, based on a redefinition of the notion of people in terms of social strata, professional groups, and their representation in the soviets. The Left SRs, which until 1918 continued to cooperate with the Bolsheviks occupying institutional positions, were the main representatives of this pluralistic trend. In a draft constitution emanating from the Commissariat of Justice in January 1918, a federated republic was proposed, whose members were to be the "land workers, industrial workers, employees of trading institutions, employees of the state, and employees of private persons."[51] The federalism that was emerging in the Soviet Republic was not based on territorial decentralization of power but, rather, on the existence of a pluralism of power in the hands of professional organizations and the soviets. These groups constantly practiced their power. This is nonsense for the jurist who looks at reality through the prism of the modern Western state and its unquestionable monopoly on power.

Beyond the centralization–decentralization dualism, there were other issues at stake for the Bolsheviks and the Socialist-Revolutionaries (SRs): for the latter, there was the pluralization of power; for the Bolsheviks, there was the "need" to have a quick and efficient decision-making center. For these same reasons, the SRs were suspicious of the plan to formulate a constitution that, from their perspective, could essentially be reduced to a charter defining "the mutual relations which must exist between different organs of power."[52] It was not about dividing the power of the state but, rather, about expressing the interests of the different strata of workers who, in their organizations, already exercised political power. The tension was between this democratic excess and its constitutional domestication. Mikhail Reisner, who participated in the drafting commission of the Constitution in April 1918, stated that "our federation is not an alliance of territorial governments or states, but a federation of social-economic organizations. It is founded not on the territorial fetishes of state power, but on the real interests of the working classes of the Russian republic."[53]

This tendency toward autonomy and pluralism should not be too quickly taken as a centrifugal force in the dissolution of the state but, rather, as an attempt, in the field of political experimentation opened up by the revolution, to identify the territorial extent most appropriate to democratic self-government. The objection that direct democracy and democratic self-government would perhaps be compatible with the small magnitude of the ancient *polis*, but totally incompatible with the scale of the great national states, has been noted. This objection, repeated as if it were commonplace, really sees things upside down. The nation is not a fact that is preexistent to the state; rather, it is the product of the state, which defines it by placing boundaries and defining the identity criteria of a political grouping. In other words, it is the state that gives dimension to the nation, and not vice versa.

And the dimension of the state is not a metaphysical entity. Real post-national politics, as experienced by the Soviet Republic, presents itself as a redefinition of the spatial measure of politics in its most appropriate scale. The soviets were searching for this new balance—a search that must be taken seriously if we do not want to raise the nation-state to a metahistoric dimension of human coexistence. At the same time, there is no historical vector teleologically oriented from the smallest to the largest, from the *polis* to the *cosmopolis*. The soviets, as had already been done in the Paris Commune, reactivated municipal and local political traditions. Soviet federalism was the continuation of the Commune of 1871.

If, in the United States, the Federalist Party was for a strong central authority—so much so that Hamilton opposed the Bill of Rights because he did not see the need to defend the people from the government, which expressed the will of the people[54]— in the French Revolution, the constitutional conflict was between the tendencies toward the fragmentation of the authority of the Girondins and the centralism of the Jacobins. But neither the Jacobins nor the Girondins called into question the monopoly power of the nation-state: the divergence concerned the administration of that power, not its unity. There is, however, another legacy that connects the Parisian sections of 1792–93 to the communal organization of 1871, and so to the Russian constitution of 1918.

The federalism proclaimed by the RSFSR was of a particular nature because it essentially questioned the assumptions of liberal constitutional law. Article 8 of the Declaration of Rights of the Working and Exploited People states that the "Third Congress of Soviets confines itself to promulgating the fundamental principles of the federation of Soviet republics of Russia, leaving it to the workers and peasants of each people to decide the following question." Soviet federalism not only provided for a right to self-determination even so far as secession, as in the case of Finland, but also combined federal decentralization with the anticentralism of the soviets. These two aspects were nothing but the expression of a suspension of the fundamental principle of modern statehood. The Declaration does not speak of the unity of the sovereign people, but of workers and peasants. It does not speak of a citizen who has rights guaranteed by the state, but of collectives who defend their freedoms. In other words, the subject of the Declaration is not the nation, the singular collective *das Volk*, but of the plural "working people." This semantic-conceptual shift, as it results from the Constitution of 1918, leads to a different notion of citizenship that is expanded until it makes the nation-state concept fade away. The term "federal" would disappear in the most famous denomination of 1922: the Union of Soviet Socialist Republics (USSR). This is an index of the tension between the pluralism of power and unity: the Socialist Federated Soviet Republic and the Union of Soviet Socialist Republics. As of 1924, the right to secession would also become more myth than reality, as an instrument for legitimizing the nationalism of political unity.

BEYOND PRIVATE-PROPERTY RELATIONS

If one considers the anomalies of the Soviet Constitution from the point of view of another trajectory of modernity, they cease to be anomalies and become new configurations of the enormous legal, political, and economic material inherited from different traditions. Only from the historicist perspective of a teleological conception of history are representative democracy, the nation-state, and private property necessary stages of human development—normative elements that have long justified Western colonialism. Instead, the alternative trajectory that I have shown allows one to see the field of possibilities that opens up beyond the crisis of the nation-state and representative democracy. It also allows one to think of different property relations. Indeed, Soviet democracy could not fail to question property relations. These two elements are intertwined. At issue was not so much the capacity of ownership; this road is the simplest and also the most trod. It leads to putting ownership of land and means of production into the hands of the state, which manages it in the name of the community. This handing over of ownership hardly changes anything in property relations, however. The dispute between Soviet jurists, in particular Evgeny Pashukanis and Peter Stuchka, regarding the nature of law was articulated on this point.[55] Initially, the discussion was about the nature of law, whose abstractness, according to Pashukanis, was to be understood in relation to commodities and merchant relations. Without deepening Pashukanis's theory, though articulate and worthy of attention, the political implication of his speech is obvious: the juridical system in its abstract form, along with the concept of a juridical subject, would be an expression of commercial or bourgeois economic forms. At stake politically was the survival of legal forms, not only in the Civil Code of 1923, which, despite the supremacy of the state in civil law relations, was basically similar to classical liberal civil law, but also the transition to socialism, the role of the state and law itself. To put it drastically, if Pashukanis was right, Russia was stuck in merchant relations, and the survival of law and the state were witness to it. The confrontation increased in intensity at the end of the 1920s, when massive state intervention and collectivization were presented as definitive steps toward socialism. The official position was expressed by A. K. Stalgevich,[56] who claimed that the law is of a class character and corresponds to the interests of the class possessing the means of production, so that it is through the Soviet state that the extinctions of the state and of law are realized. This was the theory of law functional to the concentration of political power by the state.

However, another trajectory was possible. Indeed, right after the revolution, the council democracy, hinging on how to use the land and the means of production, rewrote property relations with a different grammar. To see this, we have to start over again from the Declaration of the Rights of the Working and Exploited People, written in January 1918.

Declaration of the Rights of the Working and Exploited People, January 1918

Chap. 2, Art. 3.

a. In effecting **the socialization of land, private ownership (*chastnaya sobstvennost'*) of land is abolished** and **all land is declared the possession of the entire people (*obschenarodnoe dostoyanie*)** and turned over to the working people without compensation on the basis of equal rights to its use.

b. All nationally important forests, minerals and waters, as well as all livestock and farm implements, model estates, and agricultural enterprises, are declared the **possession of the nation (*natsional'noe dostoianie*)**.

The Declaration speaks of the socialization of land and the abolition of private property, making a distinction between two different concepts of property: *chastnaia sobstvennost'*, which is private property as understood in modern Western law, and *obschenarodnoe dostoianie*, which would be better translated as "common people's possession."[57] *Dostoianie* expresses a completely different notion of property, a conception that recalls the notion of inalienable possession, specific to the peasant tradition of the village community. In the First Party Congress of 1906, the SRs clarified that in their plan, focusing on the socialization of land, the latter is to be understood as common people's possession (*obschenarodnoe dostoianie*). They aimed to replace the property term of Western origin (*sobstvennost'*), which had emerged in Russia only in the late eighteenth century, with common possession (*dostoianie*).[58] That is, the Russian Revolution tried in an original way to combine the peasant tradition of common ownership and local self-government with the experiment and tradition of the soviets, dating back to the Commune of Paris and the French Revolution.

It has been noted that the "councils, soviets and *Räte*" emerge in every genuine revolutionary experience and express "a completely different principle of organization" that springs from "the very experience of political action."[59] This experience, explains Hannah Arendt, "has ever appeared in history, and has reappeared time and again. Spontaneous organization of council systems occurred in all revolutions, in the French Revolution, with Jefferson in the American Revolution, in the Parisian Commune, in the Russian revolutions, in the wake of the revolutions in Germany and Austria at the end of World War I, finally in the Hungarian Revolution."[60] The list could go on. Except that Arendt is missing the main point, which was not missed by either Tocqueville or Jefferson. Tocqueville wrote that the "real object of the Revolution was less a new form of government than a new form of society."[61] Jefferson wrote in defense of small property in order to limit the concentration of capital and the conflict of the industrial proletariat.[62] The council system is not just about making "our voice heard in public" or having "a possibility to determine the political course of our country."[63] It is, rather, something that questions the order separating the public from the private, the asymmetries and the dominion relationships that structure the social. And this cannot happen without questioning property relations at the same time.

The practice of democratic excess of the councils, assemblies, and soviets, from the French Revolution to those of the 1900s, has always questioned property relations, which were limited and redefined beginning with common deliberations on the use of this good. In other words, the democracy of the councils, which were essentially working councils, was concerned with labor conditions and production itself, trying to limit the absolute right of property of the owner. In Marxian terms, one could say, it overturned the relationship between use value and exchange value, putting the priority of use value in terms of workers' democratic decisions on *how* to produce, *how much* to produce, and *what* to produce. It is this democratic excess that is found in the documents of the Commune and of the soviets, and it redefines the nature of property by establishing a vertical division of ownership based on use of the means of production and reproduction.

The rallying cry of the Commune of Paris, in one of its most famous declarations, expressed a dual task: "universalization of politics and property."[64] The connection between the Paris Commune and Russia is evident in the writings of the newspaper *Obshchina* (Commune), founded in Geneva in 1878 by Z. Ralli and N. Zhukovsky, and whose plan considered communalizing all means of production and organizing them "within a free union of autonomous *obshchinas*."[65] In an article commemorating the Paris Commune, translated into Russian with Paris *Obshchina*, the manifesto Aux Travailleurs des Campagnes of 1871 was referenced, translated in terms of the transfer "of all private property, factories, shops, and the land, 'into the collective property of the *obshchina*.'"[66] This tradition was put into effect in the SR's plan for socialization of land, later taken up in the Decree on Land of 1917 and in the 1918 Declaration of the Rights of the Working and Exploited People. It is useful to retrace the steps of this development.

Indeed, in the First All-Russian Congress of Peasants' Soviets (May 26, 1917), which was dominated by the Socialist Revolutionary Party, the abolition of private ownership of land was a central issue and was to be handled by the land committees.[67] At the same congress, the Resolution on the Agrarian Question, which laid the foundations for a new agrarian code, was also passed.[68] Among the worthy principles to be highlighted, there are at least a couple: the principle that land disposition "must belong to all people managing it through democratic organs of self-government, beginning from the *volost zemstvo* (rural institution of self-government) and ending with the central national authorities."[69] Furthermore, in accordance with the abolition of private property, the Resolution refers to "rights of users, individual as well as collective." The concepts of property and proprietor are substituted with those of "usage" and the "rights of users," in accord with the widespread idea among the peasants that land is not owned by anybody except those who use it. This is not determined from above but, rather, by the rural population through its own self-governing bodies. In this way, the SRs articulated their socialist plan by beginning with the actual country, the very high peasant majority, and existing traditions and institutions—namely, common land ownership and self-government of village communities. In fact, at the time of the debates on land until the early 1920s, no less than 95 percent of Russia's peasant households lived in its 380,000 peasant communes.[70]

The SR's agrarian plan was adopted by the Bolshevik government and translated into a decree on land on November 8, 1917. In addition to the abolition of private property, it envisaged the right to use land by those who cultivate it (Article 6) and the "periodical redistribution" of land among peasants (Article 8), as was the tradition of the rural communes.[71] Two elements characterized the SR's agricultural policy, including the Left SRs, and would soon lead to a break with the Bolsheviks. The first concerned the *obshchina's* peasant tradition which, despite its revival in 1917, for the Bolsheviks was an obsolete element to be replaced with a more rational agricultural economy, while for the SRs it was a vital element in ensuring the transition from collective village ownership to socialism. The other element of friction was the concept of property. For the Bolsheviks, property should be removed from the hands of individuals, collectivized, and put into the hands of the state. For the SRs, private property should be abolished without passing through the state; those who worked the land would define property relationships according to the tradition of *mir* (village commune).

These two alternatives also differed terminologically, with the *socialization of land* on one side and the *nationalization of land* on the other. The difference between these two terms was divided into different levels: the *nationalization of land* takes place from above, the *socialization* from below; the *nationalization of land* transfers land to the central power without questioning the very nature of the concept of property, the *socialization of land* does not transfer the land anywhere since it abolishes the concept of property itself; within the framework of the *nationalization of land*, the distribution of land takes place by means of administrative decisions by the state, in the *socialization of land* instead, individual users have a right to land through their labor.[72]

The SRs, in this and many other cases, expressed the socialist nature of the peasant tradition of *mir*, as could be found in many protocols of village committee meetings. One of these protocols, dated June 8,

1917, stated: "But the land belongs to the peasants' commune (*mir*), to the working community. This land cannot be sold, cannot be an object of buying and selling. . . . As an object created not by the hands of man, land in the people's view is like air, like the sun, it cannot belong to anyone. It is an object for all mankind."[73] Not only can land not be the exclusive property of an individual, but since it does not belong to anyone in particular, if not to present, past, and future humanity, land can be used only with respect, borrowed from past generations and returned to those to come later.

The Decree on Land of November 1917, in taking up the program of the Socialist Revolutionaries, also responded to the immediate demands of the peasants and harmonized with their uses and customs.

The Decree on Land, November 1917

Art. 1 **The right of private ownership (*pravo chastnoi sobstvennosti*) of land is abolished forever**. Land cannot be sold, bought, leased, mortgaged, or alienated in any manner whatsoever. All lands—state, crown, monastery, church, factory, entailed, private, public, peasant, etc.—are confiscated without compensation and become **the possession of the people (*vsenarodnoe dostoianie*), and are turned over for the use of those who cultivate them.**

Art. 2 All the underground resources, minerals, petroleum, coal, salt, etc., as well as forests and water of national importance, are transferred to the state for its exclusive use. **All small streams, lakes, forests, etc., are transferred to the communes (*obshchinam*) for their use on condition that they be administered by the organs of local self-government.**

Art. 3. . . . Small household land in cities and villages with orchards or vegetable gardens **remain in the possession of their present owners.**

AN INSURGENT CONSTITUTION | 155

The Decree on Land, November 1917

Art. 4. Stud farms, state and private farms for breeding thoroughbred stock, poultry, etc. are confiscated, **become the property of the whole people** (*vsenarodnoe dostoianie*), and, depending upon their size and importance, turned over for the **exclusive use of either the state or the commune.**

Art. 5. The entire inventory and livestock of confiscated lands, depending upon size and importance, is turned over without indemnification for the exclusive **use of the state or the commune** (*gosudarstva ili obshchiny*)....

Art. 6.... **Hired labor is not permitted.**

Art. 7. The use of the land (*zemlepol'zovanie*) is to follow the principle of equality, i.e., **the land is to be divided** among the toilers in accordance with the consumption-labor standard and in relation to local conditions....

Art. 8.... **The land is subjected to periodical redistribution.**...

These are principles that largely formalized existing practices among peasants, such as land division and redistribution. The abolition of private property is defined in a constellation of lands by which the right to land ownership gives way to land use (*Zemlepol'zovanie*). Reference to the people's possession (*vsenarodnoe dostoianie*), instead of the property of the state (*sobstvennost' gosudarstva*) as initially proposed by the Bolsheviks, is due to the intervention of the SRs.[74] Similarly, the Fundamental Law of Land Socialization, enacted by a decree of the Central Executive Committee on February 19, 1918, and brought about as a compromise between the Left SRs and the Bolsheviks, continued to refer to the tradition of *mir*. It was an experiment with Russia's future and present.

> **The Fundamental Law of Land Socialization, February 1918**
>
> Art. 1. **All private ownership of land**, minerals, waters, forests and natural resources within the boundaries of the Russian Federated Soviet republic **is abolished forever.**
>
> Art. 2. Henceforth **all the land is handed over** without compensation (open or secret) **to the toiling masses for their use.**
>
> Art. 3. With the exceptions indicated in this decree **the right to the use of the land belongs to he who cultivates it with his own labor.**
>
> Art. 4. **The right to the use of the land cannot be limited on account of sex, religion, nationality, or citizenship.**
>
> Art. 12. The **distribution of land** among toilers should be made on an equal basis and in accordance with the ability to work it.
>
> Art. 13. The basic **right to the use of agricultural land** is individual labor.
>
> Art. 21. Land is given in the first place to those **who wish to cultivate it** not for personal profit but **for the benefit of the community.**

Here property relations are defined on a basis of the right of use, and this in turn is defined as "for the benefit of the community" rather than "for personal profit." If the trajectory of modern European private-property rights had set this as an absolute right of disposition on the matter, the noncapitalist set of peasant-property relationships would have defined property on a nonindividualistic basis and in a network of reciprocal limitations.

But in August 1918, Lenin claimed that the Bolsheviks had passed the Decree on Land without even sharing its spirit, as a concession to the middle peasant.[75] Lenin attacked the *socialization of land* for being a desire or a trend, but not something that could be realized immediately—especially not in the form of the concessions the SRs wanted to make for the middle peasant and their forms of self-government. For Lenin, in accordance with his vision of history, the ultimate goal was certainly the systematic passage "to collective common ownership of land and to socialized farming,"[76] which, however, would not have been possible by skipping the bourgeois-democratic revolution.[77] The *nationalization of land*, by dismantling the existing archaic commune and passing property "under the control of the federal government," was the means by which to accelerate Russian progress toward a system of large-scale farming.[78]

In 1918, with a decree from the Soviet Government (*Sovnarkom*), the *zemstvo*, which in November 1917 had been engaged for the organization of the land committees, were abolished and their ownership passed to the Supreme Council of National Economy. In December of the same year, Yu Larin, a member of the *Sovnarkom* and the Supreme Council of National Economy, expressed "the necessity of introducing state control over agricultural production" and the gradual appropriation by the national working-class government "of the estates of the former landlords."[79]

Pursuant to the vision of the historical stages to be achieved along the road to socialism, local forms of self-government were considered by the Bolsheviks as archaisms to be torn down. The civil war against the white armies and kulaks, a more fictional than real social category used to designate the inner enemy, justified the acceleration toward a growing centralization of power, the alignment of the soviets to central power, the repression of the Left SRs, and the nationalization of land, which should have ensured the surplus value needed to trigger the process of capitalist accumulation.

Mir had resisted the attacks of the 1906 Stolypin Reform, which sought to dismantle common property relations by introducing private land ownership among the peasants. The peasants' aversion to the reform could not have been more obvious. The peasants reacted, even violently, defending *mir* and collective ownership.[80] Indeed, by January 1917, "only 10.5% of all peasant households had been settled in new individual enclosed forms of holding."[81] Immediately after the revolution, there was a revival of the commune (*mir*), which remained the actual organ of local self-government for a long time thereafter. By about 1927, 95.5 percent of the holdings were in communal ownership, 3.5 percent were farmed as enclosed farms outside the commune, and only 1 percent operated as cooperatives.[82] These numbers mean that, in practice, the principle governing the distribution of land actually cultivated by farmers was that initially advanced by the SRs and incorporated into the Decree on Land of 1917.

The *mir* crisis began when the Bolshevik government tried to control the agricultural economy and, in the 1920s, enacted a concentration of local soviets which in 1923 totaled 80,000 but by 1929 became 55,340.[83] Until the enactment of the principle of land tenure promulgated on December 5, 1928, the situation in the countryside was characterized by a sort of two-level authority between the *mir* and the local soviets (*sel'sovet*), whereby the former had the upper hand over the latter.[84] It was not just a dual authority but also an intersection of two different perspectives that involved both power and property relations. The situation changed with the beginning of collectivization, however. The two questions of property and power were at stake. Power was transferred to the soviets and, at the same time, property ceased to be administered in communal form as *mir*. Collective farming, unlike what was sometimes imagined by the Bolsheviks, did not develop a communism of the commune into a more organized form, nor did the communal attitude of the peasants take hold. On the contrary, collective farming introduced principles that were strange to the peasants and a discipline alien to their way of life. Often, the chairman of the new *kolkhozy* was a member of the party and came from the city. The tradition of *mir* could not overlap with that of collectivization. For the peasants, it was the self-government of the *mir* and not the state that decided the total amount of land to be allocated to each household, which was then responsible for regulating the system of crop rotation and for determining the best and most efficient use of the land.[85] Collectivization succeeded where the long war by private-property interests against *mir* had failed. The commune was destroyed: "The *mir* was to perish in the holocaust of collectivization."[86] Until then, the communes had remained organs of local self-government.[87] The result of this process would be the concentration of property in the hands of the state, as repeatedly sanctioned by Articles 5, 6, 7, 8, and 10 of the Constitution of 1936.

1918. Declaration of the Rights of the Toiling and Exploited People	1936. Constitution of the USSR
Chap. 2, Art. 3. a. In effecting the socialization of land, **private ownership (*chastnaia sobstvennost'*) of land is abolished** and all land is declared the **possession of the entire people (*Obshchenarodnoe dostoianie*)** and turned over to the working people without compensation on the basis of equal rights to its use. b. All nationally important forests, minerals and waters, as well as all livestock and farm implements, model estates, and agricultural enterprises, are **declared the possession of the nation (*natsional'nym dostoianiem*)**."	Art. 5. **Socialist ownership (*Sotsialisticheskaia sobstvennost'*) in the USSR shall have either the form of state ownership (*gosudarstvennoi sobstvennosti*)** (the wealth of the people) or the form of cooperative-collective farm ownership (*sobstvennosti*) (ownership of individual collective farms and ownership of cooperative associations) Art. 6. The land, its minerals, the waters, forests, plants, factories, mines, and quarries, rail, water and air transport, banks, means of communication, large state-organized agricultural enterprises (state farms, machine-tractor stations, etc.), as well as municipal enterprises and bulk of housing in towns and industrial sites, **shall be in state ownership (*gosudarstvennoi sobstvennosti*)**, that is, the wealth of the whole people (*vsenarodnym dostoianiem*) Art. 10. **The rights of personal ownership (*pravo lichnoi sobstvennosti*)** by citizens of their income and savings from work . . . **shall be protected by law.**

The political and terminological-conceptual transition between the two constitutions is significant. The term "common possession" or "belonging" (*dostoianie*) leaves room for the modern concept of property (*sobstvennost'*), understood as something held privately that one has the right to dispose of according to one's will. The former, explicitly wanted by the SRs as an alternative to Roman law and included in the first Soviet documents, leaves room for the concept of private property. Roman law and private-property relations, which were avoided by the first Soviet trajectory of law, were introduced into the Constitution of 1936 because they were more a practical way of concentrating power in the hands of the state. The Declaration of 1918 abolished private property; the 1936 Constitution passed it into the hands of the state (Arts. 6 and 10) and individuals. The reference to common possession, traditionally anchored in *mir* and destroyed by collectivization, remained a simple rhetorical reference in line with Article 6. What now counted was the often reiterated "state ownership." It did not matter if private property ended up in the hands of the state or of individuals. Soviet jurists, using Roman law categories, transferred ownership to the state and separated *jus possidendi*, left to individuals, from the *dominium*, concentrated in the hands of the state.[88]

The process of Romanizing ownership relations began with the Civil Code of 1923, which defined the right of the owner as that "of possessing, using and disposing of his ownership" (Art. 58).[89] The Soviet trajectory was aligned with that of the French Revolution and of the modern state, completing the demarcation of the concept of *dominium*, which if originally in medieval Europe and rural Russia merged ownership and lordship, now separated them through the concentration of state power. The alternative trajectory of collective possession could have developed from a different articulation of *dominium* and, hence, a different relationship between land use and power. This trajectory was interrupted, even terminologically, with the introduction and formalization of the concept of *sobstvennost'*, which implied the individual right to dispose of things according to one's will—an unthinkable right in the concept of *dostoianie*, which instead recalled the tradition of *mir* defended by the SRs.

The Bolsheviks mistook the crisis situation, owing to the war and the post-revolutionary context, for an inescapable sign of the inefficiency of the agricultural system of rural municipalities.[90] They imposed a nationalization of land, and state control over the agricultural economy and grain requisitions, thereby aggravating the situation and provoking violent reactions from peasants. The decree of July 1920, which obliged the peasants to turn over surpluses of wheat, even from previous years, produced a violent rebellion in Siberia, which led to the dissolution of Bolshevik power and the establishment of new soviets as an alternative to the Bolshevik ones. In other cases, as in the province of Tambov in 1920, the insurgents demanded restoration of the Constituent Assembly and full implementation of the law on socialization of land that had been wanted by the SRs. The revolt continued until June 1921 when Mikhail Tukhachevsky, the conqueror of Kronstadt, defeated the Tambov Republic by resorting to gas warfare against the peasants. War Communism and civil war devastated the existing Russian agricultural system. The NEP ended the forced grain requisition, instituted a tax on the peasants, and allowed them to trade some of their products. The NEP also ended the civil war between city and countryside, Bolsheviks and peasants, and so the process of capitalist accumulation could continue on bases other than those of nationalization and requisitions.

The NEP had produced a substantial transfer of private property to individuals; the 1922 Criminal Code had to seal those new relationships. The Civil Code, which went into effect in 1923, sanctioned the right of private individuals to transact and to enter into contracts.[91] The appearance of socialism was present in the state's constant primacy in property relationships and, starting from the mid-1930s, with the legal recognition that use of property could create power relations over other individuals. Power, monopolized by the state, had privatized the social by destroying the soviets' forms of autonomous power. Private property was only apparently abolished; actually, the state was creating the conditions for it to flourish again as soon as bargaining could occupy the sphere of personal dominion relationships—that is, contractual labor relations.

But at this point we have to rewind and return to the early months of 1918, when different roads were still open. In January 1918, at the All-Russian Congress of Land Committees, Maria Spiridonova stated that if the Bolsheviks were opposed to the socialization of land, the Left SRs would join the right-wingers to pass the law. In July 1918, Spiridonova condemned Lenin's agricultural policy because, if applied, it would have turned the peasantry away from soviet power. For Socialist Revolutionary Maria Spiridonova, only the peasants and their forms of self-government, which among other things were changing in the revolutionary process, could save the Soviet Republic. On several occasions Maria Spiridinova stressed the need to combine political change with moral transformation: "Because the main great strength of the revolution is . . . its moral side, the denigration and deprecation of this side is more dangerous than a loss of quantitative revolutionary strength, and would lead to degradation, self-destruction."[92] On November 15, 1918, at the All-Russian Central Executive Committee of Soviets, Spiridinova greeted the entry of peasant deputies with these words: "We shall attain our ideal not just through hatred but also through feelings of pity for all who suffer and love for all who are oppressed. . . . We must cast off the last traces of slavery in our psychological outlook. . . . We must become better, purer, more sincere, so that no one should dare say that our insurgency is bringing forth hatred and evil. Upon the ruins of the old society there is being born, hidden from our eyes, a new society of justice and love."[93] The formation of this new society not only required principles different from those of terror but, first and foremost, it was based on the connection between the soviets and democracy. This connection, in turn, reflected the pluralism of powers that the Bolshevik's race to control the state machine was undermining.

On several occasions the Left SRs charged the Bolsheviks for their obsessive verbal and political adherence to the French Revolution, particularly to the Terror, and their will to control the state apparatus instead of establishing new forms of social life. In this way, "by thoughtlessly forcing the pace of revolution, the Bolsheviks are taking the wrong road," Mstislavsky told Trotsky, who invoked Terror and the guillotine against enemies.[94] The Left SRs sought to bring the country in line with the rhythms of the local forms of peasant self-government and the workers' soviets, without imposing from above a speed of change altogether alien to the population. But behind these various temporal registers was a different way of understanding the social fabric, and particularly the Russian peasant: for the Bolsheviks, the existing forms of peasant self-government were archaic forms to be cut down and replaced with new forms brought down from above. That is why they needed control over the entire state machine. For the Left SRs, these were forms capable of developing in a socialist direction, and that had to have ample autonomy, thus making state power recede. Maria Spiridinova very clearly expressed the position of the Left SRs in this respect: "The socialization of land corresponds with the peasant economic system which exists among the peasantry and with the endless search for justice, which also exists in great abundance, in the soul of the Russian peasant."[95] It was not a naive optimism about the peasant's soul but, rather, the conviction that only harmony between the rhythm of change and peasant morality could give the hoped-for results. The distrust of peasants, on the contrary, could only produce centralized control and a strengthening of the state apparatus.

It was clear to the SRs that the socialization of land, introduced in their agrarian plan, indicated a different trajectory: "This Roman law, in essence, is totally foreign to the people. . . . Today's private-property right in Russia is no older than a century and a quarter, and has developed very slowly and weakly. It has not had time to permeate the whole life of the people; that explains the strength of the popular conception that land is a common holding."[96] They considered Roman law an aged form, which was not suitable for the existing Russian rural communities. Resistance to Roman law was resistance to legal property relations that were being defined by the French Revolution and the Civil Code. Alternatively, the Declaration continued, in Russia "new legal concepts of socialism have appeared against the bourgeois legal principles just when these principles had not yet got the best of the popular conception of labor and law."[97] There are different temporalities that instead of being synchronized in the course of capitalist accumulation, produce creative anachronisms of new possibilities: the legal conceptions of socialism combine with the traditional ones of *mir*, removing both Roman law and bourgeois legal principles. The one-dimensional image of linear historical time, which like a stone crusher reduces any qualitative difference to quantity, delay, and progress, is replaced by the multi-dimensional image of a building with many windows: "We do not think that light passes only through the window of capitalism. . . . We do not have that other brake, that other limit to revolutionary action, which exists for Social Democrats, namely the insufficient maturity of capitalism as such."[98] The first limit is the quality and quantity of socialist forces, which include the industrial proletariat and the "noncapitalist independent producers." The second limit concerns the conception of social democratic history, the model of historical stages, and, hence, the steps that cannot be skipped. Historical jumps are possible, but they must not be understood as forward accelerations passing the predetermined course of history but, rather, as lane changes. This is not an abstract conception; it is deeply rooted in Russia's reality of the time. What was abstract, rather, was the social democratic conception of history, which put the actual country in a Procrustean bed of theory.

OBSHCHINA AS ANACHRONISM

In his critique of the *narodniks*—that is, the Russian populists—Lenin made fun of the populist idea of "different paths for the fatherland."[99] He maintained that "the path has already been chosen," and it was the capitalist path already trod by England. It was only a matter of developing large-scale capitalism and its antagonisms, whereas "to dream of different paths means to be a naive romanticist."[100] A few years later, in *The Development of Capitalism in Russia* (1899), making a very selective use of statistics, read and interpreted in the light of an inevitable historical trend, Lenin wrote that capitalism had already created "large-scale agricultural production" in Russia and praised the progressive "destructive work" of agricultural capitalism, which was destroying all the "obsolete institutions" that provoked a "tremendous delay in social development as a whole."[101]

The Bolsheviks had inherited from Plekhanov a conception of history according to which there would be archaic forms to be destroyed and historical stages to accelerate in order to recover the Western European trajectory in the race toward socialism; the SRs continued the populist tradition and saw in the peasant reality fruitful anachronisms that could open different paths toward socialism. From this tension between the Bolsheviks and the SRs—but particularly between the country ideally designed according to a philosophy of capitalist development and the real country based on a multiplicity of small-scale agricultural holdings; between a predetermined path and a multiplicity of alternative trajectories to that of Western Europe—the documents and decrees on property relations of 1917–18 took form. The idea of "different paths" was not at all romantic. It connected a *non-capitalist* legal, economic, and political structure that existed in the vast majority of the country with the possibility of its recombination in a socialist sense. The accusation of romanticism arises only where a normative conception of history is assumed, so that non-capitalist forms are degraded to residual pre-capitalist forms, which were worthy of disappearing. But looking toward *mir* did not mean looking back down the great avenue of universal history; rather, it required looking at different paths.

The Decree on Land, the Declaration, and the Constitution of 1918 did not invent new property relations, but did review and reconfigure existing alternative traditions to fit that of capitalist modernity. The Protocol of a Meeting of a Village Committee, dated June 8, 1917, stated that "land belongs to the peasant commune (*mir*), to the working community. This land cannot be sold, cannot be an object of buying and selling . . . land cannot belong to anyone."[102] It was a peasant, Semyon Martynov, in August 1917 who expressed the religious sense of this notion of ownership: "The land we share is our mother. . . . [S]elling land created by the Heavenly Creator is a barbaric absurdity. The principal error here lies in the crude and monstrous assertion that the land . . . could be anyone's private property. This is just as much of violence as slavery."[103] This trajectory of property relations did not follow the trajectory of the 1804 Napoleonic Code Civil.

From here we should not draw the easy conclusion, shared by many liberals and Marxists, that the Russian peasant tradition was a remainder of premodern times. Those property relations did not fall behind the normative claim of universal modern Western temporality but, rather, they expressed a different temporality. On the one hand, there is the tradition of the rural commune and land understood as a common possession of those who use and work it as an inalienable right. On the other hand, there is European private law, which, by reclaiming and reinventing Roman law,[104] defines the new concept of property in terms of "unrestricted, illimitable" and as the right to dispose of things according to one's liking.[105]

The concept of *obshchina* takes shape within this tension. Often the terms *mir* and *obshchina* are used as synonyms by both Western and Soviet scholars. The two terms indicate an assembly of peasant householders, who organize periodic redistribution of the arable land.[106] The English used to translate both terms as "Russian commune" or "rural commune." But a differentiation between the two terms is possible and gains political significance as soon as one observes that the peasants referred to their own village communities in terms of *mir*, while the word *obshchina* took shape around 1840 to denote a community where property is common (*obshchestvennye*). Slavophiles use *obshchina* in this sense; and starting with the writings of Saburov and Khomiakov, the political meaning of *obshchina* as an egalitarian peasant community was forged.[107] This idealization was controversial, however, as it was in opposition to the symmetrical idealization of nascent private-property relations in the West. For example, Alexander Herzen wrote that the "commune (*obshchina*) has saved the Russian people from . . . imperial civilization, from the Europeanized landlords and the German bureaucracy. The communal system, though shattered, has withstood the interference of the authorities; it has successfully survived to see the development of socialism in Europe. This circumstance is of infinite importance to Russia."[108] If we grasp the sense of this difference, we can understand that the idealization of *obshchina*, if one can speak of idealization, had nothing to do with romanticism, or the vision derived from an understanding of European history. The concept of *obshchina* is situated, instead, in the clash between two alternative trajectories of modernity. Calling it "residual" is the extreme gesture of a Eurocentric and stadial philosophy of history.

When Marx was studying the origin of private-property relations in Germany by reading G. L. Maurer,[109] he began to grasp two important points: he understood that "private property in land only arose later"; and from this, he developed an interesting parallel for Russia. That is, "the Russian manner of re-distributing land at certain intervals (in Germany originally annually) should have persisted in some parts of Germany up to the 18th century and even the 19th."[110] This allowed him to embrace the *obshchina* as a nonexclusively Russian structure of common property, which Slavophiles tended to do. The parallel with Germany could be developed because here, the centenary war against common forms of property was dotted with repeated political and legal interventions aimed at imposing a new property regime. As repeatedly supported by Chernov and other SRs, in Russia the Roman law had not been introduced, or was being introduced only with difficulty. The clash between two different legal concepts was still on, but Russia was not obliged to follow Europe in moving toward private property—a direction that had been questioned by several parties.

The clash between legal forms and different property relations in the European context dragged on for several centuries. Law schools acted like the theoretical outposts of this long war. For example, in Germany, Karl Salomo Zachariä, in a text of 1832 entitled *The Struggle of Landed Property Against Domains*, defined property as "an essentially unlimited and illimitable right"; Georg Friedrich Putchta referred to it as "absolute power on things."[111] This was the new outlook being imposed, and to thread its way through the culture, there required a new anthropological constitution based on the unlimited will of the individual. German jurisprudence was translating the results of the French Revolution into the German context, engaging in a battle between community structures and collective ownership of land. To do this, it separated the concept of private property from every other form of dominion—meaning public authority—and redefined property as an inalienable and unlimited right of the individual.

In Russia, the vitality of *mir* and the extraneousness of Roman law kept open an alternative path. In 1861, the abolition of serfdom corresponded to a transfer of peasant land into communal ownership (*obshchinnaia sobstvennost'*), which was transformed from a customary institution into a legal one.[112] The commune was defended by the Slavophiles and the conservatives in order to contain the rise of pauperism. Only a small group of liberal economists, writing in the journal *Ekonomicheskii ukazatel'*, expressed strong opposition to the commune, considering it an obstacle to the process of modernizing Russian agriculture.

The word *obshchina* had assumed a more political meaning than a descriptive one: either it was an obstacle to remove in order to establish Western-style private property relations, or it was a form of village community self-government to be defended against the atomization of social relations. Conservative German August von Haxthausen's book on Slavic communal institutions in Russia makes sense in light of this clash. His book is often accused of being inaccurate, and even of having invented an ideal of *obshchina*, later embraced by populists such as Alexander Herzen and Nikolay Gavrilovich Chernyshevsky.[113] But what is at stake in Haxthausen's book is a conservative alternative to capitalist modernization. Haxthausen talked about Russia as indicating a different path for Europe: "At the present time in particular, the organization of the Russian commune is of immense political value to Russia. All the Western European nations are suffering from an evil which threatens to destroy them and for which no cure has been found: pauperism and 'proletarianism.' Protected by its communal organization, Russia escapes this evil. Every Russian has a home and his share of communal land."[114] The interesting thing is that his writings on *obshchina*, collected during trips to Russia between 1844 and 1845, along with other pieces on the commune by Slavophiles, had produced a sort of performative description of the commune. This description began to take legal form in the Emancipation Act of 1861. To be clear, Haxthausen did not create *mir* as an organ of local self-government and communal form of landholding. Instead, Haxthausen together with the Slavophiles and the populists had built a concept of *obshchina* to counter the movement toward Western modernization. If Western Europe, from Hobbes and Locke onward, was building a political order based on a concept of the individual as market man,[115] the commune indicated a direction different from that of modernity, and was not based on possessive individualism. Obviously, modernity and private property has its own gallery, in which representatives of the Western canon of modern political theory, from Locke to Mill, are on exhibit. The portraits of Herzen and Chernyshevsky, together with those of Winstanley and Müntzer, are stored in some locked basement. It takes the right historiographic key to open that door.

The road not taken offers a different scenario. Here, the *use* of land and goods is the fundamental category: it is as if land were held in usufruct and then had to be taken care of by the user. The peasant Semyon Martynov, to whom I gladly give the floor again, stated that, "It is the property not of any generation but of all past, present, and future generations who work it and who will work it, each with their own hands, in order to feed themselves, and not according to the whim of the so-called private owners of the land."[116] The legal perspective of common ownership transcends the notion of the individual's absolute will, which is the foundation of the modern Western concept of private property. But not only that. It also expands the concept of ownership in trans-generational terms, taking away the absolute right of land ownership not just from the individual but also from the state and from a future generation. It is obvious that such a conception of land ownership would not have led to intensive exploitation of the terrain and natural resources, but on the contrary, it would have allowed us to bridge the gap with many indigenous practices of common ownership of land outside of Europe.

At the end of his pathbreaking book, C. B. Macpherson raises the question of "whether the actual relations of a possessive market society can be abandoned or transcended, without abandoning liberal political institutions."[117] The *obshchina* was an answer to this question—and the answer was no. European theories on the social contract took inspiration from an atomistic conception of individual liberty that must necessarily result in a state of nature in order to justify the state. Here the a posteriori—that is, the state and conception of possessive individualism—became the guiding principle of the a priori, which in turn works performatively on the a posteriori. The *obshchina* was the image that broke this cycle, establishing a different foundation for the relationships between owner, individual, and politics.

Chernyshevsky's position on this is interesting. In his defense of the *obshchina*, Chernyshevsky discards both the conservatives' position, which in the 1850s favored the preservation of communal ownership of land in order to prevent revolutionary uprisings, and the progressive position of Russian and foreign economists, who instead defined communal ownership of land as a primitive form that was inadequate with respect to development of social and property relations.[118] Chernyshevsky's position is articulate and, as is well known, would fascinate Marx. In essence, Chernyshevsky presents a series of binary oppositions and then goes on to show the possibility of a third, non-Hegelian path. The first dichotomy that he undermines is that which is dear to the Slavophiles and also to Herzen, contrasting Western European history with the commune as a specifically Russian political-economic form. For Chernyshevsky, communal ownership is not a typically Slavic form; it has existed "with all European peoples" and the form of individual agrarian property is only the most recent layer of historical sedimentation.[119] In this way, Chernyshevsky intended to drop the East–West binary, showing the common ground of political intervention that, in order to be crossed, needs to abandon another binary opposition—that between progress and preservation. The *obshchina* was not a structure to be preserved against the process of modernization characterized by the nation-state, private property, and the capitalist mode of production. The *obshchina* could instead be presented in a third way, a different model of social development based on common property and local self-government. To this end, Chernyshevsky—passing over another dichotomy, this time a philosophical one between Hegel and Schelling—introduced the possibility of historical jumps. Given that European development was advanced in scientific and technological terms, Chernyshevsky thought that this relative advantage could be combined to the benefit of the communal form of land ownership offered by the *obshchina*. In other words, European socialism could be combined with the socialism of the commune, without Russian history having to go through the stages of European development. These jumps became possible because the objectified information in the technology could be universally used: following one of Chernyshevsky's many examples, every technical-scientific innovation was to be understood as an inheritance offered to everyone. So, for a country that did not have railroads, there was no need to invent them, just to use them.[120] Having abandoned the universal philosophy of history that forces all people to go through the same stages, Chernyshevsky presented an image of history as different levels of development, where leaps were possible by virtue of the universality of knowledge, objectified in technology.

Chernyshevsky's vision of history allows us to grasp a third possibility in the *obshchina*, not just beyond the opposites of progress and preservation but also the opposites of laissez-faire and state interventionism. Chernyshevsky suggests this are only apparent because laizzez-faire, which results in selfish and competitive behavior, produces conflicts that must constantly be regulated by the state. On the other hand, the *obshchina*, which is not idealized as conflict free, is a more efficient system of self-government and self-regulation.

THE HIDDEN LETTER: ON USING ANACHRONISMS IN POLITICS

The *obshchina* indicated a trajectory of non-capitalist modernity. Chernyshevsky showed Marx the possibility of political uses of anachronisms and making historical jumps. But to think about this alternative, Marx needed to free himself of the universal philosophy of history, according to which each country has to pass through the European stages of primitive accumulation of capital. From this perspective, which was embraced by a certain Marxist orthodoxy, from Plekhanov to Lenin, to many anticolonial movements of the twentieth century, the commune was a remnant of the past to be wiped away.

Vera Zasulich put the question directly to Marx in 1881:

> Nowadays, we often hear it said that the rural commune is an archaic form condemned to perish by history, scientific socialism and, in short, everything above debate. Those who preach such a view call themselves your disciples par excellence: "Marxists." ... So you

will understand, Citizen, how interested we are in Your opinion. You would be doing us a very great favor if you were to set forth Your ideas on the possible fate of our rural commune, and on the theory that it is historically necessary for every country in the world to pass through all the phases of capitalist production.[121]

Marx replied on March 8, 1881. In the meantime, he had written four long drafts of his answer, full of corrections and additions, demonstrating that Vera Zasulich's question was intriguing from both a theoretical and a political point of view. Theoretically, the issue concerned the fate of the rural commune and, more generally, the possibility that it could constitute the basis for socialism in Russia without going through the phases of capitalist accumulation. Thus, the question stood for the Russians.

But the question went deeper. It was about confirming or denying the dominant interpretation of the Marxian pages on accumulation, according to which the stages described for the most developed countries would necessarily apply to the least developed countries as well. From a political point of view, Vera Zasulich was implicitly asking Marx if her positions were closer to the Russian "Marxists"—that is, at the time, mainly to Plekhanov and the Social Democrats, or to their opponents, the populists.

It was breathtaking. And not just for Marx. Vera Zasulich, in fact, copied out Marx's response and sent it to the "father of Russian Marxism," Plekhanov. However, Plekhanov not only concealed it but also said that he had never seen it when David Ryazanov, the curator of the Marx-Engels Archiv, asked for clarifications after he found the draft of Marx's answer in 1911. Ryazanov also turned to Zasulich, who denied the existence of that letter as well. In the 1924 introduction to the volume in which the four drafts of the letter were published, along with the original sent by Marx to Vera Zasulich on March 8, 1881, Ryazanov annotated with sarcasm: "We have seen that Plekhanov and the addressee, V. Zasulich, forgot the letter just as thoroughly. It must be said that, precisely in view of the exceptional interest which the letter must have aroused, such forgetfulness has a very strange quality. For specialized psychologists, it is probably one of the most interesting examples of the remarkable inadequacy with our memory functions."[122] What was so disturbing for the Russian "Marxists" in that letter? So disturbing as to ask for the intervention of "specialized psychologists" able to explain the occult parricide by Russian Marxists toward the latter-day Marx?

In reply to Zasulich, Marx wrote that the analysis of *Capital* "provides no reasons either for or against the vitality of the Russian commune. But the special study I have made of it . . . has convinced me that the commune is the fulcrum for social regeneration in Russia."[123] In the first draft of the letter, Marx wrote that Russia is not constrained to pass through the "the fatal dissolution of the Russian peasants' commune,"[124] which could instead become "an element of collective production on a nationwide scale."[125] If we keep going back in history, we find another of Marx's letters that had been shelved. In this letter, written in 1877 and addressed to the editorial staff of the populist newspaper *Otechestvennye Zapiski*, there is the same constellation of problems in question: *obshchina*, primitive accumulation, the conception of history. The question was "whether Russia . . . must begin by destroying the rural commune in order to pass on to the capitalist regime, or whether, on the contrary, it may develop its own historical foundations (*ses propres données historiques*) and thus, without experiencing all the tortures of this regime, nevertheless appropriate all its fruits."[126] In this letter, Marx debated an article by N. Mikhailovskii, who expressed his support for the latter hypothesis, while accusing Marx of drawing, in his chapter on primitive accumulation, a historical sketch on the genesis of capitalism in Western Europe, and then having it transformed into a "historic-philosophical theory of the general course fatally imposed on all peoples."[127] Marx replied using some historical examples and stated that "events of striking similarity, taking place in different historical contexts, led to totally disparate results," and success in their analysis "will never come with the master-key of a general historic-philosophical theory, whose supreme virtue consists in being supra-historical."[128] In these lines, Marx intersected two levels: a theoretical one that questions the conception of universal history, in which the historical stages that Western Europe passed through must also be passed through by any other population, and a political one where he shows greater affinities with the Russian populists than with the "Marxists." At the heart of these tensions was the *obshchina*.

It is no surprise, then, that when Marx's letter was found by Engels in March 1884 and a copy sent to Plekhanov's Group for the Emancipation of Labor for publication, the letter remained shelved. Although Vera Zasulich had promised Engels to translate it into Russian and publish it, the letter was only published in December 1886 by the populist newspaper *Vestnik Narodnoi*. It is not rash to say that the concealment of those letters and the faulty memories in relation to their vicissitudes were largely the plot of nascent Russian Marxism. And perhaps, in part, its destiny. The question was not about the different formulations of stage theory but, rather, an alternative trajectory of modernity that was not destined to retrace the stages of European Western capitalist modernization. Here Marx was more in agreement with Chernyshevsky and the *narodniks* than with the Russian Marxists and, if I may use an anachronism, with the future Bolsheviks. The *obshchina* was not an obstacle in the course of history but, instead, a happy anachronism capable of steering the process of modernization in a different direction, saving collective ownership and the rural commune's forms of self-government. Thus, in 1924, the SRs welcomed Ryazanov's publication of Marx's letter to Vera Zasulich. Vladir Zenzinov, a member of the Socialist Revolutionary Party and a deputy of the Constituent Assembly in 1918, wrote that the letter proved that, with regard to the future of the peasant commune, "Marx was definitely on the side of Populism."[129] Similarly, Chernov wrote that the publication of the letter to Zasulich, "which has been stored under a paperweight for more than 40 years," proved that the "programme described in this letter is exactly what forms the foundation of the SRs' theory of peasant revolution, agrarian demands and rural tactics."[130] But it was too late for a change of course. It was 1924, and most of the SRs were already in prison or in exile.

The influence of populists and historical studies on property[131] echoes in the third book of *Capital*, published posthumously by Engels in 1894. Here Marx wrote that, from the point of view of communist society, "the private property of particular individuals in the earth will appear just as absurd as the private property of one man in other men. Even an entire society, a nation, or all simultaneously existing societies taken together, are not the owners of the earth. They are simply its possessors, its usufructuaries (*Nutznießer*), and have to bequeath it in an improved state to succeeding generations, as *boni patres familias*."[132] No subject, individual or collective, that is "of one's own epoch" is owner of the earth. Indeed, to attribute absolute right of property to a collective subject, be it the state or the nation, does not change anything in the relationship. The Marxian image transcends the spatiality that links property to a nation, as well as the temporality that links property to the present. The trans-temporal dimension produces a double semantic slippage: ownership becomes usufruct, and the right to things becomes the "duty" to pass the earth onto successive generations in an improved condition, as *boni patres familias*. The juridical term "usufructuary" has the advantage of referring to a limited right to enjoy the thing according to the use to which it is destined, without alienating or destroying it. This right was familiar to the Russian peasants and their forms of communal self-government.

BAKU 1920: "THE RED FLAG IN THE EAST"

Article 5 of the 1918 Declaration affirms: "With the same aim in view the Third All-Russian Congress of Soviets insists on a complete break with the barbarous politics of bourgeois civilization which built the prosperity of the exploiters in a few chosen nations upon the enslavement of hundreds of millions of the toiling population in Asia, in colonies in general, and in small countries." Article 4 reiterated the principle of "self-determination of nations," along with the principle of "fraternization among the workers and peasants of the belligerent countries." Here we find three axes that would lead to the Congress of the Peoples of the East, or Baku Congress, of 1920: the break with the barbarity of Western colonial civilization, the principle of self-determination of nations, and transnational brotherhood among workers and peasants. Delegates came from former tsarist colonies, from Turkey, Persia, China, India, and Korea, together with British, French, American, German, and Italian delegates, for a total of 1,891 delegates, 55 of whom were women and of these, 3 were included in the presidium: Bulach, from Daghestan; Najia Hanum, from Turkey; and Shabanova, from Azerbaijan.[133] In her speech, Shabanova translated and summarized Najia's speech. Najia differentiated the women's movement beginning in the East from the standpoint of "those frivolous feminists who are content to see woman's place in social life as that of delicate plant or an elegant doll." She stated that the "women of the East are not fighting merely for the right to walk in the street without wearing the *chador*, as many people suppose. For the women of the East, with their high moral ideals, the question of the *chador*, it can be said, comes last in priority."[134] What the women lay claim to, continued Shabanova addressing the participants at the congress, is the commune effort and labor to realize new forms of social life, which, "however sincere and however vigorous your endeavors may be, will be fruitless unless you summon the women to become real helpers in your work."[135]

The congress, which was held in Baku in September 1920, was an experiment and an attempt to combine the numerous anticolonial struggles that took shape in national, pan-Islamic, and pan-Asian terms into a common perspective that was not limited to the war on imperialism but, rather, prefigured local socialist institutions. An example were *shuras*, or institutional principles of self-government rooted in the Qur'an which provide for collective deliberation and mutual consultation. Before and during the Russian Revolution, the terms *shura* and *soviet* had become translations of each other.

In Baku, Article 5 of the Declaration of 1918 implied a possible implementation. In his speech, Karl Radek reiterated that "capitalist civilization means death to civilization of every kind. Capitalism is unable to ensure us even the lot of an animal that is at least fed. The sooner that that civilization perishes, the better."[136] If the capitalist civilization was denounced as barbarous and destructive, it was also to show an alternative route that, as the representative of Dagestan Anatolii Skachko stated, would have saved the Eastern countries "from penetration by industrial capital" and led the national liberation movements toward "a great federation of free workers' and peasants' Soviet republics."[137] Only this path required a new articulation of existing social and economic forms based on small-scale holdings of peasants, and not their destruction by means of political and economic structures dropped from above and alien to the indigenous peoples.

If there was a real obstacle to the first—and as it turned out, the last—Baku Congress, it was not so much the babel of languages that required long translations of long speeches into the many different languages of the participants. The real obstacle lay in what apparently constituted Baku's strength and what certainly frightened the colonialist countries: anti-imperialism. The London *Times*, for example, oscillated between two apparent extremes: on the one hand, it ridiculed participants at the congress by writing that the "Eastern Communists Congress has simply shown that Orientals like pilaff," which was served for free by the Bolsheviks "at the expense of the Baku population."[138] But that was hysterical irony. On the other hand, the British were seriously concerned about the "Red Flag in the East" and used every means to sabotage the results, from insinuating that it was a plot hatched by Jews such as Grigory Zinoviev, who presided over the assembly,[139] to maintaining a maritime patrol along the northern Turkish sea coast in order to "prevent the Turkish delegates from reaching Baku across the Black Sea" and using British airplanes to bombard the delegates from Persia who reached the Caspian Sea.[140] There seems to have been something more at stake than eating pilaff at the expense of the local population.

Anti-imperialism as a common denominator of anticolonial and national struggles certainly constituted a powerful unifying element in the war against the imperialist countries that threatened Russia. And Zinoviev's emphasis on the war against imperialism probably contained some element of instrumentalism, in that, from the Russian perspective, anticolonial struggles could diminish the pressure exerted by the Western powers. More than just linguistic differences, the main obstacle in the road at Baku was the opposing dynamics of the war on imperialism, which meant that even an equivocal and anti-communist character like Enver Pasha, the Turkish executioner of the Armenian people, was present at Baku, though not as a delegate—to the perplexity of and complaints by many communists.[141]

The war on imperialism, which in the Manifest to People of the East was emphatically called the "holy war for the ending of the division of humanity into oppressor peoples and oppressed peoples,"[142] contained an underlying ambiguity. This constituted a common element for an anti-imperialist alliance founded only in reference to a common enemy. In this way, if it could trigger a highly polemical potential, it did not emerge from the classic conception of Western politics, and thus free from the trajectory that goes from Hegel to Schmitt. Hegel, in his lessons on the philosophy of law of 1824–25, had questioned the Kantian designs of alliances between states that reminded him of the Holy Alliance following the Napoleonic Wars: "Hence, if a number of states constitute a family, then this league, as an individuality, must create a juxtaposition, must create an opposition, an enemy, and that of the Holy Alliance could be the Turks or the Americans."[143] Hegel showed that such an Alliance can work as long as the principle of exclusion and enmity is rerouted toward a common enemy outside the alliance. Finding an enemy then becomes a vital requirement; it takes on an element of the alliance itself, which crumbles if missing. Developing the same line of thought, Carl Schmitt applied the friend/enemy opposition to a fundamental category of politics, showing that the concept of humanity as all-encompassing fails to become a political concept because the "enemies of humanity" might only be aliens. But at the same time, Schmitt observed that the translation of a moral vocabulary into the political grammar of war can lead, pursuant to the opposition of good/evil, to a surplus of legitimacy by those who use it, as well as to the destruction of legally institutionalized limits on political or military confrontation. In other words, if one of the parties in a war assumes the banner of humanity, politicizing it and transforming it into a powerful concept capable of dehumanizing the enemy, it gains the justification for a war without quarters against its enemy: "the most terrible war is pursued only in the name of peace, the most terrible oppression only in the name of freedom, the most terrible inhumanity only in the name of humanity."[144] Schmitt made these observations from the point of view of Germany's defeat in World War I and aimed it at Anglo-American imperialism.

The appeal, launched in the Manifest to People of the East, for a holy war against imperialism did not escape this binary logic. Sooner or later, the Baku project would collapse in the face of that binary view, reinvigorated after World War II in terms of the Cold War. "Good versus evil" was the Cold War language used by Ronald Reagan in his speech on March 8, 1983.

The binary logic of imperialism/anti-imperialism applied not only in international relations but also internally. At the Baku Congress, twenty-one delegates of Persia, India, Kalmyk, Turkestan, and the Mountain peoples submitted a resolution for correcting the abuses of Soviet power in Asia. The delegates denounced the centralization of Soviet power in various agricultural areas of the Russian Socialist Federated Soviet Republic and the lack of respect for the "autonomies of the Eastern peoples," whose institutions, instead of being developed were put into the hands of government officials.¹⁴⁵ This handover took place under the control of the secret police, the Cheka, which "generally recruits the most negative elements, and . . . shows a disrespectful attitude to the local people's residual religious customs, and persecutes indigenous workers with special zeal."¹⁴⁶ The result of this centralization was the estrangement of the local population from the Soviet government and a growing hostility to the Cheka and the Russian Red Army, whose units moved "into the East in order to artificially create a revolution in the neighboring countries."¹⁴⁷ What the Baku delegates asked the Soviet government was no different from what the peasants in Russia were asking: that "the authority and weight of the local government, local soviets, and indigenous Communists . . . be increased" against the dictatorial power exercised by some commissioners appointed from above.¹⁴⁸ Soviet anti-imperialism was working inwardly with the logic of imperialism: in the name of centralization and control, it was destroying local autonomy and local forms of self-government, which sought to lead the "struggle against patriarchal-feudal relations" following the paces and modes of the indigenous peoples.¹⁴⁹ The Red Army was increasingly seen as an army of occupation—an army that, owing to the distrust of local populations, did not recruit among the indigenous people. The Bolsheviks were deaf to appeals by the locals. And there was no second Baku Congress.

However, the Asian delegates to Baku had indicated an alternative to the centralization of power and the instrumental appeal for a holy war against imperialism. One of these alternatives recalled mention of the division between the oppressed and the oppressors, present in both the Declaration of 1918 and the Manifest to People of the East. There, though, this distinction was not limited to distinguishing between "oppressed and oppressor nations"¹⁵⁰ but also rearticulated the sense of national belonging and the very concept of the people as a homogeneous unit. In this sense, Baku's politics, in the meeting between West and East, showed political trajectories that could go beyond modern categories of this political sphere. Inherent in the binary concepts of oppressed and oppressor meant emphasizing the relational nature of political identities, built not in a national sense but on the basis of dominion relationships. Mikhail Pavlovich, founder of the newspaper *The New Orient* (*Novyi Vostok*), in 1922 described the Orient in such relational terms, such as the colonial world as comprising Asia, Africa, and Latin America.[151] In his speech to the Baku Congress, Pavlovich responded to the European socialists who accused the Bolsheviks of being an exclusively Asian phenomenon, claiming instead that "all communists—Russian, French, British, Italian, and so on—have now become Asians."[152] By focusing on dominion relationships, Pavlovich had deconstructed the category of "Asian," which now included the extra-European and European colonized and oppressed. Thus, colonization was viewed as both foreign and domestic policy within the European nations. Pavlovich and the other delegates gathered in Baku had hit upon an important point: not only was the category of Asia redefined politically to include the colonized peoples, but the lines of colonization also streaked through the West. Baku had built the bridge between the colonized peoples of Asia, Africa, and Latin America and those in Europe and the West.

From the point of view of the oppressors, external colonization served to relieve internal pressures, which were articulated and hierarchized through colonial devices based on racism, gender, and religion. But from the point of view of the oppressed, the exclusive identity of national groupings could be avoided in the practice of anticolonial politics, aimed not at building an independent nation against colonizers but, rather, at questioning the existing dominion relationships on every continent. In this sense, the category of "Asians" could be expanded, not to oppose that of "Europeans," because now those colonized inside Europe were also Asians.

In relation to the 1918 Russian Constitution, the exclusion of oppressors was never essential, the way it was for Carl Schmitt: the oppressor may stop being such by simply ceasing to exploit others' work. The distinction between oppressed and oppressor does not immediately overlap with class relations as usually defined by Social Democrats and Bolsheviks. For the latter, class differentiation was determined by ownership of the means of production, which is why it adapted poorly to ownership relations in the countryside, where class differentiation had not taken place, where dominion relationships were interwoven with those of property, and where communal ownership was interwoven with individual forms of possession. The Bolsheviks' insistence on ownership of the means of production, besides not grasping the existing social and economic structure of the countryside, ended up representing socialism as a national monopoly on those means of production, creating opposition from peasants even where there had been none.

Insistence on maintaining the oppressed/oppressor relationship, far from being purely binary, allowed a whole series of dominion relationships to be questioned, not just regarding work but also in terms of gender and religion. In her speech on behalf of women, the Turkish delegate Najia Hanum claimed full equality of civil and political rights in order to realize "new forms of social life" in which women would cease occupying the social position usually attributed to them.[153] Again, the question was about dominion relationships because "the women of the East are exploited ten times worse than the men."[154] In this perspective, Najia Hanum stated that the question of the *chador* is last in priority. On this, men and women in Baku agreed: religion—Islam, in this case— was not an obstacle to emancipation. Indeed, as Skachko stated in his speech, the principle according to which land belongs to the one who tills it is a principle affirmed by both Russian peasants and the *shariat*.

The road ahead as envisioned by the Baku Congress would have allowed various articulations of dominion relationships to be questioned—property, religion, ethnicity, gender, and, of course, colonization. At Baku, the stereotypes of Western colonialism were dismantled. The Azerbaijan delegates presented a document denouncing colonial politics based on two incorrect assumptions: that the "white race" represented all of humanity, and that the East as immoble—in short, decrying the misunderstanding of ways of life other than Western ones. Today, one would say that these assumptions were the result of an Orientalist and Eurocentric vision of the world. If there was a "halt" in Eastern development, it occurred because of the "violence of the European conquerors."[155]

This "postcolonial" criticism at Baku would not have been complete without criticism of historicism, which confined the Asian populations to the waiting room of history. In his speech, Béla Kun, from Hungary, responded to the objection that "the people of the East are not yet mature enough to decide their fate for themselves; they need to pass through the phase for bourgeois democracy in order to acquire the capacity for self-government." Kun countered, saying, "if the people are to wait, they will wait for centuries."[156] Of course, the delegates at Baku often referred to the Eastern countries in terms of their backwardness. We cannot expect these speeches at Baku, always in need of multiple translations, to have the refinement we see in more recent postcolonial literature; but the questions posed in Baku showed theoretical and political possibilities that would have allowed their speakers to go beyond the binary oppositions typical of modern politics. That's not bad for the peasants who went to Baku just to eat pilaff.

PLAYING WITH TIME

Another conception of history is necessary here—a conception that does not periodize and universalize history into phases that all peoples must necessarily go through. From the point of view of a unilinear and teleological conception of history, we can see that the different temporalities of the historical-temporal bush are nothing but branches that are dry, dying, or worthy of dying. From this viewpoint, the chronotones are nothing but obstacles to be synchronized in name of the most advanced theory of an advanced vanguard.

On many occasions, the Russian populists showed an alternative conception of history, not Lenin's. Rather, Chernyshevsky's *What Is to Be Done?* presented a conception of the future and of political practice based on the idea of anticipation:

> you know the future. It is bright, it is beautiful. Tell everybody. Here is what it is to be! The future is bright and beautiful. Love it! Seek to reach it! Work for it! Bring it nearer to men! Transfer from it into the present whatever you may be able to transfer. Your life will be bright, beautiful, rich with happiness and enjoyment, in proportion as you are able to transfer into it the things of the future.[157]

This is pre-figurative practice, which anticipates "the things of the future" in the present. But it is also about working with the possibilities contained in historical anachronisms— that is, in the presence of nonsynchronized temporalities that can show and anticipate alternative trajectories of modernity. In other words, the transfer into the present of the things of the future is possible when the times are combined. Not only does the present contain futures that are activated in prefigurative practice, but there are also chronotones that let futures erupt from the past. The Kronstadt Commune, strongly pro-Bolshevik in the first months of the revolution, was an example of how different temporalities intertwine, creating new forms of life. Kronstadt was "the democratic arena of Anchor Square where crucial decisions were noisily hammered out in the open air, was akin to the tradition of the village *mir*, the Cossack assembly (*krug*), and the ancient town *veche*."[158] The reactivation of different institutions, similar to those in use among the peasants, led to the formation of numerous communes of forty to fifty people, workers, sailors, and intellectuals, who took their fate into their own hands and reshaped the present by playing with time.

1994: ZAPATISTAS AND THE DISPOSSESSED OF HISTORY

> I consider that our agrarian problem has a special character due to an indisputable and concrete factor: the survival of the Indian "community" and of elements of practical socialism in indigenous agriculture and life.
>
> —JOSÉ CARLOS MARIATEGUI[1]

"WE ARE THE PRODUCT OF 500 YEARS OF STRUGGLE"

There is a dominant history of modernity that began five hundred years ago. It is the history of the conquest of the America. This history includes colonialism, the development of the nation-state, the evolution of the capitalist mode of production, and the origin of the concept of private property, which have been legitimized with great names of the Western canon of dominant modernity. In this arena, the concepts of equality and freedom have been redefined legally, based on the conceptual political structure of the modern state. But there are other historical and temporal trajectories. The struggle of the Zapatistas is also one for history. Indeed, colonial violence not only dispossesses colonized populations of land, water, and future but it also destroys memory. The Zapatistas are aware of this: "We are the dispossessed of history."[2] Their Fourth

Declaration (1996) asserts, "Our fight is for history and the bad government proposes to erase history." It is not about writing stories of the excluded, or of erecting monuments and embalming pieces of the past in a museum that individuals are free to visit. The Zapatistas are clear on this point: "Our dignity is imprisoned in statues and museums."[3] The history that is erased is that which lives on in indigenous institutions and in a different path toward modernity. Modernity is not hostile to the kind of history that can be embalmed in a museum. Indeed, the more modernity is disconnected from the past, the more it invests in museums. It is hostile to everything that questions its claim to being universal and inevitable.

The first Zapatista Manifesto claims one of these alternative trajectories for itself:

> We are the product of 500 years of struggle: first against slavery, then during the War of Independence against Spain led by insurgents, then to avoid being absorbed by North American imperialism, then to promulgate our constitution and expel the French Empire from our soil, and later the dictatorship of Porfirio Díaz denied us the just application of the Reform Laws, and the people rebelled and leaders like Villa and Zapata emerged, poor people just like us.[4]

The start of this manifesto is important. "We are the product of 500 years of struggle." It echoes the first Article of the Gathering "500 Years of Indian Resistance" in which indigenous peoples rejected "the Quincentennial celebration" of the conquest of the America and aimed to turn that date into a struggle towards liberation, self-determination (Art. 2), defense of indigenous "forms of spiritual life and communal coexistence" (Art. 3), traditional exercise of Common Law (Art. 7) and the right to land (Art. 8).[5] The Zapatista Declaration ties into a different trajectory of modernity, one rooted in the struggles of Zapata, on the one hand, and in the forms of self-government and communal possession of land of indigenous peoples, on the other. A similar history was fought in Europe. It is the history of the Diggers for the defense of the commons in England, of the 1525 German peasants' insurgency for the defense of communal possession, and of the numerous peasant revolts scattered throughout the sixteenth and seventeenth centuries. There is a legacy that has its roots in those struggles; but it is not just the expression of resistance against oppressive power, nor is it an anachronistic defense of "the way things always were" against the historical necessity of modernity. In short, it is a different trajectory of modernity.

The Zapatista insurgency is also situated within a different trajectory of modernity, which intersects with the remaking of customs and practices of indigenous communities in Chiapas, in the Lacandon Jungle. It would be easy to object that this tradition is not only hierarchical but often also discriminatory toward women. In this regard, we must point out that the indigenous Zapatista women themselves quickly amended the first Zapatista Declaration with a Women's Revolutionary Law (December 31, 1993) and also assumed the title of Comandante. With this, indigenous Zapatista women have claimed their active role in the struggle against hierarchies and patriarchal relationships within indigenous traditions and communities.[6]

Tradition is not the mere repetition of the past; it is, rather, a dynamic net of practices that hold different generations in what is understood as a common legacy. It can be said that the vitality of a tradition lies in its ability to change to meet new challenges.[7] This means that a tradition is open to different outcomes; the political challenge lies in considering change as a field of possibilities for opening up alternative trajectories of modernity—just as the Zapatistas have done, and as the Zapatista women did in May 1994, in San Cristóbal de las Casas, in a workshop entitled "The Rights of Women with our Customs and Traditions." Their approach has two particularly important elements. First, it takes inspiration from the agency of individuals and groups, rather than assuming women to be passive subjects or victims to be protected and integrated into the institution—no less violent—of the Western state and its system of individual rights. Second, it assumes the dynamic character of tradition. The Zapatistas, referring to indigenous traditions, show us that tradition is a living thing that can link a political experiment of the present with forms of life that are alternative to the trajectory of capitalist modernity.[8] Evoking the indigenous tradition and the Mexican Revolution of 1910, the Zapatistas gather energy for their current experiment with democracy to complete what was interrupted in the first Mexican Revolution: authority vested in local councils and property relations configured according to "custom and the usage of each pueblo," which goes beyond private ownership and nationalization.[9] Indeed, the Zapatistas refer to a history that dates back to the Mexican Revolution, to agrarian reform, to the spread of the *ejido*—a form of peasant community that was institutionalized after the Mexican Revolution—and to the indigenous communities. It is a history that, as a different temporal layer, overlays the history that began five hundred years ago with the conquest of the Americas, the establishment of the nation-state, and the beginning of the capitalist mode of production. For this reason, the first declaration claims a tradition not of victimhood but of struggle for a different trajectory of modernity. What is essential in the Zapatista insurgency is the call to a legacy—as energy for reimagining the present.

The Zapatistas know they are not alone—not just because of the solidarity of international groups and associations but, most important, because they revive past attempts at liberation that are finally free to achieve, in the present, what was repressed in the past. "The dead, our dead, will speak through our voice, so alone and so forgotten, so dead and yet so alive in our voice and in our steps."[10] In the struggle of the present, the dead live again and take the living by the hand as their contemporaries, to bring forward a different world. What characterizes and distinguishes universality from universalism is this: universality not only refers to space in a different way but it also exceeds the provincialism of time that absolutizes the present, confining the past to museums unconcerned with how it will leave the world to future generations.

Dominant modernity has its universalism, which conceals the alternative trajectories of the "dispossessed of history."[11] From the standpoint of dominant universalism, anything that might show other historical directions becomes marginalized as a deviation, as irrational, or as premodern backwardness. But having abandoned the unilinear philosophy of history, we can see that it makes no sense to classify events as either modern or premodern ones. These events exist elsewhere with respect to the dominant modernity; and this elsewhere is not spatial nor geographical. It is above all temporal. Events are like temporal trajectories that, in their difference, share the same experiment. A Zapatista document stated that "there are different paths but one longing: Freedom! Democracy! Justice!"[12]

If it can be said that nation-states have differentiated themselves in terms of national languages and cultures, in reality the state has established itself as the sole political model, replicated in all parts of the world. Indeed, the rhythm of Western modernity is characterized by an enormous process of singularization. Not only have local histories been subsumed under the singular collective of universal history, but politically the numerous *auctoritates* have been absorbed by the centralized power of the state; the numerous and differentiated *libertates* have merged into the singular concept of freedom; communal forms of ownership have been replaced by the individual right to private property; and local and vernacular differences have been eclipsed—linguistically and culturally—by the construction of a unified national state. This obsession with unity and singularization has been pushed so far as to embody a yearning for a world state, which in essence would reproduce, as in a gigantography, the legal structure of the modern Western state.

If dominant Western modernity was established in the name of a universal history (*Weltgeschichte*) in which there is only one world (*Welt*), the Zapatistas, in their Fourth Declaration of 1996, provided the appropriate image for insurgent universality: "The world we want is one where many worlds fit." To build bridges between these worlds, we must abandon the unilinear conception of history that has characterized the last five hundred years of Western history, and embrace the plurality, not only of cultures but also of authorities and historical trajectories, as a challenge to the modern obsession with unity and binary oppositions. Universalism presumes unity to produce unity—and this unity always depends dialectically on an alterity, around which it must be possible to draw exclusions and juxtapositions. Universality has freed itself from this obsession with unity and with -isms.

TOWARD A PLURALITY OF AUTHORITIES

The Zapatistas want to change the world, at least their own, without taking power.[13] This sentence is both true and false at the same time. It is correct because they do not seek to conquer state power. It is false because their political practice aims to reform the constitution by integrating into it the plurality of indigenous community authorities. In this way, they place themselves beyond the dualism of power and its negation. Indeed, between the state and the population, there is "a third factor in power and decisions," which is articulated in councils (*consejos*) at the municipal level.[14] It is a conception of democracy that does not deny power, but does not leave power exclusively in the hands of the state, either. What the Zapatistas show in practical terms, and not as a theoretical model to be fulfilled, is a plurality of power that leaves room for the "traditional authorities of indigenous communities" that "can exist and exercise their functions with a level of legality."[15] In doing so, they activate political authorities that place themselves in front of state power, thereby limiting it.

An example of this tension is the discussion of Article 4 of the Mexican Constitution.

Mexican Constitution[16]	Zapatistas' Proposal
Art. 4. **Every person has cultural rights, has the right of access to culture and the right to enjoy state cultural services. The State shall provide the means** to spread and develop culture, taking into account the cultural diversity of our country and respecting creative freedom. **The law shall provide instruments** that guarantee access and participation of any cultural expression. **All individuals have a right** to physical culture and the practice of sports. **The State shall promote and stimulate this right** by issuing laws on the matter.	The Fourth Article of the Constitution would be reformed to acknowledge the **existence of regions populated by several ethnic groups that have their own structure.** ... What the *compañeros* are really proposing in the end is a **collective government at all levels. The need for a state governor to govern in conjunction with a group of Indigenous governors, for each ethnic group.**[17] We have asked the government to issue a broad call to discuss and approve Article Four in the Congress, as well as its regulatory law. Our proposal remains defined at a general level, but we say that said reform must consider at the least some aspects. **One of them is that the traditional authorities of Indigenous communities can exist and exercise their functions with a level of legality.**[18]

The difference is remarkable. On the one hand, Article 4 of the Mexican Constitution speaks repeatedly of individual rights and the cultural rights of the individual, which the state has the task of guaranteeing and promoting, but only as individual rights. This is the language of modern Western law. The Zapatista proposal speaks instead of "collective government at all levels" and of indigenous groups constituted as autonomous authorities and institutions. But the proposal goes further. The traditional authorities of indigenous communities must be able to exercise functions of penal law, thus taking away one of the state's most important functions: the right to judge and punish. In the indigenous communities, the assembly not only has political authority but also penal authority, which it exercises in accord with local practices. When the assemblies "decide to punish a crime, the problem is solved inside the community. But then society or the state imposes or overimposes on the person a new punishment based on its own codes and laws. We say that if the community has already punished, there is no reason for another punishment. And that should be established by law."[19] The right to punish is taken out of the hands of the state and managed according to local forms of justice.

This is a legacy that recalls both the common experience of indigenous communities and the Mexican Revolution. Indeed, "Zapata never organized a state police," although "law enforcement . . . remained the province of village councils."[20] Here is how the Zapatistas reshape that juridical legacy:

> If you kill someone in an indigenous community, it is almost certain that the community will apply the punishment of making you work for the widow. That is your sentence. The justice of the *mestizos* puts you in jail, which leaves two widows. That is something they cannot understand. If you go and do damage to the pig or the house of another, *mestizo* justice puts you in jail. The justice of the communities sets you to repairing the damage: You even have the right to eat the pig, since you have already paid for it. There is, then, a logic that is very logical, which is in conflict with the penal code.[21]

Justice is regulated according to customs and practices of the "cargo system,"[22] and the penalty is assessed and administered in relation to the needs of the communities, and not in view of prevention or punishment of the offender. Of course, it is a system in which local penal law can lead to great prejudice, especially when one assumes that the central power is more progressive. But the opposite can also be valid: a local legal system can resist or act differently from the central government's authoritarian policies. A case like this today could be that of sanctuary cities or institutions that, harking back to a nonstate tradition, practice immigration policies that are often in conflict with those of the state. It is not a question of deciding between what is progressive and what is regressive, but of keeping the tension between the two and working toward a plurality.

The Zapatista indigenous communities in Chiapas have not eliminated crime; they simply handle justice in an alternative way. Politically, the question is articulated through institutional forms that redefine not only the sense of crime and its punishment but also the entire logic of modernity's penal law and the state monopoly on punishment. The former is replaced with the customs of the community; the latter is called into question in the plurality of powers. From here, meaningful political implications are derived, thereby producing a system aimed at reforming the constitution that knocks it off the political trajectory of the Western modern state. The communities, as holders of authority not derived from the state but, rather, asserted before the state, also hold veto power and the right to recall representatives, even the president: "When the president of the Republic is no good, he should be automatically removed."[23] In other words, the mandate is always revocable if the mandatories do not perform their duty. This control is exercised at all levels and is a democratic way of controlling representatives. The mandatories relate not to a mass of individuals who lose all real control over them after having elected them but, instead, to a society articulated in communities that collectively deliberate and exercise political authority. The mandatories do not represent the nation, as happens in the modern representative state, but, rather, are single assemblies that operate in a gradation of authority that includes representation of the entire political body—that is, the president of the Republic. The president's power is limited not by a system of checks and balances but, instead, by the plurality of authorities before her or him. In this configuration, *mandar obedeciendo* (govern by obeying) takes form, which is an indigenous idea. As explained:

> The Indian communities have used the cargo system for a very long time. This system has worked because they are constantly taking account of what the person does in this position. In order to *mandar*, you have to be able to serve. And the one who doesn't serve, well, they get rid of him. There are even severe punishments for the one who can't serve the people. Sometimes they even expel him from the community. At the very least, they get rid of him and put someone else in his place without any problems.[24]

It is an institution with remarkable similarity to the imperative mandate, or the alternative to the representative state that has been repeatedly experimented with in the European legacy of insurgent universality. A rough translation of *mandar obedeciendo* could be "leading we obey" or "our authorities receive orders."[25] In this phrase, the accent must be placed on the community, the "we," as the source of authority: "In the community it is we, the *comuneros*, who control our authorities (*En la comunidad somos nosotros, los comuneros, que controlamos a nuestras autoridades*)."[26] The rulers are not commanders because the community constitutes the authority and it can authorize the mandatories to speak on its behalf. If, from the point of view of the modern representative state, the accent is placed on the representatives, the leaders and their charismatic qualities, from the point of view of Mayan culture, from which *mandar obedeciendo* derives, the *nosotros* takes priority—the "we" of the community is structured in assemblies and councils.

The contrast with the dominant trajectory of modernity could not be greater: the *nosotros* exists without being represented, and it expresses its authority in the entirety of a community of communities. In the modern state tradition, in contrast, the nation exists as unity and totality only by virtue of the representative nature of the representative. In the words of Hobbes, a "multitude of men are made one person when they are by one man, or one person, represented. . . . For it is the unity of the representer, not the unity of the represented, that maketh the person one."[27] In modern terms, Zapatista politics, like the politics of the French Communards, does not need leaders because it does not need the charisma, or the "absolutely personal devotion, and personal trust in revelation, in heroism or in other leadership qualities of an individual."[28] This is an expression of the theological nucleus embedded in the concept of representation as that which makes visible the invisible and present the absent—that is, the nation as unity. An act that is magical and that, despite the degree of secularization that the modern state attributes to itself, requires a strong dose of belief. And where faith fails, violence takes over.

The differences between the dominant trajectory of modernity and that of the Zapatista insurgency are apparent on many levels. For the indigenous and the Zapatistas, "democracy is not just going to vote"; it also concerns the autonomy of the forms of government and the indigenous authorities in a context of real "legal pluralism."[29] It is a system that "is very different than representative democracy."[30] In this context, participation is central—not as individuals with political and civil rights before the state but, rather, as members within communities and assemblies.[31] Democracy is the responsibility of the leaders toward the community and, more important, of members of the community toward the community itself and its leaders. If in Western democracy the decision made by a majority is often only a sublimated form of war to impose the winner's will on the rest of the population, in the Mayan indigenous practice, consensus is founded as an authority that does not impose a decision. Authority, rather, recalls the original, etymological sense of *augeo*, not so much the act of increasing as that of creating something new from fertile soil and of mediating the historical level with a level that is unachievable—and therefore not at someone's disposal.[32] The bearers of authority can only mediate between these levels, but they cannot abolish the distance between themselves and what they mediate, and therefore they cannot embody authority, which is instead present in every member of the community to the extent that each member mediates and manifests a common truth from a distinct and unique—and therefore essential—point of view.

In this reference to the original meaning of the term "authority," clearly the authority of the community we are talking about has to do with a different way of understanding consensus, which is not the decision that separates the majority from a minority but, rather, a practice that connects the members of the community with each other and with the past generations.[33] This plurality is not to be understood in a liberal sense, as a plurality of points of view within an area juridically circumscribed by the state. The plurality we are talking about reaches out to include past and future generations, and is a condition for mediating the historical level of the present with the unavailable level of justice. In the Western individualistic conception, formally free and equal individuals count as a mass to constitute a majority; in the indigenous community, the individual counts as expressing a singular and unique perspective. Each individual, insofar as she or he occupies a certain position in the world, has a partial vision of the world. Hence, the complementarity of points of view is understood to have a political implication. Each vision, one could say with Platonic categories, participates in the same overall vision, the totality of which remains unachievable. Equality, in this conception, is not a starting point but, rather, a result based on difference. Equality—with respect to totality—exceeds and transcends every particular perspective. Everyone participates in this universality in different forms and ways, but each complementary to the other, in order to have some plausible vision of the whole togetherness. If in the Western juridical conception individuals are abstractly equal, in the indigenous vision individuals are equal because their difference is essential for the life of the community. Thus, we discover a conception that, precisely because it assumes the priority of the community over the individual, also appreciates individual differences to the utmost degree.

The plurality of points of view, of authorities, and of worlds constitutes the intersection of labyrinthine alleys and passageways in which experiments with justice take place. Consensus is not a compromise between different positions that remain firm in their alterity while waiting to renegotiate the previous agreement. Instead, consensus has to do with translation as a practice in which each language transforms itself in relation to a language that is inaccessible to each single language.[34] The practice of consensus has an analogous purpose: everyone questions her or himself and transforms her or himself. This practice of consensus also has a different temporality. In the modern representative state, the speed of decision-making is so important that it sacrifices the democratic procedures themselves, which are bypassed by continuously resorting to government decrees. In the indigenous assembly, discussion requires patience and it continues until an agreement is reached, because what really counts is the complementarity of different points of view. It is about "two different forms of decision-making."[35]

In an interview, Subcomandante Marcos affirmed that, "Voting will not solve the problems of social decomposition.... Hence, we have to organize society, not so it can make demands on the government—that is why we distance ourselves from populism—but rather in order to solve problems."[36] Here the distance is declared both from the representative democracy of the modern state and from the populist alternative that challenges and influences the government through demands. In both cases, the state takes responsibility for "the problems of social decomposition"—a problem that the state itself causes. The Zapatista alternative starts from society and stimulates social and communal institutions in order to solve common problems. Of course, this process requires patience over long periods of time, during which community members reciprocally learn other ways of living politics and of being together,[37] hence the Zapatista principle of "walking at a slower pace." In fact, community assemblies can take hours or even days to reach a decision. The Zapatistas interrupt the dominant temporality of the state and capital to establish a different temporal regime. This asynchronicity has caused numerous misunderstandings between the government and the Zapatistas. Ironically, Comandante Tacho commented on these misunderstandings by saying, "They haven't learned. They understand us backwards. We use time, not the clock."[38] It is the "rhythms, forms of understanding, of deciding, of reaching agreements"[39] of the indigenous who are not backwards, but who live time in a different way, placing priority on achieving agreement, rather than on rapid decision-making that reduces to mere majority wins.

ANOTHER WAY OF DOING POLITICS: THE ZAPATISTA INSTITUTIONS

The Zapatistas do not want to abolish the constitution. As claimed in numerous documents, what they want is to reactivate the true spirit of the constitution. For this reason, the appeal to reform the constitution is always accompanied by reference to Article 39, which reads: "National sovereignty resides essentially and originally in the people. All public power originates in the people and is instituted for their benefit. The people at all times have the inalienable right to alter or modify their form of government." It is by virtue of this article that the Zapatistas, in the First Declaration, declare the incumbent federal government illegitimate and "ask that other powers of the nation (*otros Poderos de la Nación*) advocate to restore (*restaurar*) the legitimacy and stability of the nation by overthrowing the dictator."[40]

The language they use is important. As we have seen, the appeal to other powers of the nation does not make reference to a system of checks and balances to contain the power of Carlos Salinas de Gortari. The Zapatistas refer to the spirit of Article 39 "in which the people have, at all times, the inalienable right to alter or modify the form of their government."[41] Their declaration speaks of restoring (*restaurar*) the legitimacy and stability of the nation by deposing the government that is acting illegitimately. To draw a parallel with European constitutional history, the categories employed by the Zapatistas have resonance not with modern theories of revolution[42] but, instead, with nonmodern doctrines of *ius resistentiae*. In these conceptions, perhaps inherited from the proto-modern Spanish law and reconfigured in their encounter with local juridical forms, resistance is the right and/or duty exercised by other authorities to *restore* order that has been unjustly violated by the tyrant, who is the true subversive. What emerges is a tension between different temporalities and historical trajectories.

Modern revolutionary temporality is oriented toward a future to be realized and, once realized, will be the basis for justifying the revolutionary practice that led to it. If the revolutionaries win, this story will be written in the future tense: the revolutionaries will be legitimated by the new constitution that they will put into place, and they will be glorified as heroes for having driven out the previous government. If the federal army wins, the same story will be told as a reflection in the mirror: the government will be reconsolidated and justified for having made a clean sweep of those who undermined public order. Kant perfectly grasped the temporality of this revolutionary logic. "There is hardly a doubt that if the revolts by which Switzerland, the United Netherlands, or Great Britain attained their much-acclaimed constitutions had failed, the reader of the history of these uprisings would see in the execution of their now so celebrated initiators nothing other than the deserved punishment of persons guilty of high treason."[43] If the result of the American Revolution had been favorable to the kingdom of Great Britain, George Washington would not be remembered as a founding father but, on the contrary, as a criminal hanged after a court-martial.

The restorative temporality instead looks at an order that has been violated and must be restored. But it is not a return to a past order, as one would be tempted to say if applying modern Western categories. Rather, the order to be restored is set in the unavailable dimension of an original order that we must constantly look at again in order to modify an imperfect existing order. In other words, in the first case, the practice of revolutionaries is legitimized ex post facto; in the second case, the justification is in the reference to an authority and practice in which the constitution is a living word, constantly recalled to be interpreted and updated in light of new challenges and experiments with democracy.

When the Zapatistas say that the "Constitution that exists doesn't reflect the popular will of the Mexican people,"[44] they are not trapped in the dualism of constituted power and constituent power of the people; rather, they indicate the *tertium datur* beyond the dualism that sees the Zapatista Army of National Liberation (Ejército Zapatista de Liberación Nacional, or EZLN) and the federal army in opposition. In an interview with *La Jornada* on February 23, 1994, Marcos stated that the alternative was not between "I want the Zapatistas to win, or, I want the Federal Army to win," but included a third possibility: "civil society has shown its maturity."[45] Society is mature when its members are able to handle the anxiety that comes from insecurity and instability. That insecurity arises when power is not monopolized in the hands of the state; the instability arises when the change of a political and social order is addressed. The plurality of powers as a democratic practice is the maturity of society and its members. Reference to Article 39 paradoxically aims at disarticulating the constituent power into a plurality of powers that will configure what, in 2003, would be called the Juntas de Buen Gobierno (Committees of Good Government).[46]

The Zapatistas, perhaps in part for strategic reasons, have continued to speak in terms of constitutional reform, but the political grammar of their reform represents a challenge to the logic of the state. This is why the Senate, in December 2000, when it was concretely discussing the reform proposed by the indigenous peoples and Zapatistas, rightly stated that the reform would have meant changing the entire legal order.[47] The constitutional reform initiative, elaborated by the Comisión de Concordia y Pacificación (Cocopa),[48] was the result of the San Andrés Accords, unilaterally broken by President Zedillo in December 1996 and resumed in 2000, when Vicente Fox was elected president. It was only at this point that the Senate took the Cocopa law into consideration. For the Zapatistas, the Cocopa law "reflects another way of doing politics, that which aspires to make itself democratic,"[49] whereas for the Senate, it represents an attack on the unity of the nation-state. The Senate reaffirmed that the principle of free determination of the indigenous people cannot become a constitutive element for the creation of a state within the Mexican state. The Senate's statement went on to say that the request for autonomy must therefore be contained within the constitution and made compatible with the spirit of Articles 40 and 41 of the Constitution, which define the nature of national sovereignty and the powers of the union. Despite the Zapatista attempt to translate the political proposal for indigenous autonomy into the legal language of the constitution, what emerges is a clash of incompatible trajectories. In fact, looking at the constitutional reform from the point of view of the state, the Senate could only define it as "unconstitutional."[50] The state cannot abdicate its legal-political assumptions.

Cocopa Law[51]	Mexican Constitution[52]
Art. 4. The **Indigenous peoples have the right to free determination and**, as an expression of this, **to autonomy as part of the Mexican State, to:** Sec. I. **Decide their internal forms of coexistence**, as well as their social, economic, political and cultural organization; ... Sec. III. **Choose their authorities and exercise their internal forms of government according to their rules on autonomy;** Sec. IV. Strengthen their participation and political representation according to their cultural specifics; Sec. V. **Collective access to the use and enjoyment of the natural resources of their lands and territories;** Art. 73 Sec. IX. **Indigenous communities as public law entities (***entidades de derecho público***)** and municipalities that recognize their belonging to an Indigenous people will have the authority (*facultad*) to freely associate in order to coordinate their actions.	Art. 2. **The Mexican Nation is unique and indivisible.** ... Indigenous people's right to self-determination **shall be subjected to the Constitution in order to guarantee national unity.** A. This Constitution recognizes and protects the Indigenous peoples' right to self-determination and, consequently, the right to autonomy, so that they can: Sec. I. Decide their internal forms of coexistence, as well their social, economic, political and cultural organization. Sec. II. Apply their own legal systems to regulate and solve their internal conflicts, **subjected to the general principles of this Constitution.** ... The law shall establish the way in which judges and courts will validate the aforementioned regulations.

Cocopa Law[51]	Mexican Constitution[52]
	Sec. IV. Attain with preferential use of the natural resources of the sites inhabited by their indigenous communities, **except for the strategic resources defined by this Constitution.** The forgoing rights shall be exercised **respecting the forms of property ownership and land possession established in this Constitution** and in the laws on the matter as well as respecting third parties' rights.
	Sec. VIII. The constitutions and laws of the States and the Federal District shall establish those elements of self-determination and autonomy that may best express the conditions and aspirations of indigenous peoples in each State, as well as the rules, according to which **indigenous communities will be defined as public interest entities**.

The text, approved by the Senate in 2001 and inserted into Article 2 of the Mexican Constitution, reaffirms the unitary character of the Mexican nation, transforming the plurality of communities from "public law institutions" into cultural entities of public interest. Similarly, the reference to collective rights and, especially, to the collective access to the use of land, is denied, individualized, and delimited in accord with the forms of property ownership.[53] There are two trajectories of modernity straining against each other: the dominant one, which individualizes rights and property; and the other, which recognizes the indigenous community institutions, offering fertile ground for the reinvention of politics. Similarly, one offers the formal freedom of possessive individuals, while the other reflects the collective collaboration for communal tasks and community self-government. The social-political emancipation experimented by the Zapatistas passes through these political structures without having to follow the path of individual rights characteristic of the modern West.

In March 2001, when the proposed constitutional reform was discussed in the Mexican Congress, Comandanta Esther did not fail to underline the difficult situation of indigenous women. She upset the legalistic discourse in her response to the legal language of formal equality granted by the government, which implied that the Cocopa bill legalized the marginalization of women. However, what was discriminatory, affirmed Esther, was the legal discourse of the government, which, with formal equality, individualized community relations and treated women as passive subjects or potential victims to be protected. Esther, instead, upheld the active role of women in the struggle and in the community. She stressed their role in modifying community relations, establishing a plan of equality and participation by women *in* the communities, and not in the abstract sphere of legal equality, which left hierarchies and power relations to subsist in the social sphere. "It is not our custom, but the dominant law that requires a man—the "head of the family"—to sign property titles. It is the dominant law that requires personalizing rights (*personalizar el derecho*), individualizing property and land tenure (*individualizar la propiedad o posesión*) and it is this same law that takes women into consideration with different levels of participation, lower than those of men."[54] Similarly, María de Jesús Patricio showed Mexican deputies the different grammar of indigenous politics: "Women have been participating from within the family, because in indigenous peoples, it is not man or woman, rather it is the entire families. And here, women participate in decision-making; so when the man goes to a communal assembly or *ejidal* assembly to put together ideas, the man's participation includes the woman's participation. But as I said, it is not exclusively man–woman, but rather that of the whole family."[55] Political relations are conceived and practiced not in terms of individuals who are abstractly equal before the state but, instead, start from groups and collectives, to which families also count as units. In this case, emancipation passes not through formal and political equality recognized by the state but, rather, in social and political practice that is articulated within each indigenous community, giving a different meaning to political life in common. In this context, Comandanta Esther insisted that she wanted both to transform and to preserve indigenous tradition.[56] She stated that indigenous women and men want "recognition for our ways of dressing, of talking, of governing (*de gobernar*), of organizing, of praying, of working collectively (*trabajar en colectivos*), of respecting the earth, of understanding nature as something which we are part of."[57] These requests are not written in the mere tone of cultural recognition. That is, the reference to culture is not to a timeless entity but, rather, only makes sense within a different proprietary regime, and therefore also is in relation to the territory. The term "territory" is not neutral. Indeed, an indigenous territory "is conceived based on a relational model—as a fabric, not as areas."[58] The destruction of these institutions would be the price to pay for full citizenship in the nation-state as the only large community, in which power is centralized in the hands of the state and individuals are holders of rights, that can guarantee them the freedom to practice their culture and religion in the private sphere. But once those institutional dimensions are destroyed, the native epistemologies and cosmologies become empty shells—new-age phrases available in the multicultural market.

Tension with the Mexican state, therefore, takes place on a different level from the merely cosmological one. The state can, in fact, allow the richest proliferation of cults, beliefs, cosmologies, and lifestyles, as long as they are confined to the private sphere—that is, to a sphere without public authority. This is the way in which Westerners often look at indigenous cosmology—as a different epistemology and a different way of relating to nature that can be individually embraced without questioning property relations and the monopoly of state power. Yet it is precisely these assumptions that are questioned theoretically and practically by the Zapatistas. To put it in terms familiar to modern Western concepts, in their political practice, the Zapatistas updates Marx's early conception of emancipation by intertwining, instead of putting in succession, political, social, and human emancipation. This intertwining reconfigures the political structure by interrupting the trajectory that sees a necessary stage of civil progress as the individual rights of formally free and equal proprietors. The indigenous tradition intervenes as a different trajectory that, in its tension with the modern dominant legal-political-economic trajectory, opens up new possibilities and new fields of experimentation.

The dialogue for constitutional reform having failed, the Zapatistas continued their journey toward construction of autonomous institutions with their Sixth Declaration in 2005. They decided "to carry on, alone and on their own side (unilateral, in other words, because just one side), the San Andrés Accords regarding indigenous rights and culture."[59] If in the Fifth Declaration of 1998 the Cocopa law was presented as "another way of doing politics," which was a tall order on the level of constitutional law, the Sixth Declaration of 2005 stated, "we are going to try to build, or rebuild, another way of doing politics." The same expression now assumed a different meaning: the autonomy of indigenous communities and institutions is practiced outside of legal recognition, not against the constitution, but as the living language of the constitution founded on the "method of autonomous government" and the "self-governance of the communities." Instead of entering the arena of military confrontation, into which the government wanted to push the Zapatistas with the provocations of 1997, the Zapatistas redefined their politics by working to build a better social and political fabric in the villages. It is important to remember that in the first ten years of the Zapatista insurgency, 800 community health centers, 300 schools, 18 clinics, and 2 hospitals were built. In just one year, 50 schools were built.[60]

Writer Carlos Antonio Aguirre wrote that the Other Campaign (*La otra campaña*), begun with the Sixth Declaration, is a "long-lasting revolution (*revolución de larga duración*)," which is distinguished by another temporality and another form of politics that implies multiple breaks with traditional forms of politics.[61] The Zapatista experiment, like the numerous experiments carried out regarding other Latin American insurgencies, is an experiment with time and institutions. It is a different temporality taken from the indigenous world, in which past, present, and future are not dimensions juxtaposed in the unilinear vector of historical time; rather, they intertwine. [62] This intertwining makes it possible to imagine and practice a time in which everyday life blends with the time of rupture and tradition, giving rise to anticipations in the present of new forms of life. Western political theories of revolution have worked extensively on the historical rupture and destruction of existing institutions, but they have often been found impotent when required to shape a new institutional fabric. In indigenous Zapatista insurrectionary practices, however, a rupture is not viewed in destructive terms but, rather, as construction of new institutions that reinvent traditional forms of autonomy, self-government, and collective access to land. This will emerge clearly in the Other Campaign that we analyze next.

THE OTHER CAMPAIGN

Instead of opposing the state in order to take its place, the Zapatista insurgency occupies the space left empty by the state. Neoliberalism—this rather vague term nevertheless used by the Zapatista insurgency—is defined as a field of possibilities that opens up in a process in which the state redefines its functions. On the one hand, the state retracts itself to make room for the market; and on the other, it intensifies its presence by keeping alive the primordial functions of sovereignty—that is, security, control, and boundaries. This is what remains of the state when the decision-making mechanisms are decentralized and, in many respects, relocated to the supranational level. The Zapatista insurgency no longer demands state and public intervention; instead, it seeks to direct autonomy and decentralization in a different direction, through new types of institutions that arise at the community level. This is why the grammar of the Zapatista practices is not crushed by the binary oppositions typical of dominant modern conceptuality. "Individual" and "collective" are not opposing terms; they are dimensions that integrate and implement each other. Private property is not set against public or state property; it is a different regime of possession. Local institutions of self-government do not oppose the state in order to take control; they modify the fundamental concepts of the modern state, such as national sovereignty, unity, and monopoly of power.

The Zapatista experiment takes shape in society, which is not the desert of individual atoms produced by the state and theorized by modern political philosophy; rather, it is full of units, groupings, communities, associations, and forms of life held in common. When the tide of state power withdraws, it is not the desert that remains but, rather, a plurality of life forms. The Zapatistas are addressing these forms. The Sixth Declaration invites

> all indigenous peoples, workers, *campesinos*, teachers, students, housewives, neighbors, small-business persons, small-shop owners, micro-business persons, pensioners, handicapped persons, religious men and women, scientists, artists, intellectuals, young persons, women, old persons, homosexuals and lesbians, boys and girls—to participate, whether individually or collectively, directly with the Zapatistas in this NATIONAL CAMPAIGN *for building another way of doing politics*, for a program of national struggle of the left, and for a new Constitution.[63]

What unites these layers of civil society is not the simple opposition to neoliberal modernity. An identity built in opposition to a common enemy would not be *another way of doing politics*—an enemy, moreover, that would be difficult to identify. *Another way of doing politics* begins when different temporalities are not violently synchronized either by a party or by the global market but, rather, experiment in practice with different forms of life and coexistence.

It would be wrong to think that the Other Campaign was the beginning of a journey toward individual civil rights, in the way these terms are understood in the liberal constellation of the modern state. At the base of the Sixth Declaration and the Other Campaign is autonomy and local self-government. There is a plurality of authority rather than the denial of any authority or the assumption of a state monopoly of power; there are collective rights rather than individual human rights; the production of use values has priority over the valorization of value and the production of goods for the global market; and there is a different regime of proprietary relations rather than the individual and absolute right of property introduced by the reform of Article 27.

The Other Campaign has been misunderstood in different ways by the Left. On the one hand, an orthodox Marxist Left considered the contribution of "backward" indigenous people to be irrelevant and the cross-class reference to civil society to be vague, if not politically suspect. On the other hand, the postmodern Left has been ready to embrace openness to differences and, at times, even indigenous cosmology, but without questioning property relations and the representative state. Those latter two pieces of the Left, both postmodern and dogmatic though apparently opposed, are like two sides of the same coin. During a meeting with the indigenous associations, a representative of Nación Purépecha hit the nail on the head when he said that "the left has not completely understood the indigenous movement; they are illiterate in terms of autonomy and that we as indigenous people are fundamental to the fight against capitalism."[64] This statement addresses the two sides of the Left position: one cannot understand Indigenous autonomy and self-government; the other is not able to bring together indigenous culture, the practice of differences, and criticism of property relations. The Zapatistas, instead, combine these aspects in practice: autonomy, plurality, different property regime.

TRANS-LOCAL INSURGENT UNIVERSALITY

The Zapatistas have been walking the road that was abandoned in Russia by the Bolsheviks: the road on which revolutionary politics combines with indigenous communities. Their isolation has been taken by the Zapatistas not as premodern backwardness but as an opportunity. In fact, precisely their separation from national power "provoked the development of another type of 'state,' a state to deal with the survival of the collective, of a democratic collective with two characteristics: The leadership is collective and it is removable."[65] This different type of state and democracy do not consist in the implementation of democratic procedures in the constitutional framework of the representative state. When the Zapatistas say that "there is no democracy or freedom in Mexico,"[66] this statement is made from the point of view of an entirely different democratic practice. This alternative democracy is "not about raising your hand or putting a check-mark for one option or the other. You have to debate and analyze the pros and the cons."[67] If democracy is limited to putting a marked ballot in the ballot box, sooner or later the population will get tired of that gesture, which reduces political participation to something in which the individual, among millions of other individuals, acts politically for a fraction of a minute every few years. Abstentionism is not indifference to politics; rather, it is a clear sign of dissatisfaction with a procedure that is insufficient for the demands for democracy in a mature society.

In Zapatista practice, as in many other political experiences with insurgent universality, an important step is outlined: moving from resistance to the construction of new institutions and of a new social and political fabric that originates from the communities. If the temporality of resistance is still reactive with respect to the dominant temporality of the state and the capitalist mode of production, and thus follows that rhythm, the configuration of new institutions proceeds with a different temporality, with a different rhythm and along a different path.

Political life in these institutions is marked by another way of understanding democracy, consensus, and citizenship. Concrete political experiences in Latin America, such as the El Alto insurgency in Bolivia, show a practice of citizenship in which "nested affiliations shape *vecinos*' citizenship."[68] Here the term *vecinidad* recalls something more akin to the Ancien Régime than to the modern individual ownership of a set of rights guaranteed by the state. This reference to the Ancien Régime is not meant as a reference to a premodern context, however. It would be such only from the point of view of a unilinear and teleological conception of historical time. From our perspective, it is a reference to a nonmodern horizon, which shows political possibilities alternative to those imposed in the dominant modernity. The insurgent citizenship of El Alto is to be understood as agency that starts from the neighborhood, not as an abstract place but rather, is "concrete, territorialized and rooted."[69]

Unlike what happens on the scene of modern Western political concepts, the starting point is not abstract; it is concrete and rooted in the practices of local institutions. In this vernacularization of citizenship and democracy, the question is not about size. Insurgent universality is not stretched to scale up toward international forms. Nor is it limited to the local. The space in which it takes place is trans-local:[70] a network of relations between different worlds. As stated earlier, unlike the image of the Sieyès circle, in insurgent universality there is no circumference that delineates the political form. The problem is not the extension of the diameter. Plurality consists of a multiplicity of units that aggregate and disaggregate in the common experiment of the world.

AGRARIAN LAW AND PEASANTS' COMMUNITIES

As mentioned, agrarian reform, and therefore Article 27 of the Mexican Constitution, is the cornerstone of the Zapatista insurgency.[71] The story began in February 1992, when the Salinas government approved a new agrarian law that modified property relations by incentivizing the privatization of *ejidal* lands in several ways, thus distorting the very social structure of the *ejidos*.[72] Starting in December 1991, protests began against agrarian reform. In December 1992, the diocese of San Cristóbal hosted a workshop on the reform, inviting different organizations that had denounced the reform for being part of a strategy to privatize the land and concentrate it in just a few hands. When the results of the reform began to be felt, discontent in the countryside grew.

In the first few months of 1994, "some 340 private farms representing over 50,000 hectares were seized."[73] Article 27 had become a chronotone, the point where different temporalities came into tension with each other. On the one hand, capitalist modernization was desired by the government; on the other hand, there were forms of social and political life that avoided their own destruction. The story that I follow here is neither on the side of modernization nor a romantic defense of existing traditions. This alternative is false at the very moment at which those two trajectories collide. Rather, it is a matter of showing the field of possibilities that opens up in that tension, when friction causes the temperature to rises, and the elements that constitute both can be reconfigured in a different form. That is what the Zapatistas did when they pointed their finger at Article 27 in order to direct the agrarian reform and the constitution itself in a different direction, reactivating the original spirit of the 1917 Constitution. The government, instead, aimed to complete the project of privatization of communal land begun under the Constitution of 1857 and interrupted by the Mexican Revolution.

1857 Constitution	1917 Constitution[74]
Art. 27. **Private property shall not be taken without the consent of the owner**, except for reasons of public utility, indemnification having been made. The law shall determine the authority to make the expropriation and the conditions on which it shall be carried out. No religious corporations and institutions of whatever character, denomination, duration or object, nor civil corporations, when under the patronage, direction or administration of the former, or of ministers of any creed shall have legal capacity to acquire title to, or administer, real property, other than the buildings **immediately and directly destined to the services or purposes of the said corporations and institutions.**	Art. 27. **The ownership of lands and waters comprised within the limits of the national territory is vested originally in the Nation,** which has had, and has, the right to transmit title thereof to private persons, thereby constituting private property. **The Nation shall have at all times the right to impose on private property such restrictions as the public interest may demand** as well as the right to regulate the development of natural resources, which are susceptible of appropriation, **in order to conserve them and equitably to distribute the public wealth.** For this purpose, necessary measures shall be taken to divide large landed estates; **to develop small landed holdings; to establish new centers of rural population with such lands and waters as may be indispensable to them; to encourage agriculture and to prevent the destruction of natural resources**, and damages against property to the detriment of society.

While recognizing the right to property, Article 27 of the 1917 Constitution limited this right to make room for the forms of common possession in village communities.[75] The same article spoke of restitution of land to indigenous communities and expropriation of large private holdings in favor of landless people.[76] But what is most interesting, especially in light of the Zapatista insurgency, is that Article 27 indicated an alternative way for modern relations of private property in the autonomy of village communities. "Only members of the commune shall have the right to the lands destined to be divided, and the rights to these lands shall be inalienable so long as they remain undivided" (Art. 27, Sec. VII).

If we look instead at Article 27 as amended following the agrarian reform of November 1991, sought by President Salinas,[77] we can see that Section VII, while speaking of the protection of "indigenous groups' land," constantly refers to the intervention of the state to define the right of the indigenous peoples on the land. "The law shall regulate the exercise of indigenous peoples' rights over their land and of joint-title farmers" (Art. 27, Sec. VII). In this way, through constant reference to the law and to state intervention, the reform pushed toward an individualization of the common land, and granted members of the *ejidos* the right to sell their individual plots.

From the very first months of the uprising, the Zapatistas demanded "the nullification of the agrarian reforms of 1991 and 1992" and the "return to the spirit of Article 27 approved in Querétaro in 1917."[78] With this, the Zapatistas intended to reactivate not the words of the 1917 Mexican Constitution but its spirit. In an interview with the Comité Clandestino Revolucionario Indígena-Comandancia General inf February 1994, they expressly said, "we have to make new laws to divide up the land, maybe different from how Zapata said. . . . We need another form of working, of organizing ourselves. But ownership of the land should pass into the people's hands."[79] These few lines contain an entire political project: relationship with tradition, agrarian reform, new institutions, and new property regime.

1917 Mexican Constitution	Mexican Constitution Salina's amendments to Art. 27[80]	1993 Zapatista's Revolutionary Agrarian Law
Art. 27 Sec. II. The religious associations known as churches, irrespective of creed, **shall in no case** have legal capacity to acquire, hold or administer real property or loans made on such real property.... Sec. III. Public and private charitable institutions for the sick and needy, for scientific research, or for the diffusion of knowledge, mutual aid societies or organizations formed for any other lawful purpose **shall in no case acquire, hold or administer loans made on real property, unless the mortgage terms do not exceed ten years.**	Art. 27 Sec. II. Religious associations, created in accordance with the terms provided in Article 130 and its regulatory law, **can acquire, possess or manage, properties** essential for their religious activities.... Sec. III. Public and private charitable institutions for the sick and needy, for scientific research, or for the diffusion of knowledge, mutual aid societies or organizations formed for any other lawful purpose **cannot acquire other real estate than that which is essential to fulfill their objective, according to the regulatory law.**	Art. 3. All poor-quality land in excess of 100 hectares and all good-quality land in excess of 50 hectares will be subject to the Revolutionary Agrarian Law. **The landowners whose lands exceed the aforementioned limits will have the excess taken away from them, and they will be left with the minimum permitted by this law. They may remain as small landholders or join the cooperative** *campesinos'* **movement,** *campesino* **societies, or communal** lands (*tierras comunales*). Art. 5. **The lands** affected by this agrarian law **will be distributed to the landless** *campesinos* **and the agricultural laborers** who request it **as collective property (PROPIEDAD COLECTIVA)** ...

1917 Mexican Constitution	Mexican Constitution Salina's amendments to Art. 27[80]	1993 Zapatista's Revolutionary Agrarian Law
Sec. IV. Commercial stock companies **shall not acquire, hold, or administer rural properties.** Sec. VII. . . . All laws of restitution enacted by virtue of this provision shall be immediately carried into effect by the administrative authorities. **Only members of the commune shall have the right to the lands destined to be divided, and the rights to these lands shall be inalienable so long as they remain undivided**; the same provision shall govern the right of ownership after the division has been made. . . .	Sec. IV. Commercial stock companies **can own rural lands, but only in the extension necessary to fulfill their objective.**	Art. 7. In order to better cultivate the land for the benefit of the poor *campesinos* and the agricultural laborers, the expropriation of large estates and agricultural/livestock monopolies will include the expropriation of means of production such as machinery, fertilizer, stores, financial resources, chemical products and technical expertise Art. 12. **Individual hoarding (*acaparamiento individual*) of land and the means of production will not be permitted.** Art. 13. Zones of virgin jungle and forest will be preserved. There will be reforestation campaigns in the principal zones.

1917 Mexican Constitution	Mexican Constitution Salina's amendments to Art. 27[80]	1993 Zapatista's Revolutionary Agrarian Law
(a) In each State and Territory there shall be fixed **the maximum area of land which any one individual or legally organized corporation may own**. . . .	Sec. VII. **The law** shall regulate the exercise of commoners' (*comuneros*) rights over their land and of joint-title farmers over their parcels, respecting their will to adopt the best conditions for the use of their productive resources. **The law shall establish the procedures whereby the** members of an *ejidos* and commoners (*ejidatarios y comuneros*) may: associate among themselves or with the State or with third parties; grant the use of their lands; **transfer their land rights to other members of their rural community, in the event of farming cooperative.**	

1917 Mexican Constitution	Mexican Constitution Salina's amendments to Art. 27[80]	1993 Zapatista's Revolutionary Agrarian Law
(f) The local laws **shall** govern the extent of the family patrimony, and **determine what property shall constitute the same on the basis of its inalienability**; it shall not be subject to attachment nor to any charge whatever.	The law shall also set forth the **requirements and procedures whereby the *ejidal* assembly shall grant their members (*ejidatario*) private rights (*dominio*) over land.** In cases of **transfer of ownership**, the right of preference set forth by the law shall be respected.	Art. 14. The riverheads, rivers, lakes and oceans are the collective property of the Mexican people (*propiedad colectiva del pueblo mexicano*), and **they will be cared for by not polluting them** and by punishing their misuse. Art. 16. The *campesinos* who work collectively will not be taxed. Nor will the *ejidos*, cooperatives or communal lands be taxed.

The conflict is articulated on different levels. In fact, the change introduced by the Salinas reform not only introduces a market economy into agricultural land but also gives shape to a new possessive mentality. While recognizing the "legal personality of the nuclei of the *ejidos* population" (Art. 27, Sec. VII), the reform individualizes the legal relations in the peasant community by means of constant reference to the state law which, on the one hand, protects the "wholeness of the indigenous groups' lands" and, on the other, "shall regulate the exercise of commoners' (*comuneros*) rights over their land and . . . set forth the requirements and procedures whereby the *ejidal* assembly shall grant their members (*ejidatario*) private rights (*dominio*) over land" (Art. 27, Sec. VII).

Although it is possible to distinguish between *ejido* and *comunidad*, the 1992 reform, even in the language used, tends to conflate the two terms. "In order to promote respect and strengthening of the community life of farming cooperatives and communal land (*la vida comunitaria de los ejidos y comunidades*), *the law* shall protect the lands for human settlements and *shall regulate the uses of communal lands, forests and waters.* The law shall implement actions to improve the quality of life in such communities. *The law*, by respecting the will of the *ejidatarios* and *comuneros* to adopt conditions that best suit them in the use of their productive resources, *will regulate the exercise of the rights of comuneros on the land and of each ejidatario on its parcel*" (Art. 27, Sec. VII). If, originally, the *comunidad* referred to a preexisting entity regulated by internal rules and customs, its legal regime was now equated with that of the *ejido*.

The transition is not innocent. In the case of the *ejido*, the state maintains the title on the land and grants the members of the *ejido*, called *ejidatarios*, the right to cultivate the land both in collective form and in the form of individual *parcelas*. By equating the *comunidad* to the *ejido*, the former was subjected to the legal regime of the latter, thus paving the way for state intervention, individualization, and private-property relations.

In the 1917 Constitution, the collective law of the *ejido* had priority over individual law, so that the *ejidatarios* could not sell or rent the land but could only transmit the right of usufruct on it. With the 1992 reform, however, an *ejido* could confer individual title to land to individual *ejidatarios*, who could maintain the ownership of the land even without working it. The *ejidatarios* could thus rent or sell the land and form partnerships with private entrepreneurs. The process of capitalist modernization sought by Salinas was configured as a process of synchronization with the market and its legal regime.

From a theoretical point of view, it is interesting to note that when *ejidos* and *comunidades* are *recognized* as having "legal status" (*personalidad jurídica*), the price to pay for this recognition is the erosion of common possession and collective forms of self-government. In other words, the destruction of the indigenous communities' autonomy is one with their legal recognition. It is a story that has been repeated countless times in the course of modernity. Recognition gives rise to a new juridical universal in which the authority that is exercised within a community is negated and, at the same time, is lifted up to the level of *dominio*, which is thereby reconfigured through recognition by the state that *regulates "the exercise of the rights of comuneros on the land and of each ejidatario on its parcel"* (Art. 27, Sec. VII). This is how the *ejidatario* acquires private rights (*dominio*) over land (Art. 27, Sec. VII). With legal *recognition* the community receives the right of private property for its members and entry into the sphere of the legal regulation of contractual relations. If you start with recognition, you end with the state. Recognition is the death sentence for every alternative trajectory to the modern state. Hence, there are the skepticism of indigenous peoples toward the declarations written in the language of individual human rights,[81] their criticism of legal citizenship[82] and the rejection of the logic of recognition.[83]

Recognition is the solvent of community relations and the engine that runs the movement "from status to contract."[84] This, in Maine's words, is the "progressive societies" movement. It gives rise to contractual relations between juridical individuals who recognize each other as such. The individual, in the words of Hegel, "behaves, therefore, towards others in a manner that is universally valid, recognizing them—as he wishes others to recognize him—as free, as persons."[85] Progressive society cancels the dissymmetries, the personal relationships of an authoritative type, and establishes relationships between proprietor individuals who exchange things through mediation by law: contractual relations. In other words, the "progressive societies" movement and the movement toward private-property relations are one.

Civil law is the outpost of Western colonial civilization. The *dominium*, this term that in medieval times included both the concepts of power and of property, is dichotomized by removing authority from the community, which is reconfigured as power in the hands of the state and property in the hands of individuals.

This demarcation has been repeated countless times, in Europe and outside Europe, and is the common matrix of colonialism and the so-called primitive accumulation of capital. Indeed, the alternative to private property is not state property, as often, both on the Left and on the Right, one is led to think. State ownership of land, water, and subsoil resources is an inheritance of colonialism, both within and outside of Europe. State violence has destroyed the indigenous alternative of common possession, which cannot be equated with a right of land ownership in the hands of a community. Rather, in the expression "common possession," the accent has to be put on the first term. Possession is common because use is common, and thus nobody owns the privilege of abusing the land. What makes the term "common" so important is its link with democracy. Indeed, the way communities use land and the means of production are matters of democratic decision based on the self-government of communities, villages, and neighborhoods.

In Mayan indigenous tradition, common possession of the land is configured in a legal constellation whose center is *not* the individual will, but the territory, understood as a network of ecological units, which cannot be subdivided or alienated.[86] On April 25, 2007, in San Cristóbal, Comandanta Kelly recalled that "for indigenous peasant and rural peoples, land and territory (*la tierra y el territorio*) are more than work and food: they are also culture, community, history, ancestry, future dreams, life and mother. But for two centuries, the capitalist system has de-ruralized, expelled peasants and indigenous people, changed the face of the Earth, dehumanized it."[87] Territorial right embraces many different elements, such as culture, spirituality, and collective dignity. The territory is a collective good, it is trans-personal, and it is trans-generational, since it "transcends the present generation's legal will, making the territory unavailable (*inalienable, unseizable*) and conceptually indivisible."[88] The modern concept of private property, be it individual or state, is incompatible with the indigenous concept of territory and territorial right. At the basis of the concept of territory there is, in fact, its preservation as a space for life shared by past, present, and future generations.

IN LIEU OF A CONCLUSION

Trajectories of Possession

BY COMPARING THE EXPRESSION "TIERRA y Libertad" of the Mexican revolutionaries to "Zemlja i Volja" (Land and Liberty) of the *narodniks*, it is perhaps possible to draw lines of connection between the end of the nineteenth century in Russia and the beginning of the twentieth century in Mexico. But this connection is made possible at a deeper level—the layer that led Marx to suppose that common possession was almost a universal form. "A ridiculous presumption has latterly got abroad that common property in its primitive form is specifically a Slavonian, or even exclusively Russian form. It is the original form (*Urform*) that we can prove to have existed amongst Romans, Teutons, and Celts, and which indeed still exists to this day in India, in a whole range of diverse patterns, albeit sometimes only as remnants."[1]

Marx was still missing an appropriate conceptual historical representation for what he had grasped. Concepts do not evolve progressively along a historical-temporal line; rather, they are temporally stratified, and different historical sedimentations correspond to each layer. To arrive at this historical vision, we must replace the image of linear development with that of a historical multiverse. Common possession of land constitutes one of these strata, which, among other things, spans an enormously greater historical time than does capitalist modernity. There are social, political, and economic forms of life based on common possession that have been experimented with for a very long time, all over the globe. From this point of view, capitalist modernity is nothing more than a tiny historical-geographical fragment. Among the many possible roads, it was the one taken. By virtue of a unilinear philosophy of history, an alleged superior efficiency of private property over common property, and a robust dose of economic and extra-economic violence, this trajectory has asserted itself as universal and dominant.

Initially, European colonialism, through the concept of *terra nullius*, denied the indigenous ownership of land. Subsequently, the legal framework was redefined based on the idea that, with the conquest of the New World, the indigenous peoples lost ownership of all lands, so that these people's legal status changed from being owners to being tenants. The conquest of the New World conferred title on lands to the European states, which later was transferred to the United States. In this way, as resulted in decisions in the case of *Johnson v. M'Intosh* (1823), Native Americans could not purchase land and the colonizers could obtain the tribal lands cheaply.[2] Behind the scenes of this colonial violence, Western legal concepts such as private ownership came to the fore as universal and metahistorical.[3]

The conceptual arsenal for the modern enterprise of private property is consecrated in the canon of Western political theory. Its history goes back to John Locke's denunciation of common possession of land as an anachronism of un-civility: "the wild Indian," wrote Locke, "knows no inclosure, and is still a tenant in common."[4] By establishing a dual dichotomy, spatial and temporal, Locke provided ideological instruments for colonialism and the war against the commons. The enclosures represent civilization, while the common possession becomes, temporally, an anachronism and, spatially, something that disregards the faraway "wild Indian(s)." These Indians, according to Locke's puritan ethic of labor, would also be responsible for leaving their land uncultivated. And according to the modern theory of private property that Locke was outlining, the cultivation of land and its appropriation are intertwined. This was an equation that did not apply to commoners and diggers. The purpose of that equation was to individualize property.

The so-called Western civilization divides the world synchronically and diachronically into barbarians and moderns, imposing a mentality that bends toward modern Western views of property and values. This mentality—that is, of the *Homo proprietarius*— is based on new kinds of relationships between individuals and between *individual will* and nature. It is on the latter dichotomy, not on the distinction between human and nature, that modern relations of private property are founded—in the words of Hegel, on humankind's "absolute right to appropriate all that is a thing."[5] Hegel condensed the basis for the juridical anthropology of the modern *Homo proprietarius* in the definition of the person as infinite free will— a form which he developed in the concept of private property.[6] Pursuant to this opposition between will and nature, the latter becomes, in Locke's terms, "almost worthless materials"[7] and, in Hegel's, a thing on which individuals impose their own will, their ends and soul.[8] From this position, it follows that human beings have "the absolute *right of appropriation*" over all things.[9] This right makes the human being the "lord over all of nature."[10]

Modern property relations even had their own morbid poetry. The English magnate and prime minister of Cape Colony Cecil Rhodes lyrically stated: "To think of these stars that you see overhead at night, these vast worlds which we can never reach. I would annex the planets if I could; I often think of that. It makes me sad to see them so clear and yet so far."[11] This dominant trajectory of modernity finds a timely counterpoint in another legacy. In 1649, forty years before the publication of Locke's *Second Treatise*, the Diggers' declaration was published: *A Declaration from the Poor Oppressed People of England*. Here, the Diggers contested the trajectory of "particular propriety" in the name of a different tradition and a different way of understanding possession: "For the earth, with all her fruits of corn, cattle and such like, was made to be a common storehouse of livelihood to all mankind, friend and foe, without exception."[12] The practice of the commons defended by the Diggers reconfigured the notion of possession in nonexclusive and nonnational terms. It instead referred, in egalitarian terms, to "all the nations of the world"[13] and to all generations: "For we shall endeavour by our righteous acting not to leave the earth any longer entangled unto our children by self-seeking proprietors; but to leave it a free store-house and common treasury to all, without respect of persons."[14]

The language of the English Diggers in 1649 echoes that of the German peasants of 1525. Indeed, insurgent peasants presented their program in the famous Twelve Articles, which defended common property, agrarian communism, and a form of rule based on participation and self-government.[15] The Twelve Articles endorsed the communal possession of land in an antifeudal sense, oriented toward a nonhierarchical communalism; they supported the imperative mandate as a practice of community power, as well as universal equality and brotherhood as a way of being.

This alternate legacy of modernity reemerges during the French Revolution, in the Manifesto of the Enragés of 1793 and again in the Manifesto of the Equals in 1796: "We are aiming at something more sublime and more equitable: the *common good* or the *community of goods!* No more individual property in land, *the land belongs to no one.* We demand, we want the common enjoyment of the fruits of the earth: the fruits belong to all."[16] These written works and the names of Gerrard Winstanley, Thomas Müntzer, Jacques Roux, and François-Noël Babeuf, among others, are marginalized in the canon of modern political theory. But the task of critical history is to read these words line by line, parallel to classics such as those of Locke and Hegel. What emerges is not an intellectual competition but, rather, a clash between alternative theoretical and political trajectories.

The price paid by the defeated is not just their exclusion from the canon. That would be a little thing and, to remedy this, it would be enough to add a few pages to school textbooks. But the defeated are such because the winners have absolutized the political and economic concepts of modernity, to the point at which those concepts have become common sense and make any alternative trajectory marginal or residual; thus, a real alternative to state and capitalist modernity becomes almost unthinkable.

The concept of property has become a sort of ubiquitous human institution that can be found in all places and at all times—a sort of anthropological constant that is reproduced in every human grouping at different levels of development. This universalization is undoubtedly ideological, in the sense that it indefinitely expands the dominant modern Western categories to the extent of naturalizing them; however, this universalizing movement is not just the result of bad faith or ignorance. That tendency is inherent in modern concepts that are universalized by linear development. There is still much work to do in this direction, to break the spell that transforms modern Western concepts into universal and quasi-natural concepts.

The clash with indigenous temporality calls into question the universalizing claim of modern Western concepts and shows a third possibility—one that goes beyond the binary opposition of progress by capitalist modernization and the romanticism of community. In Chiapas, the Zapatista insurgency is not for peasant ownership of the land; it stands against individualization and for common possession, democratically regulated in local self-government. In Bolivia, the Coalition for the Defense of Water and Life has redefined its authorities and property relations beyond the binary opposition of private and public. What has emerged are new forms of "social property" in which groups and associations maintain the authority to control and use resources such as water without claiming its property.[17]

Trying to understand these experiments with property relationships using the grammar of Western modern concepts can easily lead to great misunderstandings. The legal language of property rights conflicts with that of indigenous communities, who consider the territory not as a natural resource but as a natural relative, employing a different grammar of possession. It is possible, however, to translate the conceptual constellation of relationships regarding a common possession of land into the language of other non-capitalist contexts, which allows a closer comparison of modern and nonmodern Western categories. In abandoning the unilinear and teleological paradigm of universal history, we see that medieval juridical material could be configured differently, and this opens up possibilities for communications among the trajectories of Russian communal possession, agrarian socialism of the English Diggers, common possession of land by indigenous communities, universalization of property by the Communards, and the *dominium utile* of the European Middle Ages.

But we must be careful how the historical categories are used. The bridge does not connect the Russian *obshchina* as a "feudal archaic residue," the "pre-capitalist" indigenous agrarian communities, and the European Middle Ages. This is, after all, how Eurocentric universal history works. Instead, the temporal multiverse shows the way in which anachronisms intersect with each other and the clash between the temporalities gives rise to productive chronotones. Overcoming temporal provincialism means that it is not the European Middle Ages that show us the "feudal" nature of the *obshchina*; on the contrary, it is the latter that shows us the Middle Ages as a field of possibilities for alternative trajectories that streak across the European continent. With this spirit, the Communards retrieved medieval juridical material to activate alternative institutions for that nation-state. Similarly, the *ayllus*, the indigenous local forms of self-government in South America, instead of being an obstacle to capitalist modernization, constitute an opportunity to experiment with different forms of life and politics that connect to the Russian *mir* and the soviets, as well as the Paris Commune.[18] These forms are not relics but, rather, are social structures that have existed elsewhere since before modernity— not in remote geographical spaces or in some oceanic atoll, but in temporalities that flow alongside the dominant one of capitalist modernity.[19]

From the Middle Ages to capitalist modernity, there has not been a sole historical trajectory that can be constructed from the single outcome of European modernity. Instead, there are multiple streams that were interrupted and then reactivated in different configurations throughout history. The European Middle Ages showed us a way of possession defined, not from the primacy of the individual who exercises an unlimited and illimitable right over land, but from a rei-centric relationship in which primacy is given to the thing (*res*).[20] The modern outlook, however, sees the primacy of the sovereign subject over the thing.

The medieval conception of possession posed the primacy of the real, and was based on the connective tissue of groups that individuals were part of. In this conception, property was not modeled on the individual will but, rather, corresponded to the complexity of the real order and to the multiplicity of *dominia utilia*,[21] which limited the right of the owner. Possession, the *dominium*, was never exclusive; it was shared by those who exercised a *dominium utile*. In other words, what is relevant here is the multiplicity of *dominia utilia* that limit and define the role of the *dominus directus*—what today we would call the proprietor. The *dominus* who abused his power provoked rebellion, even very violent ones, by the peasants who redefined the sphere of dominion. Similarly, power was not monopolized but, rather, was articulated in mutually limiting authorities.

Comparison with another way of possession allows us to highlight an alternative trajectory of possession that differs from that concept of private ownership. In general terms, modernity takes shape in the clash between the limits that characterize medieval economic and power relations and the limitlessness of the individual subject's will, the right to property, and the absolute power of the state.[22] Marx showed that one of the specific characteristics of the capitalist mode of production is precisely the absence of limits in the process of valorization. In order to bring into focus this difference between limits and limitlessness, Marx needed new studies in the ethnological and anthropological fields. Thus, he read Lewis H. Morgan's *Ancient Society*, a text that can today be accused of ethnocentrism,[23] but which, in its encounter with indigenous communities, posed an essential question for our present.

Indeed, in the final pages of the book, Morgan wrote that property has become an "uncontrollable power," that humanity, like a sorcerer's apprentice, "stands bewildered in the presence of its own creation."[24] Looking at the indigenous communities, Morgan hoped that a "mere property career is not the final destiny of mankind" because "such a career contains the elements of self-destruction."[25] But an alternative possibility becomes conceivable and desirable from the encounter with the indigenous trajectory, which Morgan reads in the light of the issues opened up by modern civilization. This alternative, concludes Morgan, "will be a revival, in a higher form, of the liberty, equality and fraternity of the ancient *gentes*."

Marx, reading, commenting on, and translating Morgan's pages, writes that modern societies tend toward "a revival in a superior form of an archaic social type." He adds, "We must not let ourselves be alarmed at the word 'archaic.'"[26] Precisely. We must not be alarmed by the word "archaic" because it does not stand behind us, as in the unilinear and progressive representation of historical time; rather, it flows along as a different trajectory in the many temporal layers of modernity and configures new chronotones. Marx refers to one of these layers when he writes that, from the point of view of communist society, "private ownership of the globe by single individuals will appear quite as absurd as private ownership of one man by another. Even a whole society, a nation, or all simultaneously existing societies taken together, are not the owners of the globe. They are only its temporary possessors, its usufructuaries (*Nutznießer*), and, like *boni patres familias*, they must hand it down to succeeding generations in an improved condition."[27]

Marx's concept of property is redefined as usufruct on the part of human generations, which use the land as "*boni patres familias*." Not only does this concept denote an attitude toward common land, but also it is spatially and temporally broadened: no subject, individual or collective, even the entire humanity, that is of one's own epoch, is owner of the earth. To attribute an absolute right of ownership to a collective subject, be it the state or the nation, does not change anything in the relationship. The Marxian image transcends the temporality that links property to the present. The trans-temporal dimension produces a double semantic slippage: property becomes usufruct, and the right to things becomes the "duty" to pass the earth onto successive generations in an improved condition.

The term "usufructuary" has the advantage of referring to a right to enjoy the good according to the use to which it is destined, without alienating or destroying it. It is a right that supersedes the provincial conception of time and that is conceded to generations past and to come. It is, therefore, a right that is limited, but not limited by the state. If one moves beyond the binary opposition of private property as a right to exclude and state property, then property relations can be defined as an institution that binds the members of a community and establishes relationships, instead of making separations. The institution of usufruct drops the right of ownership to alienate the thing and, instead, considers the relationship with the good as a loan. In other words, the present generation does not inherit but, rather, borrows the good to return it to future generations after having taken care of it.

The subject is no longer an "I" but, instead, a "we" that includes present, past, and future generations. Similarly, the "good" is no longer a simple external thing but, instead, a nature toward which we have duties, and in this sense makes demands on us. These are the demands of the generations who, before us, took care of the territory. This priority of duty over right changes the whole relationship with territory. The dominant modernity has terminated these kinds of property relations, practically and theoretically. Rethinking them means learning to speak another language. An indication of this change in direction comes from Gandhi's practice of *aparigraha* (nonpossession), which encourages one to "not possess anything which one does not really need."[28] It is not a denial of property but, rather, its restriction within the concept of *proper use*.

What is at stake in the legacy of insurgent universality is the democratization of that usage through assemblies, councils, and associations, which binds the right of the proprietor. Modern private property, on the contrary, is antidemocratic by definition. If modern sovereignty and the modern right to private property arise together, both are characterized by the right to exclude; insurgent universality undoes both through a different practice of freedom and democracy, which are redefined, starting from unexplored trajectories of modernity. If, as stated in Article 4 of the 1789 Declaration, "liberty consists of doing anything which does not harm others," it is necessary to redefine the concept of freedom, as that outlined by the Communards in their Declaration of the Rights of Man Transposed to the City.[29] In that 1789 Article, freedom subsists only by means of a law that establishes borders which define the sphere of individual freedom and avoid conflict between individual liberties. Instead, by emphasizing the rights of groups, both the Communards and the Russian revolutionaries gave priority to the duties and responsibilities toward the community or the city. Not only that, those rights were understood in terms of agency, such as freedom and the political practices of associations and their members, and not just as individual rights that the state must protect.

Today, the question of different property relations is raised with urgency in relation to the environment and natural resources. During the 2016–17 Standing Rock protests concerning the Dakota Access Pipeline in the U.S. West, Chief Arvol Looking Horse expressed the different indigenous perspectives with regard to the territory:

> We, the Original Caretakers of Mother Earth, *have no choice but* to follow and uphold the Original Instructions, which sustains the continuity of Life. We recognize our umbilical connection to Mother Earth and *understand that she is the source of life, not a*

resource to be exploited. We speak on behalf of all Creation today, to communicate an urgent message that man has gone too far, placing us in the state of survival. Not heeding warnings from both Nature and the People of the Earth keeps us on *the path of self-destruction.* These self-destructive activities and development continue to cause the deterioration and destruction of sacred places and sacred waters that are vital for Life.[30]

This perspective would have sounded familiar to the Russian peasant, whose relationship with land was not of private property but of use and usufruct. The bridge that unites the indigenous communities is not built upon a cosmology that curbs the environmental disaster capitalist modernity is causing. Rather, that cosmology is the expression of a different mentality of possession and an understanding of relationship with the territory. Here the absolute right of the owner (subject) gives way to common possession and to the usufruct of land. It is, above all, a different proprietary regime, not a cosmology to be adopted by free individual choice. This conception, to the extent that it assumes a centrality of individual will, is still part of the problem.

If we start from the priority of the territory, and not of the subject, the network of property relations changes profoundly. It is defined and delimited starting from multiple relations with that territory. The individual ceases to be at the center of these relationships. But this alternative framework requires a different subjectivation, a point that starts from where the individual, both as a single person and as an entire generation, ceases to portray itself as lord of nature, and instead is a link in an intergenerational chain. And through this, nature can be restored as the common storehouse.

Thus, we see an alternative legacy in which it is possible to reveal bridges that unite different insurgencies throughout history—and not only European history. The *Sans-culottes*, the Communards, peasants, and indigenous peoples have all experimented with democracy as a practice that takes care of both the community and the land. The two sides of the *dominium*, which Western modernity has dichotomized, can be recombined differently when power is not monopolized by the state and property is not an absolute individual right. The Zapatista slogan "land to the tiller" puts the priority of use on property rights. Democracy raises the question of good use through the institutions of those who live on and till the land.

It is not about creating an entirely new world. The innumerable paths of the insurgent universality help us to provincialize the present. These alternative trajectories have faced colonialism and a long war against the commons. The translation between these alternative trajectories is what characterizes the legacy of insurgent universality. The Zapatistas' experiment teaches us, on a practical level this art of translation among multiple levels because, as the Zapatistas wrote, "there are different paths but one longing." Now, we know that the dominant modern trajectory has also been one of these paths—an experiment with the state, the capitalist mode of production, and private property. For reasons we have seen, this path has been represented as the sole, universal normative for the rest of humanity. But there are other paths and other ways of practicing universality. In this sense, for insurgent universality, one can only speak of *experiments*. Different ways of practicing and experimenting with something in common. This is what I have called "universality," which is "insurgent" because it rises up, creating tensions with the dominant layers of modernity.

NOTES

Preface

1. Ruth O'Brien, *Out of Many One: Obama and the Third American Tradition* (Chicago: University of Chicago, 2013), 6–9.

Chapter 1

1. Walter Benjamin, *The Arcades Project*, ed. Rolf Tiedemann, trans. Howard Eiland and Kevin McLaughlin (Cambridge, MA, and London: Harvard University Press, 1999), 857: O°, 5.
2. Reinhart Koselleck, "Geschichte, Historie," in *Geschichtliche Grundbegriffe: Historisches Lexikon zur politisch-sozialen Sprache in Deutschland*, ed. Otto Brunner, Werner Conze, and Reinhart Koselleck (Stuttgart: Klett-Cotta, 1992), 2:647–91; as well Koselleck's work, *Futures Past: On the Semantics of Historical Time*, trans. Keith Tribe (New York: Columbia University Press, 2005).
3. Friedrich Schiller, *Was heißt und zu welchen Ende studiert man Universalgeschichte?* (Jena: Akademische Buchhandlung, 1789).
4. August von Cieszkowski, *Prolegomena zur Historiosophie* (Hamburg: Felix Meiner, 1981 [1838]).

5. Immanuel Kant, *Critique of Pure Reason*, ed. and trans. Paul Guyer and Allen M. Wood (Cambridge: Cambridge University Press, 1998), 259, B 156.
6. Johann Gottfried Herder, *Verstand und Erfahrung: Eine Metakritik der Kritik der Reinen Vernunft* (Leipzig: J.F. Hartknoch, 1799), 120–21.
7. Koselleck, *Futures Past*, 2.
8. Reinhart Koselleck, *Zeitschichten* (Frankfurt: Suhrkamp, 2001); Reinhart Koselleck, "Wiederholungsstrukturen in Sprache und Geschichte," in *Vom Sinn und Unsinn der Geschichte* (Frankfurt: Suhrkamp, 2010), 96–114.
9. Koselleck, *Zeitschichten*, 238.
10. Ernst Bloch, "Differentiations in the Concept of Progress" (1955), in *A Philosophy of the Future*, trans. John Cumming (New York: Herder and Herder, 1970), 143.
11. Benjamin, *Arcades Project*, 456: N 1,2.
12. Walter Benjamin, "On the Concept of History," trans. Harry Zohn, in *Selected Writings, vol. 4: 1938–1940*, ed. Howard Eiland and Michael W. Jennings (Cambridge, MA: Harvard University Press, 2006), 389–411.
13. Karl Marx, *Drafts of the Letter to Vera Zasulich*, trans. Barrie Selmann, in *Marx and Engels Collected Works* (London: Lawrence & Wishart, 1989), 24:358.
14. Marx, *Drafts of the Letter to Vera Zasulich*, 367–68. See Massimiliano Tomba, *Marx's Temporalities* (Leiden: Brill, 2013), 159–86.
15. Karl Marx, *Theories of Surplus Value* (Amherst, NY: Prometheus, 2000), 3:468.
16. Harry Harootunian, *Marx After Marx: History and Time in the Expansion of Capitalism* (New York: Columbia University Press, 2015), 206.
17. Michel Serres with Bruno Latour, *Conversations on Science, Culture, and Time*, trans. Roxanne Lapidus (Ann Arbor: University of Michigan Press, 1995), 60. Serres says: "If you take a handkerchief and spread it out in order to iron it, you can see in it certain fixed distances and proximities. If you sketch a circle in one area, you can mark out nearby points and measure far-off distances. Then take the same handkerchief and

crumple it, by putting it in your pocket. Two distant points suddenly are close, even superimposed. If, further, you tear it in certain places, two points that were close can become very distant. This science of nearness and rifts is called topology, while the science of stable and well-defined distances is called metrical geometry."

18. Dipesh Chakrabarty, *Provincializing Europe: Postcolonial Thought and Historical Difference* (Princeton, NJ, and Oxford: Princeton University Press, 2000).
19. T. S. Eliot, *What Is a Classic?* (London: Faber & Faber, 1945), 30.
20. Bruno Bauer, *Geschichte Deutschlands und der französischen Revolution unter der Herrschaft Napoleons* (Charlottenburg: E. Bauer, 1846), 2:253 and 255; Alexis de Tocqueville, *The Old Régime and the Revolution,* trans. Stuart Gilbert (New York: Anchor, 1983).
21. François Furet and Denis Richet, *La révolution française* (Paris: Hachette, 1986), 9. Benedetto Croce, *Scritti e discorsi politici, 1943–1947* (Naples: Bibliopolis, 1993).
22. J. S. Mill, *On Liberty and Other Writings* (Cambridge: Cambridge University Press, 1989),13; J. S. Mill, "Considerations on Representative Government," in *The Collected Works* (Toronto: Toronto University Press, 1977), 19:335–36. Uday S. Mehta, *Liberalism and Empire: A Study in Nineteenth-Century British Liberal Thought* (Chicago: University of Chicago Press, 1999).
23. Aimé Césaire, "Letter to Maurice Thorez," trans. Chike Jeffers, *Social Text* 28, no. 2 (2010): 149.
24. Gary Wilder, *Freedom Time: Negritude, Decolonization and the Future of the World* (Durham, NC, and London: Duke University Press, 2015).
25. Tomba, *Marx's Temporalities*, 144.
26. I want to thank Prof. Simav Bargu for the beautiful conversation we had in France and his explanation of the geological phenomenon of subduction.
27. Benjamin, "On the Concept of History," 402: XVII A.
28. See Ethan Kleinberg, *Haunting History: For a Deconstructive Approach to the Past* (Stanford, CA: Stanford University Press, 2017).

29. Hayden White, *Tropics of Discourse: Essays in Cultural Criticism* (Baltimore, MD: Johns Hopkins University Press, 1978), 281.
30. Koselleck, *Futures Past*, 111.
31. Hayden White, *Metahistory: The Historical Imagination in Nineteenth-Century Europe* (Baltimore, MD: Johns Hopkins University Press, 1973).
32. Benjamin, "On the Concept of History," 394.
33. "The philosophers have only interpreted the world, in various ways; the point is to change it," quoted in Karl Marx, *Early Writings*, trans. Rodney Livingstone and Gregor Benton (London: Penguin, 1992), 423.
34. Benjamin, *Arcades Project*, 471: N 8,1.
35. Adolfo Gilly, *The Mexican Revolution* (New York: New Press, 2005), 268–73.
36. Rebecca Manski, of Occupy Wall Street, acknowledged the Zapatista influence after visiting Oventic. She said: "As soon as I arrived I saw that many of the principles, language, themes and ways of organizing Occupy Wall Street had been taken straight from Zapatista philosophy." See Duncan Tucker, "Are Mexico's Zapatista Rebels Still Relevant?," *Al-Jazeera*, January 1, 2014, http://www.aljazeera.com/indepth/features/2014/01/are-mexico-zapatista-rebels-still-relevant-20141183731812643.html.
37. G. W. F. Hegel, *Lectures on the Philosophy of World History*, trans. H. B. Nisbet (Cambridge: Cambridge University Press, 1984) 54–55.
38. Immanuel Kant, *The Contest of the Faculties*, in *Toward the Perpetual Peace and Other Writings on Politics, Peace and History*, ed. Pauline Kleingeld, trans. David L. Colclasure (New Haven, CT: Yale University Press, 2006), 150: Ak 7:79.
39. Kant, *Contest of the Faculties*, 152: K 7:81.
40. Kant, *Contest of the Faculties*, 150: K 7:79.
41. Kant, *Contest of the Faculties*, 155: K 7:85 (translation modified).
42. Richard Tuck, *The Sleeping Sovereign: The Invention of Modern Democracy* (Cambridge: Cambridge University Press, 2015).
43. The Bossales were former slaves born in Africa who constituted the majority of the population of Santo Domingo. Gérard Barthélemy, *L'univers rural Haitien: Le pays en dehors* (Paris: L'Harmattan, 1990).

44. As Susan Buck-Morss observed, the Haitian Revolution "rather than giving multiple, distinct cultures equal due, whereby people are recognized as part of humanity indirectly through the mediation of collective cultural identities, human universality emerges in the historical event at the point of rupture. It is in the discontinuities of history that people whose culture has been strained to the breaking point give expression to a humanity that goes beyond cultural limits." Susan Buck-Morss, *Hegel, Haiti and Universal History* (Pittsburgh, PA: University of Pittsburgh Press, 2009), 133.
45. Léger-Félicité Sonthonax, *Proclamation au nom de la République* (1793), in *The Haitian Revolution: A Documentary History*, ed. David Geggus (Indianapolis, IN: Hackett, 2014), 107.
46. Eduardo Grüner, *La oscuridad y las luces: Capitalismo, cultura y revolución* (Buenos Aires: Edhasa, 2010), 34.
47. Haitian Constitution of 1801, Art. 3, in Toussaint L'Ouverture, *The Haitian Revolution*, ed. Nick Nesbitt (London and New York: Verso, 2008), 46. On the degree of universality of Art. 3, see Sibylle Fischer, *Modernity Disavowed: Haiti and the Cultures of Slavery in the Age of Revolution* (Durham, NC, and London: Duke University Press, 2004), 266–71.
48. Nick Nesbitt, "Alter-Rights: Haiti and the Singularization of Universal Human Rights, 1804–2004," *International Journal of Francophone Studies* 12, no. 1 (2009): 93–108.
49. Jorge Sánchez Morales, *La Revolución rural francesa: Libertad, igualdad y comunidad* (1789–1793) (Madrid: Biblioteca Nueva, 2017).
50. Here, and in the rest of this book, I assume the definition of "institution" provided by Santi Romano: "A revolutionary society or a criminal association do not constitute law from the viewpoint of the State that they try to subvert, or whose laws they violate, just as a schismatic sect is considered antilegalistic by the Church; but this does not imply that in the above case there are not institutions, organizations, and orders which, taken per se and intrinsically considered, are legal." Santi Romano, *L'ordinamento Giuridico. Studi sul Concetto, le Fonti e i Caratteri del Diritto* (Pisa: Tipografia Editrice Cav. Mariotti, 1917), 42.

51. François Furet and Mona Ozouf, eds., *A Critical Dictionary of the French Revolution*, trans. Arthur Goldhammer (Cambridge, MA, and London: Harvard University Press, 1989).
52. Albert Soboul, *The French Revolution 1789–1799*, trans. Alan Forrest and Colin Jones (New York: Vintage, 1975), 332.
53. Michel Rolph Trouillot, *Silencing the Past: Power and the Production of History* (Boston, MA: Beacon, 1997), 70–107. See also Dale Tomich, "Thinking the 'Unthinkable': Victor Schoelcher and Haiti," *Review (Fernand Braudel Center)* 31, no. 3 (2008): 401–31.
54. Adom Getachew, "Universalism After the Post-Colonial Turn: Interpreting the Haitian Revolution," *Political Theory* 44, no. 6 (2016): 821–45; Nick Nesbitt, *Universal Emancipation: The Haitian Revolution and the Radical Enlightenment* (Charlottesville and London: University of Virginia Press, 2008).
55. Pierre Guyomar, "Discussion of Citizenship Under the Proposed New Constitution (April 29, 1793)," in *The French Revolution and Human Rights: A Brief Documentary History*, ed. Lynn Hunt (New York: St. Martin's, 1996), 133–34.
56. Alice Mazzotti, "Madri di Haiti tra schiavitù e rivoluzione (Saint-Domingue XVII-XIX secolo)," *Annali di Ca' Foscari* 48, nos. 1–2 (2008): 175–203.
57. Geggus, *Haitian Revolution*, 92.
58. Geggus, *Haitian Revolution*, 159.
59. William H. Sewell, *Work & Revolution in France: The Language of Labor from the Old Regime to 1848* (Cambridge: Cambridge University Press, 1980), 109, 138.
60. Achille Mbembe writes, in his *On the Postcolony* (Berkeley: University of California Press, 2001), 9–15: the "time of African existence is neither a linear time nor a simple sequence in which each moment effaces, annuls, and replaces those that preceded it, to the point where a single age exists within society." Instead of this,

> the peculiar "historicity" of African societies, their own raisons d'être and their relation to solely themselves, are rooted in a multiplicity of times, trajectories, and rationalities that, although particular and sometimes local, cannot be conceptualized outside a world that is, so to speak, globalized. From a narrow methodological standpoint, this

means that, from the fifteenth century, there is no longer a "distinctive historicity" of these societies, one not embedded in times and rhythms heavily conditioned by European domination.
61. Emmanuel Joseph Sieyès, "What Is the Third Estate?," in *Political Writings*, ed. Michael Sonescher (Indianapolis, IN, and Cambridge, MA: Hackett, 2003), 156.
62. Lucien Jaume, *Le discours jacobin et la démocratie* (Paris: Fayard, 1989), 318.
63. Pierre-Henri Zaidman, *Le mandat impératif de la Révolution française à la Commune de Paris* (Paris: Éditions du monde libertaire, 2008); Oskar Anweiler, *The Soviets: The Russian Workers, Peasants and Soldiers Councils, 1905–1921* (New York: Pantheon, 1974).
64. Joan Thirsk, "Enclosing and Engrossing," in *The Agrarian History of England and Wales*, ed. Joan Thirsk and H. P. R. Finberg (Cambridge: Cambridge University Press, 1967), 4:200.
65. Günther Rudolph, "Thomas Müntzer Sozialökonomische Konzeption und das Traditionsbewusstseins der sozialistischen Arbeiterbewegung," *Deutsche Zeitschift für Philosophie* 23 (1975): 562.
66. Peter Blickle, *Die Revolution von 1525* (Munich: Oldenbourg, 2004), 321–27.
67. Jacques Roux, "Manifesto of the Enragés" (June 25, 1793), in *Social and Political Thought of the French Revolution, 1788–1797: An Anthology of Original Texts*, ed. Marc Allan Goldstein (New York: Peter Lang, 2001), 211.
68. Antonio Gramsci, *Quaderni dal carcere*, ed. Valentino Gerratana (Turin: Einaudi, 1977), 2:Q 11, V.

Chapter 2

1. C. L. R. James, *The Black Jacobins* (New York: Vintage, 1989), 138.
2. Bruno Bauer, *Die Judenfrage* (Braunschweig: Druck und Verlag von Friedrich Otto, 1843), 19. See Massimiliano Tomba, "Exclusiveness and Political Universalism in Bruno Bauer," in *The New Hegelians: Politics and Philosophy in the Hegelian School*,

ed. Douglas Moggach (Cambridge: Cambridge University Press, 2006), 91–113.
3. Jack R. Censer and Lynn Hunt, eds., *Liberty, Equality, Fraternity: Exploring the French Revolution* (University Park: Pennsylvania State University Press, 2001). This print collection was accompanied by a CD-ROM of documents relating to the French Revolution, which are also available at an online archive: http://chnm.gmu.edu/revolution/. References to the documents of the French Revolution are from this source.
4. Ernst Bloch, *Natural Law and Human Dignity*, trans. Dennis J. Schmidt (Cambridge, MA: MIT Press, 1987), 186.
5. Marcel Gauchet, *La Révolution des droits de l'homme* (Paris: Gallimard, 1989), 116.
6. Pierre Manent, An Intellectual History of Liberalism (Princeton, NJ: Princeton University Press, 1994), xvi.
7. Luigi Ferrajoli, "Dai diritti del cittadino ai diritti della persona," in *La cittadinanza. Appartenenza, identità, diritti*, ed. Danilo Zolo (Rome and Bari: Laterza, 1994), 288.
8. Censer and Hunt, *Liberty, Equality, Fraternity*.
9. Lynn Hunt states that the "frames of the UN Declaration of 1948 closely followed the model established by the French Declaration of the Rights of Man and Citizens of 1789." Hunt, *French Revolution and Human Rights*, 3.
10. I cite from the text of the Declaration of Independence, found online at http://avalon.law.yale.edu/18th_century/declare.asp.
11. Costas Douzinas, *The End of Human Rights* (Oxford and Portland, OR: Hart, 2000), 87.
12. Thomas Hobbes, *Leviathan, or the Matter, Form and Power of Commonwealth, Ecclesiastical and Civil*, in *English Works of Thomas Hobbes* (London: Bohn, 1839), 3:chap. 16.
13. Joan Wallach Scott, *Parité! Sexual Equality and the Crisis of French Universalism* (Chicago: University of Chicago Press, 2005), 13. See also Paula Diehl, *Das Symbolische, das Imaginäre und die Demokratie: Eine Theorie politischer Repräsentation* (Baden-Baden: Nomos, 2015), 189–90.
14. See Carl Schmitt on political unity; Carl Schmitt, *Roman Catholicism and Political Form*, trans. G. L. Ulmen (London: Greenwood, 1996); Carl Schmitt, *Political Theology*

II: *the Myth of the Closure of Any Political Theology*, trans. Michael Hoelzl and Graham Ward (Cambridge and Malden: Polity, 1970), 71–72.

15. Paul Friedland, *Political Actors: Representative Bodies and Theatricality in the Age of the French Revolution* (Ithaca, NY, and London: Cornell University Press, 2002), 284–288.
16. Robert B. Rose, *The Enragés: Socialists of the French Revolution?* (Sydney: Sydney University Press, 1968), 89, 35.
17. Jonathan Israel, *Revolutionary Ideas: An Intellectual History of the French Revolution from The Human Rights to Robespierre* (Oxford and Princeton, NJ: Princeton University Press, 2014), 347–67.
18. Condorcet, "Projet de Déclaration des droits naturels, civils et politiques des hommes," in *Oeuvres de Condorcet* (Paris: Firmin Didot Frères Libraires, 1847), 12:422.
19. Condorcet, in *Archives Parlementaires*, February 15, 1793, 58:601, in *Archives parlementaires de 1789 à 1860: recueil complet des débats législatifs & politiques des Chambres françaises* (Paris: Librairie administrative de P. Dupont, 1862), http://purl.stanford.edu/vr741ts8017. See also Lucien Jaume, "Citizen and State under the French Revolution," in *States & Citizens: History, Theory, Prospects*, ed. Quentin Skinner and Bo Strath (Cambridge: Cambridge University Press, 2003), 138.
20. See Condorcet, *Selected Writings*, ed. Keith Michael Baker (Indianapolis, IN: Bobbs-Merrill, 1976), 150–151. Lucien Jaume, "La souveraineté montagnarde: République, peuple ed territoire," in *La Constitution du 24 Juin 1793: L'Utopie dans le droit public français?* ed. Jean Bart et al. (Dijon: Ed. Editions Universitaires de Dijon, 1997), 119–20.
21. Hedwig Hintze, *Staatseinheit und Föderalismus in alten Frankreich und in der Revolution* (Frankfurt: Suhrkamp, 1989), 417–48.
22. *Archives Parlementaires*, April 24, 1793, 63:199, trans. in *Maximilien Robespierre, Virtue and Terror*, ed. Jean Ducange, trans. John Howe (London and New York: Verso, 2007), 71.
23. *Archives Parlementaires*, April 22, 1793, 63:114–15.
24. *Archives Parlementaires*, April 24, 1793, 63:199, trans. in *Maximilien Robespierre, Virtue and Terror*, 70–71.
25. *Archives Parlementaires*, June 24, 1793, 67:139.
26. *Archives Parlementaires*, May 27, 1793, 65:393.

27. Eric Hazan, *A People's History of the French Revolution*, trans. David Fernbach (London and New York: Verso, 2014), 246. Mathiez wrote that the revolution of May 31–June 2 was made by the *Enragés* and "to save themselves and to triumph, the Montagnards were obliged . . . to lean frankly on the masses led by the Enragés"; Albert Mathiez, "Les Enragés contre la constitution de 1793," *Annales révolutionnaires* 13 (1921): 303; see Morris Slavin, *Making of an Insurrection: Parisian Sections and the Gironde* (Cambridge, MA: Harvard University Press, 1986), 127.
28. Marcel Morabito, "La résistance à l'oppression en 1793," *Revue d'histoire du droit* 72, no. 2 (1994): 235–47.
29. It is not an exaggeration to say that "both the Girondins and the Montagnards feared the Enragés" and their idea to introduce direct democracy through the mandat impératif; Slavin, *Making of an Insurrection*, 127.
30. Olivier Jouanjan, "La suspension de la Constitution de 1793," in *Droit* 10 (1993): 125–38.
31. Carl Schmitt, *Dictatorship: From the Origin of the Modern Concept of Sovereignty to Proletarian Class Struggle*, trans. Michael Hoelzl and Graham Ward (Cambridge: Polity, 2014), 119.
32. Robespierre, in *Archives Parlementaires*, December 25, 1793, 82:300.
33. Jaume, "Citizen and State Under the French Revolution," 139.
34. Shirly E. Roessler, *Out of the Shadows: Women and Politics in the French Revolution, 1789–95* (New York: Peter Lang, 1996), 195; Olwen H. Hufton, *Women and the Limits of Citizenship in the French Revolution* (Toronto: University of Toronto Press, 1992); see also Darline G. Levy and Harriet B. Applewhite, "Women and Militant Citizenship in Revolutionary Paris," in *Rebel Daughters: Women and French Revolution*, ed. Sara E. Melzer and Leslie W. Rabine (New York and Oxford: Oxford University Press, 1992), 79–101; Sophie Mousset, *Women's Rights and the French Revolution* (New Brunswick, NJ: Transaction, 2007).
35. Joan B. Landes, *Women and Public Sphere in the Age of the French Revolution* (Ithaca, NY, and London: Cornell University Press, 1988).

36. See Darline G. Levy, Harriet B. Applewhite, and Mary D. Johnson, eds., *Women in Revolutionary Paris, 1789-1795* (Urbana: University of Illinois Press, 1980), 87-96.
37. Jacques Rancière, *Disagreement: Politics and Philosophy*, trans. Julie Rose (Minneapolis: University of Minnesota Press, 1999).
38. Levy and Applewhite, "Women and Militant Citizenship in Revolutionary Paris," 88-89.
39. Yves Bénot, *La Révolution française et la fin des colonies 1789-94* (Paris: La Découverte, 1988).
40. Adom Getachew, "Universalism After the Post-Colonial Turn," in *The Making of Haiti: Saint Domingue Revolution from Below*, ed. Carolyn E. Fick (Knoxville: University Tennessee Press, 2004).
41. Susan Buck-Morss, *Hegel, Haiti and Universal History*, 147; see also Nesbitt, *Universal Emancipation*, 189; Fischer, *Modernity Disavowed*, 241.
42. Aimé Césaire, *Toussaint Louverture: La Révolution française et le problème colonial* (Paris: Présence africaine, 1960), 23.
43. Tyler Stovall, *Transnational France: The Modern History of a Universal Nation* (Boulder, CO: Westview, 2015), 33-34; Wilder, *Freedom Time*.
44. Robin Blackburn, *The Overthrow of Colonial Slavery: 1776-1848* (New York: Verso, 1988), 179.
45. Geggus, *Haitian Revolution*, 105.
46. Geggus, *Haitian Revolution*, 107-108. The text of the Proclamation of August 29, 1793, can be found at http://mjp.univ-perp.fr/constit/ht1793.htm.
47. Geggus, *Haitian Revolution*, 112.
48. Geggus, *Haitian Revolution*, 69.
49. Laënnec Hurbon, *Comprendre Haiti: Essai sur l'Etat, la nation, la culture* (Paris: Édition Karthale, 1987), 75-87.
50. Fischer, *Modernity Disavowed*, 11.
51. Victor Schoelcher, *Vie de Toussaint Louverture* (Paris: Paul Ollendorf, 1889), 264.
52. Among them, Condorcet, Lescallier, and Gregoire. See David Williams, *Condorcet and Modernity* (Cambridge: Cambridge University Press, 2004), 146; Louis Sala-Molins, *Dark Side of the Light: Slavery and the French Enlightenment* (Minneapolis: University of Minnesota Press, 2006), 17-18.

53. Nick Nesbitt, "Turning the Tide: The Problem of Popular Insurgency in Haitian Revolutionary Historiography," *Small Axe* 12, no. 27 (2008): 14–31.
54. Gérard Barthélemy, "Le rôle des Bossales dans l'émergence d'une culture de marronage en Haiti," *Cahiers d'études africaines* 37, no. 148 (1997): 846; Nesbitt, "Turning the Tide," 18–19.
55. Michael J. Drexler and Ed White, "The Constitution of Toussaint: Another," in *A Companion to African American Literature*, ed. Gene Andrew Jarret (London: Blackwell, 2013), 59–74.
56. Nesbitt, "Turning the Tide," 23.
57. Nesbitt, "Turning the Tide," 21. Gérard Barthélemy, *L'univers rural Haitien*; Barthélemy, "Le rôle des Bossales."
58. Hippolyte Taine, *Les origines de la France contemporaine: La Révolution, L'Anarchie*, (Paris: Librairie Hachette, 1904), 3:28, t. 1.
59. Jean Léger, "Babeuf et la naissance du communisme ouvrier," *Socialisme ou Barbarie* 2 (1949): 68; Maxime Leroy, *Le socialisme en Europe des origines à nos jours* (Paris: Centre de documentation universitaire, 1945).
60. Sánchez Morales, *La Revolución rural francesa: Libertad, igualdad y comunidad (1789–1793)* (Madrid: Biblioteca Nueva, 2017), 23.
61. "The rural community revolution was practically indecipherable for the Paris authorities." Morales, *La Revolución rural francesa*, 203.
62. Rafe Blaufarb, *The Great Demarcation: The French Revolution and the Invention of Modern Property* (Oxford: Oxford University Press, 2016), 52.
63. Charles-Louis Chassin. *La preparation de la guerre de Vendée, 1789–1793*, (Paris: Imprimerie de P. Du Pont, 1892), 374–75, t. III, cited in Jorge Sánchez Morales, "The French Rural Revolution 1789–1793," *Age of Revolutions*, January 29, 2018, https://ageofrevolutions.com/2018/01/29/the-french-rural-revolution-1789-1793/.
64. Florence Gauthier, *Triomphe et mort du droit naturel en Révolution: 1789-1795-1802* (Paris: Presses universitaires de France, 1992), 108.
65. Gauthier, *Triomphe et mort du droit naturel en Révolution*, 66, 97.

66. Albert Souboul, *The Sans-Culottes*, trans. Rémy Inglis Hall (Princeton, NJ: Princeton University Press, 1972), 54.
67. Florence Gauthier, "Robespierre théoricien du droit naturel à l'existence," *Le Canard républicain*, 2010, http://www.xn--lecanardrpublicain-jwb.net/spip.php?article381.
68. Alphonse Aulard, *The French Revolution: A Political History, 1789–1804*, trans. Bernard Miall (New York: Scribner's, 1910), 2:176–217, 198. Aulard states that it was "only in appearance that the Montagnards and the Girondins, in the debates on the Constitution, were divided on the question on property" (176).
69. Rose, *The Enragés*, 89.
70. Roux, "Manifesto of the Enragés," 211.
71. Roux, "Manifesto of the Enragés," 212–13.
72. Maurice Dommanget, *Enragée et curés rouges en 1793: Jacques Roux, Pierre Dolivier* (Paris: Spartacus, 1993), 130–131.
73. Walter Markov, *Die Freiheiten des Priesters Roux* (Leipzig: Leipziger Uni-Verlag, 2009).
74. Karl Marx and Friedrich Engels, *The Communist Manifesto*, trans. Samuel Moore (London: Pluto, 2008 [1848]), 78.
75. This is what Rancière calls the interruption of the police order by the politics of equals; Rancière, *Disagreement*.
76. Furet stated that since 1792, the burst of the masses onto political scene represents the *dérapage* from the revolution's true liberal character; François Furet and Denis Richet, *The French Revolution*, trans. Stephen Hardman (New York: Macmillan, 1970), 10. It is remarkable that Furet's *Critical Dictionary of the French Revolution* (1989) does not have any entries for "slavery" and "women."
77. *Archives Parlementaires*, May 27, 1793, 65:394.
78. "Avant-propos," in *Archives Parlementaires, vol.1: Etats généraux: Cahier des sénéchaussées et bailliages*, 2nd ed. (Paris: Libraire administrative de P. Dupont, 1879), 15, http://www.persee.fr/doc/arcpa_0000-0000_1879_num_1_1_1416.
79. Souboul, *The Sans-Culottes*, 97, 119.
80. Jean Varlet, *Projet d'un mandat spécial et impératif, aux mandataires du peuple à la Convention nationale* (Paris, 1792), http://gallica.bnf.fr/ark:/12148/bpt6k6255308z/f7.image. An

English translation is available as "Proposal for a Special and Imperative Mandate," in Roux, *Social and Political Thought of the French Revolution*, 153–61.
81. Michael P. Fitzsimmons, *The Remaking of France: The National Assembly and the Constitution of 1791* (Cambridge: Cambridge University Press, 1994), 49–59.
82. Martin Breaugh, *The Plebeian Experience: A Discontinuous History of Political Freedom* (New York: Columbia University Press, 2013), 117–18.
83. Varlet, "Proposal for a Special and Imperative Mandate," 159.
84. Varlet, "Proposal for a Special and Imperative Mandate," 155.
85. *Archives Parlementaires*, May 10, 1793, 64:432.
86. Jon Cawans, *To Speak for the People: Public Opinion and the Problem of Legitimacy in the French Revolution* (New York: Routledge, 2001), 93; Friedland, *Political Actors*, 288. On the repudiation of the binding mandate, see Keith Michael Baker, "Representation," in *The French Revolution and the Creation of Modern Political Culture*, ed. Keith Michael Baker (Oxford: Pergamon, 1987), 1:469–92. On the concept of representation, see Hasso Hofmann, *Repräsentation: Studien zur Wort- und Begriffsgeschichte von der Antike bis ins 19. Jahrhundert* (Berlin: Duncker & Humblot, 1974), 409; Giuseppe Duso, *La rappresentanza: un problema di filosofia politica* (Milan: Franco Angeli, 1988).
87. *Archives Parlementaires*, June 24, 1793, 67:334–35.
88. *Archives Parlementaires*, June 14, 1793, 66:530.
89. Carl Schmitt, *Constitutional Theory*, trans. Jeffrey Seitzer (Durham, NC: Duke University Press, 2008), 289.
90. On the incompatibility of imperative mandate and modern democracy, see also Ernst-Wolfgang Böckenförde, "Mittelbare/ repräsentative Demokratie als eigentliche Form der Demokratie. Bemerkungen zu Begriff und Verwirklichungsproblem der Demokratie als Staats- und Regierungsform," in *Staatsorganisation und Staatsfunktionen im Wandel: Festschrift für Kurt Eichenberger zum 60. Geburtstag*, ed. Georg Müller, René A. Rhinow, Gerhard Schmid, and Luzius Wildhaber (Basel/Frankfurt: Helbig & Lichtenhahn, 1982), 301–28.
91. Christian Müller, *Das imperative und freie Mandat* (Leiden: A.W. Sijthoff, 1966), 29–32.

92. Frank Maloy Anderson, *The Constitutions and Other Select Documents Illustrative of the History of France, 1789-1901* (Minneapolis: H.W. Wilson, 1904).
93. Varlet, "Proposal for a Special and Imperative Mandate," 153-61.
94. Müller, *Das imperative und freie Mandat*, 51. Joseph Marty wrote of the Constitution of 1793 that it is "a Constitution which in principle admits the imperative mandate"; Joseph Marty, "Du Conseil des empereurs romains depuis Auguste jusqu'à Justinien, en droit romain De la nature du mandat donné par les électeurs aux membres des assemblées législatives, en droit français," doctoral dissertation, Université de Toulouse, 1890.
95. Varlet, "Proposal for a Special and Imperative Mandate," 154.
96. Varlet, "Proposal for a Special and Imperative Mandate," 154.
97. Jaume, "Citizen and State Under the French Revolution," 135; see also Jaume, *Le discours jacobin et la démocratie*, 59ff.
98. Sewell, *Work and Revolution in France*, 60.
99. Philippe-Joseph-Benjamin Buchez and Prosper Charles Roux, *Histoire parlementaire de la Révolution française* (Paris: Paulin, 1834), 10:194; English translation found in John Hall Stewart, *A Documentary Survey of the French Revolution* (New York: Macmillan, 1951), 165-66.
100. Stewart, *Documentary Survey of the French Revolution*, 196.
101. For the individualistic model of the Declaration imposed on freedom of association, see Jaume, "Citizen and State Under the French Revolution," 135-37.
102. *Archives Parlementaires*, 23:559, http://frda.stanford.edu/fr/catalog/wz883qs5666_00_0563.
103. On November 18, 1789, the Prémontrés district claimed the imperative mandate "as a principle of natural law which subjects mandatories to their mandants" On March 1, 1790, the Cordeliers district affirmed the sovereignty of the districts in expressing their "particular interests." See Jaume, *Le discours jacobin et la démocratie*, 288-90; Zaidman, *Le mandat impératif de la Révolution française à la Commune de Paris*.
104. Jaume, *Le discours jacobin*, 299-307.
105. See Friedland, *Political Actors*, 290.
106. This absolutization of the stranger as enemy is bound up in the relationships between nation, sovereignty, and

citizenship, as Sophie Wahnich has demonstrated in her *L'impossible citoyen: L'étranger dans la Révolution française* (Paris: Albin Michel, 1997). It is thus not the result of the aegis of natural right, as argued by Dan Edelstein in his *The Terror of Natural Rights: Republicanism, the Cult of Nature, and the French Revolution* (Chicago: University of Chicago Press, 2009).

107. Sieyès, "What Is the Third Estate?," 110.
108. Sewell, *Work & Revolution in France*, 205.
109. As observable in Art. 8 of the Constitution of 1848. See Jacques Godechot, *Les Constitutions de la France depuis 1789* (Paris: Garnier Flammarion, 1979), 265.
110. Karl Marx, *The 18th Brumaire of Louis Bonaparte* (1852), in *Marx and Engels Collected Works* (London: Lawrence & Wishart, 1979), 11:159. See also Massimiliano Tomba, "Marx as the Historical Materialist: Re-reading The Eighteenth Brumaire," *Historical Materialism* 21, no. 2 (2013): 21–46.
111. See Art. 12 of the Declaration of 1789.
112. Jürgen Habermas, "The Concept of Human Dignity and the Realistic Utopia of Human Rights," in *The Crisis of the European Union*, trans. Ciaran Cronin (Malden: Polity, 2012), 71–100.
113. Hannah Arendt, *On Revolution* (London: Penguin, 1990), 46, 107.
114. Hannah Arendt, *The Origins of Totalitarianism* (New York: Harcourt Brace Jovanovich, 1979), 297. See Étienne Balibar, "(De)Constructing the Human as Human Institution: A Reflection on the Coherence of Hannah Arendt's Practical Philosophy," *Social Research* 74, no. 3 (Fall 2007): 733.
115. Arendt, *Origins of Totalitarianism*, 297.
116. Giorgio Agamben, *Homo Sacer: Sovereign Power and Bare Life*, trans. Daniel Heller-Roazen (Stanford, CA: Stanford University Press, 1998), 88. Through the concept of "homo sacer," Agamben replaces the fundamental categorial pair of "friend/enemy" that Carl Schmitt conceived as the original opposition of politics with a new pair: "bare life/political existence, zoe/bios, exclusion/inclusion." By doing so, Agamben explains modern sovereignty through an "obscure figure of archaic Roman law"—i.e., the *homo sacer*, now elevated to the rank of a meta-historical category (8).

117. Guyomar, "Discussion of Citizenship," 133–34.
118. Badiou defines this singular universality in the terms of the "droit du générique." See Alain Badiou, "Huit Thèses sur l'Universel," in *Universel, Singulier, Sujet: actes du colloque organisé par l'Institut de philosophie, Centre de recherches scientifiques (Ljublijana), et la Maison Suger, Maison des sciences de l'homme, novembre 1998*, ed. Jellica Sumic (Paris: Èditions Kimé, 2000), 11–20.
119. Patrice Higonnet, *Goodness Beyond Virtue: Jacobins during the French Revolution* (Cambridge, MA: Harvard University Press, 1998), 118.
120. On this point, see Costas Douzinas, *Human Rights and Empire: The Political Philosophy of Cosmopolitanism* (Abingdon: Routledge, 2007), 105–107.
121. Jacques Rancière, "Who Is the Subject of the Rights of Man?," *South Atlantic Quarterly* 103, nos. 2/3 (Spring/Summer 2004): 305.
122. Claude Lefort, *Democracy and Political Theory*, trans. David Macey (Cambridge: Polity, 1988), 38; Claude Lefort, "Politics and Human Rights," trans. Alan Sheridan, in *The Political Form of the Modern Society: Bureaucracy, Democracy, Totalitarianism*, ed. David Thompson (Cambridge, MA: MIT Press, 1986), 258.
123. Étienne Balibar, "Ambiguous Universality," in *Politics and the Other Scene*, trans. Christine Jones, James Swenson, and Chris Turner (London: Verso, 2002), 146–76.
124. Balibar, "Ambiguous Universality," 166.
125. Balibar, "Ambiguous Universality," 173.
126. Étienne Balibar, "Citizen Subject," trans. James Swenson, in *Who Comes After the Subject?*, ed. Eduardo Cadava, Peter Connor, and Jean-Luc Nancy (New York and London: Routledge, 1991), 47.
127. See Peg Birmingham, "Revolutionary Declarations: The State of Right and the Right of Opposition," in *The Aporia of Rights: Explorations in Citizenship in the Era of Human Rights*, ed. Anna Yeatman and Peg Birmingham (London: Bloomsbury, 2014), 159–81.
128. Roessler, *Out of the Shadows*, 197; Levy and Applewhite, "Women and Militant Citizenship in Revolutionary Paris," 81. This feminist legacy reemerged in the nineteenth century in the form of a "revolutionary humanism which challenged

hierarchies at all levels of social existence," a "wholesale transformation of private and public life." See Barbara Taylor, *Eve and the New Jerusalem: Socialism and Feminism in the Nineteenth Century* (New York: Pantheon, 1983), 275.
129. Joan Wallach Scott, *Only Paradoxes to Offer: French Feminists and the Rights of Man* (Cambridge, MA: Harvard University Press, 1996), 33.
130. E. Lairtullier, *Les femmes célèbres de 1789 à 1795 et leur influence dans la révolution* (Paris: La Librairie Politique, 1840), 93; in a *réponse* to Robespierre, de Gouges defined herself as "plus homme que femme"; Lairtullier, *Les femmes célèbres de 1789 à 1795*, 127. See Scott, *Only Paradoxes to Offer*, 33.
131. Théodore Dézamy, *Code de la Communauté* (1842) (Paris: Éditions d'Histoire Sociale, 1967), 285.

Chapter 3

1. Benjamin, *Arcades Project*, 789: k 1,3.
2. Pierre Sorlin, "La Commune: Cent ans après," *Études* 334 (1971): 707–18.
3. Sorlin, "La Commune," 715.
4. Henri Guillemin, *L'avènement de M. Thiers et réflexions sur la Commune* (Paris: Gallimard, 1971), 139.
5. Sorlin, "La Commune," 715. Volker Hunecke, "La Comune di Parigi del 1871," *Primo Maggio* 2 (1974): 57–72.
6. Vladimir Borisovich Lutsky, *Modern History of the Arab Countries*, trans. Lika Nasser, ed. Robert Daglish (Moscow: Progress, 1969), 266.
7. Lutsky, *Modern History of the Arab Countries*, 268.
8. *Journal Officiel de la Commune*, March 29, 1871.
9. *Actes du Gouvernement de la Défense Nationale, du 4 Septembre 1870 au 8 Février 1871* (Paris: Librairie des Publications Législative, 1876), 3:205.
10. Lutsky, *Modern History of the Arab Countries*, 269.
11. Claude Martin, *La Commune d'Alger (1870–1871)* (Paris: Editions Heraklès, 1936).

12. Lutsky, *Modern History of the Arab Countries*, 273. Mohammed Brahim Salhi, "L'insurrection de 1871," in *Histoire de l'Algérie à la période coloniale*, ed. Abderrahmane Bouchène, Gilbert Meynier, and Tahar Khalfoune (Paris: La Découverte, 2014), 103–109.
13. Lutsky, *Modern History of the Arab Countries*, 273.
14. Louise Michel, *La Commune* (Paris: Editions Stock, 1971), 278.
15. Louise Michel, *The Red Virgin: Memoirs of Louise Michel, écrits par elle-même*, ed. and trans. Bullitt Lowry and Elizabeth Ellington Gunter (Tuscaloosa: University of Alabama Press, 1981), 66.
16. Karl Marx, *The Civil War in France* (1871), in *Marx and Engels Collected Works* (London: Lawrence & Wishart, 1986), 22:334.
17. Antonio Negri, *Insurgencies: Constituent Power and The Modern State*, trans. Maurizia Boscagli (Minneapolis: University of Minnesota Press, 1999).
18. On the need for institutions in the present moment, see Michael Hardt and Antonio Negri, *Assembly* (New York: Oxford University Press, 2017), 38, 289.
19. Santi Romano, *L'ordinamento Giuridico: Studi sul Concetto, le Fonti e i Caratteri del Diritto* (Pisa: Tipografia Editrice Cav. Mariotti, 1917), 42.
20. See Louis M. Greenberg, "The Commune of 1871 as a Decentralist Reaction," *Journal of Modern History* 41, no. 3 (1969): 304–18.
21. Anderson, *Constitutions and Other Select Documents*.
22. Anderson, *Constitutions and Other Select Documents*.
23. Karl Marx, "The Constitution of the French Republic Adopted November 4, 1848," in *Marx and Engels Collected Works* (London: Lawrence & Wishart, 1978), 10:577.
24. "Déclaration au Peuple Français," in *Commune de Paris*, no. 170, April 19, 1871. English translation available in Anderson, *Constitution and Other Select Documents*.
25. *Journal Officiel de la Republique Française*, no. 79, March 20, 1871, in *Réimpression du Journal Official de la Republique Française sous la Commune* (Paris: Victor Bunel, 1871), 4. Arthur Arnould, *Histoire Populaire et Parlementaire de la Commune de Paris* (Lyon: Éditions Jacques-Marie Laffont, 1981), 104.
26. *La Commune*, no. 8, March 27, 1871.

27. Georg Wilhelm Friedrich Hegel, *The Philosophy of History*, trans. J. Sibree (New York: Dover, 1956), 30–31.
28. Marx, *Civil War in France*, 341.
29. Kristin Ross, *Communal Luxury: The Political Imaginary of the Paris Commune* (London and New York: Verso, 2015).
30. Club Saint-Ambroise, in *Le Prolétaire*, May 19, 1871, in Stewart Edwards, ed., *The Communards of Paris, 1871*, trans. Jean McNeil (Ithaca, NY: Cornell University Press, 1973), 98.
31. Stewart Edwards, *The Paris Commune, 1871* (Chicago: Quadrangle, 1973), 280.
32. I have shown elsewhere how this phenomenon emerges today in the temporal conflict between the decision-making processes in politics and those in finance and the market. The synchronization of these two temporalities can only happen to the detriment of democracy; Massimiliano Tomba, "Clash of Temporalities: Capital, Democracy, and Squares," *South Atlantic Quarterly* 113, no. 2 (2014): 353–66.
33. Henri Lefebvre, *La Commune: dernière fête populaire*, in *Images of the Commune*, ed. James A. Leith (Montreal: Queen's University Press, 1978), 33–45.
34. Ross, *Communal Luxury*, 58.
35. Arnould, *Histoire Populaire*, 104.
36. Louis-Auguste Blanqui, *Eternity by the Stars: An Astronomical Analysis*, trans. Frank Chouraqui (New York: Contra Mundum, 2013), 125.
37. "Séance du 19 mai 1871," in *Procès-Verbaux de la Commune de 1871*, ed. Georges Bourgin and Gabriel Henriot (Paris: Lahure, 1945), 2:426; for an English translation, see "The Debate in the Commune on the Control of Theaters," in Edwards, *The Communards*, 152.
38. Arnould, *Histoire Populaire*, 275–86.
39. Arnould, *Histoire Populaire*, 276.
40. Michel, *Red Virgin*, 66.
41. Jacques Rougerie, *Paris libre 1871* (Paris: Seuil, 1971), 213.
42. Rougerie, *Paris libre 1871*.
43. *Le peuple souverain, journal des travailleurs*, March 26, 1848. See Roger V. Gould, *Insurgent Identities: Class, Community, and*

Protest in Paris from 1848 to the Commune (Chicago: University of Chicago Press, 1995), 42.
44. "Keep to your role of mere attendants . . . do not pretend to be sovereigns." This was the relationship that the clubs had with the Communal Council. See *Le Prolétaire*, May 19, 1871, in Edwards, *The Communards*, 98.
45. Stewart, *Documentary Survey of the French Revolution*, 165–66.
46. See also Sewell, *Work & Revolution in France*, 91.
47. Sewell, *Work & Revolution in France*, 162.
48. Alexis de Tocqueville, *The Ancien Régime and The French Revolution*, trans. Arthur Goldhammer, ed. Jon Elster (Cambridge: Cambridge University Press, 2011), 61, 183.
49. Poster of March 22, 1871, in *Journal officiel*, March 25, 1871.
50. "Manifeste du Comité des Vingt Arrondissements," in *Le Cri du Peuple*, March 27, 1871; also in Rougerie, *Paris libre 1871*, 137. Similarly, the paper *La Commune* "spoke of the news from the provinces as 'greatly resembling the liberating of the communes that occurred in identical fashion seven centuries ago.'" See Edwards, *Paris Commune*, 175.
51. *Le Père Duchêne*, no. 38, April 22, 1871.
52. *Le Père Duchêne*, no. 38, April 22, 1871.
53. *La sociale*, no. 23, April 22, 1871.
54. Carolyn J. Eichner, *Surmounting the Barricades: Women in the Paris Commune* (Bloomington: Indiana University Press, 2004), 10, 99.
55. Eichner, *Surmounting the Barricades*, 10.
56. Eichner, *Surmounting the Barricades*, 3; Edith Thomas, *The Woman Incendiaries*, trans. James Atkinson and Starr Atkinson (New York: G. Braziller, 1966).
57. Nic Maclellan, ed., *Louise Michel* (New York: Ocean, 2004), 20–21.
58. Cesare Lombroso, by looking at 50 photographs of Communards, found that eleven show some anomaly and 47% in general are show of criminal and inferior types. Vincenzo Ruggiero, *Understanding Political Violence: A Criminological Analysis* (New York: Open University Press, 2006), 40–41.
59. Thomas Hobbes, *Leviathan* (Oxford: Oxford University Press, 2009 [1651]), 96.

60. Niccolò Machiavelli, *Discourses on Livy*, trans. Harvey C. Mansfield and Nathan Tarcov (Chicago: University of Chicago Press, 1996), 1:58, 115.
61. Machiavelli, *Discourses on Livy*, 1:5, 18.
62. "Declaration of Principles of the Club Communal of the Church Saint-Nicolas-des-Champs," published in *Bulletin Communal*, May 6, 1871, in Edwards, *The Communards*, 99.
63. Rougerie, *Paris libre 1871*, 221.
64. Eugène Varlin, March 3, 1871, in Rougerie, *Paris libre 1871*, 93.
65. Arnould, *Histoire Populaire*, 218, 256.
66. "Declaration of Principles of the Club Communal of the Church of Saint-Nicolas-des-Champes," 99.
67. "Declaration of Principles of the Club Communal of the Church of Saint-Nicolas-des-Champes," 99.
68. Gustave Lefrançais, *Étude sur le mouvement communaliste à Paris, en 1871* (Neuchatel: G. Guillaume Fils, 1871), 22–23.
69. The Manifeste du Comité des Vingt Arrondissements, published in *Le Cri du Peuple* on March 26, 1871, reiterates together with the principle of communal autonomy of all federate communes, the centrality of the imperative mandate as a "limitation of the power of mandatories," together with the principle of their permanent revocability. See Rougerie, *Paris libre 1871*, 138.
70. Lefrançais, *Étude sur le mouvement communaliste à Paris*, 23.
71. Declaration of Principles of the "Vigilance Committees of a Revolutionary Socialist Party," dated February 20 and 23, 1871, in Edwards, *The Communards*, 54.
72. Rougerie, *Paris libre 1871*, 218.
73. Schmitt, *Constitutional Theory*, 289.
74. Anderson, *Constitution and Other Select Documents*.
75. "Manifeste du Comité des Vingt Arrondissements," *Le Cri du Peuple*, March 27, 1871.
76. *Journal Officiel*, no. 110, April 20, 1871.
77. Gustave De Molinari, *Les clubs rouges pendant le siège de Paris* (Paris: Garnier Frères, 1871).
78. *Le Cri du Peuple*, no. 26, March 27, 1871.
79. F. T. Perrenes, *Étienne Marcel prévot des Marchands (1354–1358)* (Paris: Imprimerie Nationale, 1874), 345.

80. Alice M. Holden, "The Imperative Mandate in the Spanish Cortes of the Middle Ages," *American Political Science Review* 24, no. 4 (1930): 886–912; on the imperative mandate in the French Middle Ages, see Müller, *Das imperative und freie Mandat*, 161–204.
81. Johannes Althusius, *Politica* (Indianapolis, IN: Liberty Fund, 1995 [1603]), XVIII, §66.
82. Althusius, *Politica*, V, §§8–10.
83. Althusius, *Politica*, XVIII, §84.
84. Thomas O. Hueglin, *Early Modern Concepts for a Late Modern World: Althusius on Community and Federalism* (Waterloo, ONT: Wilfrid Laurier University Press, 1999).
85. Martin Phillip Johnson, *The Paradise of Association: Political Culture and Popular Organizations in the Paris Commune of 1871* (Ann Arbor: University of Michigan Press, 1996), 89; Jean Bruhat, "Pouvoir, Pouvoirs, État en 1871?," *Le Mouvement Social* 79 (1972): 157–71.
86. Johnson, *Paradise of Association*, 173. Donny Gluckstein, *The Paris Commune: A Revolution in Democracy* (Chicago: Haymarket, 2006), 91.
87. Johnson, *Paradise of Association*, 134.
88. Otto Brunner, *Land and Lordship: Structures of Governance in Medieval Austria* (Philadelphia: University of Pennsylvania Press, 1992).
89. Reinhart Koselleck, *Preußen Zwischen Reform und Revolution* (Stuttgart: Enrst Klett, 1967); Arno J. Mayer, *The Persistence of the Old Regime* (New York: Pantheon, 1981).
90. Blaufarb, *Great Demarcation*.
91. Blaufarb, *Great Demarcation*, 52.
92. Blaufarb, *Great Demarcation*, 128.
93. Blaufarb, *Great Demarcation*, 55.
94. Jacques-Nicolas Billaud-Varenne, *Les Éléments du républicanisme* (1793), English translation found in Goldstein, *Social and Political Thought of the French Revolution*, 163.
95. Goldstein, *Social and Political Thought of the French Revolution*, 183.
96. John Oswald, *Le gouvernement du peuple, ou Plan de constitution pour la République universelle* (Paris: Imprimerie des Révolutions de Paris, 1793), 11.

97. Arnould, *Histoire Populaire*, 290.
98. "Your sovereignty is hereby returned to you in its entirety, and belongs to you completely: profit from this precious, perhaps unique moment to seize the communal liberties—enjoyed by the humblest villages—of which you have been deprived for so long." In *Journal officiel de la République française*, no. 84, March 25, 1871.
99. Gustav Graf von Schlabrendorf, *Bonaparte and the French People Under his Consulate* (London: Tipper and Richards, 1804), 13.
100. Louis Napoleon Bonaparte, *The Political and Historical Works of Louis Napoleon Bonaparte* (London: Office of the Illustrated London Library, 1852), 1:102–103.
101. Adolphe Thiers, *The Rights of Property: A Refutation of Communism & Socialism* (London: Groombridge, 1848), 10.
102. Blaufarb, *Great Demarcation*, 208; Marcel Waline, *L'individualisme et le droit* (Paris: Montchrestien, 1949), 334.
103. Marc Bloch, "La lutte pour l'individualisme agraire dans la France du XVIIIe siècle. Première partie: l'œuvre des pouvoirs d'ancien régime," *Annales d'histoire économique et sociale* 2, no. 8 (1930): 544.
104. Pierre-Joseph Proudhon, *What Is Property?*, ed. and trans. Donald R. Kelley and Bonnie G. Smith (Cambridge: Cambridge University Press, 1994), 35.
105. Proudhon, *What Is Property?*, 35.
106. Robert Joseph Pothier, *Traité du droit de domaine de propriété* (Paris: Debure, 1772), 6.
107. See Shael Herman, "The Uses and Abuses of Roman Law Texts," *American Journal of Comparative Law* 29, no. 4 (1981): 671–90.
108. Thomas Rüfner, "The Roman Conception of Ownership and the Medieval Doctrine of Dominium," in *The Creation of the Ius Commune*, ed. John W. Cairns and Paul J. du Plessis (Edinburgh: Edinburgh University Press, 2010), 127–42.
109. "Quemadmodum theatrum cum commune sit, recte tamen dici potest ejus esse eum locum quem quisque occuparit," in Cicero, *De Finibus*, III. 20, 67; Proudhon, *What Is Property?*, 44.
110. Proudhon, *What Is Property?*, 44.
111. Proudhon, *What Is Property?*, 66.

112. Robert Tombs, *The Paris Commune 1871* (London and New York: Longman, 1999), 92.
113. Tombs, *Paris Commune*, 92.
114. "Séance du 18 mai 1871," in *Procès-Verbaux de la Commune de 1871*, 2:426; an English translation can be found in Edwards, *The Communards*, 152.
115. *L'ouvrier de l'avenir*, no. 3, March 19, 1871.
116. Sewell, *Work & Revolution in France*, 138.
117. Paolo Grossi, *La proprietà e le proprietà nell'officina dello storico* (Naples: Editoriale Scientifica, 2006), 70–74.
118. Paolo Grossi, "Proprietà," in *Enciclopedia del diritto* (Varese: Giuffré Editore, 1988), 37:226–54; Grossi, *La proprietà e le proprietà nell'officina dello storico*; Dieter Schwab, "Eigentum," in *Geschichtliche Grundbegriffe: Historisches Lexikon zur politisch-sozialen Sprache in Deutschland*, vol. 2, ed. Otto Brunner, Werner Conze, and Reinhart Koselleck (Stuttgart: Klett-Cotta, 1992), 75–76.
119. Grossi, *La proprietà e le proprietà*, 84–86. C. B. Macpherson, *The Political Theory of Possessive Individualism from Hobbes to Locke* (Oxford: Oxford University Press, 2011).
120. Bloch, "La lutte pour l'individualisme agraire," 329–30.
121. Bloch, "La lutte pour l'individualisme agraire," 330.
122. Rougerie, *Paris libre 1871*, 213.
123. Rougerie, *Paris Libre 1871*, 228.
124. Séance du 19 mai 1871, in *Procès-Verbaux de la Commune de 1871*, 2:426; English version in Edwards, *The Communards*, 152.
125. According to Oxfam, in 2017, eight men in the world own the same wealth as 3.6 billion people; see https://www.oxfam.org/en/pressroom/pressreleases/2017-01-16/just-8-men-own-same-wealth-half-world.
126. Report of a meeting in the women's club of the Trinité Church, May 12, 1871; in Edwards, *The Communards*, 106.
127. Report of a meeting in the women's club, 106.
128. Report of a meeting in the women's club, 106.
129. Regulations of the Louvre armaments factory cooperative, May 3, 1871, in Edwards, *The Communards*, 127.
130. Edwards, *Paris Commune*, 259.
131. Edwards, *Paris Commune*, 260.

132. Bourgin and Henriot, *Procès-Verbaux de la Commune* 1:542–53; English translation in Edwards, *The Communrds*, 138. See Gluckstein, *Paris Commune*, 17–18.
133. Arnould, *Histoire Populaire*, 169; Lefrançais, *Étude sur le mouvement communaliste*, 298–99.
134. *La Révolution politique et sociale*, no. 3, April 16, 1871.
135. Barère, on behalf of the Public Health Committee, in *Le Moniteur Universal*, no. 250, May 29, 1794, 584. See Roman Schnur, *Revolution und Weltbürgerkrieg* (Berlin: Duncker & Humblot, 1983), 86.
136. *Le Père Duchêne*, no. 30, April 15, 1871.
137. Marcel David, *Fraternité et Révolution française 1789–1799* (Paris: Aubier, 1987), 64–76.
138. Edwards, *Paris Commune*, 302.
139. Michel, *La Commune*, 221.
140. Ross, *Communal Luxury*, 23.
141. *La Révolution politique et sociale*, no. 3.
142. *Le salut public*, no. 6, May 22, 1871.
143. *La Révolution politique et sociale*, no. 3.
144. *La Commune*, no. 23, April 11, 1871.
145. *Le Père Duchêne*, no 30.
146. Anacharsis Cloots, *Bases Constitutionnelles de la République du Genre Humain* (Paris: De L'imprimerie Nationale, 1793), 43. See Alexander Bevilacqua, "Conceiving the Republic of Mankind: The Political Thought of Anacharsis Cloots," *History of European Ideas* 38, no. 4 (2012): 550–69; Francis Cheneval, "Der kosmopolitische Republikanismus: Erläutert am Beispiel Anacharsis Cloots," *Zeitschrift für philosophische Forschung* 58, no. 3 (2004): 373–96.
147. Cloots, *Bases constitutionnelles*, 1.
148. Cloots, *Bases constitutionnelles*, 29.
149. Schnur has shown this to be the crux of the totalization of the modern concept of war; Schnur, *Revolution und Weltbuergerkrieg*.
150. Cloots, *Bases constitutionnelles*, 24.
151. Oswald, *Le gouvernement du peuple*.
152. Oswald, *Le gouvernement du peuple*, 8–9.
153. Oswald, *Le gouvernement du peuple*, 12.
154. Gould, *Insurgent Identities*, 27, 150.

155. *Le Père Duchêne*, no. 17, April 2, 1871.
156. Fred Dallmayr, "'Asian Values' and Global Human Rights," *Philosophy East and West* 52, no. 2 (2002): 173–89.
157. Thomas, *Women Incendiaries*, 142.
158. Léon Michel Gambetta, *June 1, 1874, Discours et playdoiers politiques de M. Gambetta*, ed. J. Reinach (Paris: G. Charpentier, 1881), 4:155.
159. It is the opposite of what Hannah Arendt maintains in "On Humanity in Dark Times: Thoughts About Lessing," in *Men in Dark Times* (New York: Harcourt, Brace, & World, 1968), 25.

Chapter 4

1. Quoted in John L. H. Keep, *The Debate on Soviet Power: Minutes of All-Russian Central Executive Committee of Soviets* (Oxford: Clarendon Press, 1979), 132.
2. Steklov's Speech at the Fifth All-Russian Congress of Soviets, July 10, 1918, in *Intervention, Civil War, and Communism in Russia, April-December 1918*, ed. James Bunyan (Baltimore, MD: Johns Hopkins Press, 1936), 504.
3. G. W. F. Hegel, *Hegel and the Human Spirit: A Translation of the Jena Lectures on the Philosophy of Spirit (1805-06) with Commentary*, trans. Leo Rauch (Detroit, MI: Wayne State University Press, 1983), 155.
4. Oskar Negt, "Ernst Bloch, the German Philosopher of the October Revolution," trans. Jack Zipes, *New German Critique* 4 (Winter 1975): 7.
5. Susan-Buck Morss, *Dreamworld and Catastrophe: The Passing of Mass Utopia in East and West* (Cambridge, MA: MIT Press, 2000), 37.
6. Moshe Lewin, *The Making of the Soviet System: Essays in the Social History of Interwar Russia* (New York: Pantheon, 1985), 294.
7. J. Stalin, *Problems of Leninism* (Moscow: Foreign Languages, 1953), 456.
8. James Bunyan and H. H. Fisher, eds., *The Bolshevik Revolution, 1917-1918: Documents and Materials* (Stanford, CA: Stanford University Press, 1934), 559.

9. Bunyan, *Intervention, Civil War, and Communism*, 457–82. On the collectivization as the institutional logic of authoritarian high modernism, see James C. Scott, *Seeing Like a State: How Certain Schemes to Improve the Human Condition Have Failed* (New Haven, CT, and London: Yale University Press, 1998), 193–222.
10. Yuri Slezkine, *Arctic Mirrors: Russia and the Small Peoples of the North* (Ithaca, NY: Cornell University Press, 1994), 220.
11. This is the position expressed, for example, by A. M. Kulisher, *Das Wesen des Sowjetstaates* (Berlin: Politik und Wirtschaft, 1921).
12. Otto Kirchheimer, "The Socialist and Bolshevik Theory of the State" (1928), in *Politics, Law and Social Change*, ed. Frederic S. Burin and Kurt L. Shell (New York: Columbia University Press), 16.
13. Kirchheimer, "Socialist and Bolshevik Theory of the State," 18–20.
14. Kirchheimer, "Socialist and Bolshevik Theory of the State," 21.
15. According to Carl Schmitt, the people as unity does not exist until it is made visible by representation: "To represent means to make an invisible being visible (*sichtbar machen*) and present through a publicly present one." See Schmitt, *Constitutional Theory*, 243.
16. Giuseppe Boffa, *Storia dell'Unione Sovietica* (Rome: l'Unità, 1990), 1:81.
17. Boffa, *Storia dell'Unione Sovietica*, 1:81.
18. Bunyan and Fisher, *The Bolshevik Revolution*, 372.
19. All the texts pertaining to the Soviet Constitutions are taken from Aryeh L. Unger, *Constitutional Development in the USSR: A Guide to the Soviet Constitutions* (New York: Pica, 1982).
20. Unger, *Constitutional Development in the USSR*, 81.
21. J. V. Stalin, "On the Draft Constitution of the USSR, 25 November 1936," in *Collected Works* (London: Red Start, 1978), 14:157.
22. Stalin, "On the Draft Constitution," 179.
23. "In the USSR there is no conflict between the interests of the working people and those of the state, of society. The interests of both coincide completely." See V. A. Karpinsky, *The Social and State Structure of the U.S.S.R.* (Moscow: Foreign Languages, 1950), 192.
24. *Le Père Duchêne*, no. 38, April 22, 1871.
25. B. F. Makin (Left SR), at the Fifth Session (November 4, 1917) of the CEC, in Keep, *Debate on Soviet Power*, 69.

26. A. L. Kalegayev (Left SR), in Keep, *Debate on Soviet Power*, 71.
27. B. F. Makin (Left SR), at the Fifth Session of the CEC, in Keep, *Debate on Soviet Power*, 75.
28. Andrey Y. Vyshinsky, *The Law of the Soviet State*, trans. Hugh W. Babb (New York: Macmillan, 1948), 318.
29. Mario Sertoli, *La costituzione Russa: Diritto e storia* (Florence: Felice Le Monnier, 1928), 63–81. Michael Eljaschoff, *Die Grundzüge der Sowjet-Verfassung* (Heidelberg: Carl Winters Universitätsbuchhandlung, 1925), 58–61.
30. Oskar Anweiler, *The Soviets: The Russian Workers, Peasants, and Soldiers Council 1905-1921* (New York: Pantheon, 1974), 225.
31. Kirchheimer, "Socialist and Bolshevik Theory of the State," 21.
32. Kirchheimer, "Socialist and Bolshevik Theory of the State," 21.
33. Giuseppe Berti, *I primi dieci anni di vita del PCI: Documenti inediti dell'archivio Angelo Tasca* (Milan: Feltrinelli, 1967), 231–232.
34. Eljaschoff, *Die Grundzüge der Sowjet-Verfassung*, 61.
35. European Commission for Democracy through Law (Venice Commission), Report on the Imperative Mandate and Similar Practices, Venice, June 12–13, 2009, Art. 11, http://www.venice.coe.int/webforms/documents/default.aspx?pdffile=CDL-AD(2009)027-e.
36. Edward Hallett Carr, *The Bolshevik Revolution 1917-1923* (New York: Macmillan, 1951), 1:131.
37. Anweiler, *The Soviets*, 223–24.
38. Leon Trotsky, *The History of the Russian Revolution*, trans. Max Eastman (Chicago: Haymarket, 2008), 149–54.
39. R. P. Browder and A. F. Kerensky, eds., *The Russian Provisional Government* (Stanford, CA: Stanford University Press, 1961), 1216–17.
40. Browder and Kerensky, *Russian Provisional Government*.
41. Browder and Kerensky, *Russian Provisional Government*, 1225.
42. Browder and Kerensky, *Russian Provisional Government*, 1224–25.
43. V. I. Lenin, "The Dual Power" (April 9, 1917), in *Collected Works* (Moscow: Progress, 1964), 24:41.
44. Trotsky, *History of the Russian Revolution*, 149.
45. Raymond Garfield Gettell, "The Russian Soviet Constitution," *American Political Science Review* 13, no. 2

(1919): 294: "Sovereignty in the Russian state, therefore, lies in the local soviets, or committees *of* delegates chosen by the local industrial, military, and professional groups, and secession of the local units from the federal union is definitely permitted."

46. T. S. Tewatia, "Soviet Theory of Federalism," *Indian Journal of Political Science* 36, no. 2 (1975): 181–182: "Whether the Soviet federalism is a true federation has been haunting the minds of the Western political thinkers since the very inception of federal system in the Soviet Union."
47. For an idea of how the local Soviets self-represented themselves as autonomous centers of power, just think that in early 1918 "some local Soviet sets up an independent republic." Lenin, cited in Carr, *Bolshevik Revolution 1917–1923*, 1:132.
48. Eljaschoff, *Die Grundzüge der Sowjet-Verfassung*, 22–33.
49. Eljaschoff, *Die Grundzüge der Sowjet-Verfassung*, 36.
50. Carr, *Bolshevik Revolution 1917–1923*, 1:147.
51. Carr, *Bolshevik Revolution 1917–1923*, 1:128.
52. This is the position of the Left SR Trutovsky at the All-Russian Central Executive Committee of Soviets (VTsIK). See Carr, *Bolshevik Revolution 1917–1923*, 1:128.
53. Carr, *Bolshevik Revolution 1917–1923*, 1:128–29.
54. Alexander Hamilton, "Federalist No. 84," May 28, 1788, in John Jay, James Madison, and Alexander Hamilton, *The Federalist*, ed. Jacob E. Cooke (Chicago: University of Chicago Press, 1961), 575–81.
55. Evgeny Pashukanis, *Selected Writings on Marxism and Law*, ed. Piers Beirne and Robert Sharlet, trans. Peter B. Maggs (London and New York: Academic, 1980), 31–32; Peter Stuchka, *Selected Writings on Soviet Law and Marxism*, ed. and trans. Robert Sharlet, Peter B. Maggs, and Piers Beirne (Armonk, NY: M.E. Sharpe, 1988).
56. Alfred K. Stalgevich, *Puti razvitija sovetskoj pravovoj mysli [Ways of Development of Soviet Legal Thought]* (Moscow: Izd. Kommunističeskoj Akademii, 1928); Vyshinsky, *Law of the Soviet State*. Pashukanis was marginalized and accused of revisionism. His self-criticism came to nothing. In September 1937 he was arrested and executed.
57. I thank my friend and colleague Dmitri Nikulin for his help and the discussion about these terms.

58. Oliver H. Radkey, *The Agrarian Foes of Bolshevism: Promise and Default of the Russian Socialist Revolutionaries, February to October 1917* (New York: Columbia University Press, 1958), 25–26.
59. Hannah Arendt, "Thoughts on Politics and Revolution," in *Crisis of the Republic* (New York: Harcourt Brace Jovanovich, 1972), 231–232; Arendt, *On Revolution*, 249.
60. Arendt, "Thoughts on Politics and Revolution," 231–32.
61. Alexis de Tocqueville, *The European Revolution and Correspondence with Gobineau*, ed. and trans. John Lukacs (New York: Doubleday, 1953), 160.
62. "The small landholders are the most precious part of a state." Thomas Jefferson to James Madison, October 28, 1785, in *Thomas Jefferson: Writings*, ed. Merrill D. Peterson (New York: Library of America, 1984), 842.
63. Arendt, "Thoughts on Politics and Revolution," 232.
64. "Déclaration au Peuple Français," in *Commune de Paris*, no. 170, April 19, 1871.
65. Alan Kimball, "The First International and Russian Obshchina," *Slavic Review* 32, no. 3 (1973): 509.
66. Kimball, "First International and Russian Obshchina," 509.
67. Resolution on the Land Question (May 26, 1917), in Browder and Kerensky, *Russian Provisional Government*, 597–58.
68. Browder and Kerensky, *Russian Provisional Government*, 604–605.
69. Browder and Kerensky, *Russian Provisional Government*, 605. Kermit E. McKenzie, "Zemstvo organization and role within the administrative structure," in Terence Emmons and Wayne S. Vucinich, *The Zemstvo in Russia: An Experiment in Local Self-Government* (London: Cambridge University Press, 1982), 34.
70. Israel Getzler, *Nikolai Sukhanov: Chronicler of the Russian Revolution* (London: Palgrave, 2002), 130.
71. Bunyan and Fisher, *Bolshevik Revolution*, 128–32.
72. Manfred Hildermeier, *The Russian Socialist Revolutionary Party Before the First World War* (New York: St. Martin's, 2000), 81–82.
73. Mark D. Steinberg, *Voices of Revolution, 1917* (New Haven, CT, and London: Yale University Press, 2001), 143.
74. Dorothy Atkinson, *The End of the Russian Land Commune, 1905–1930* (Stanford, CA: Stanford University Press, 1983), 168.

75. V. I. Lenin, "Comrade Workers, Forward to the Last, Decisive Fight!" (1919), in *Collected Works* (Moscow: Progress, 1965), 28:57.
76. V. I. Lenin, "Moscow Party Workers' Meeting, November 27, 1918," in *Collected Works* (Moscow: Progress, 1965), 28:213.
77. V. I. Lenin, *The Proletarian Revolution and the Renegade Kautsky* (1918), in *Collected Works* (Moscow: Progress, 1965), 28:314–35
78. Lenin, *Proletarian Revolution*, 308.
79. Bunyan and Fisher, *Bolshevik Revolution*, 684.
80. "Peasants were rioting on a large scale until about 1913, and much of European Russia was under martial law during the entire period." See George L. Yamey, "The Concept of the Stolypin Land Reform," *Slavic Review* 21, no. 2 (1964): 219.
81. D. J. Male, *Russian Peasant Organization before Collectivisation: A Study of Commune and Gathering 1925–1930* (Cambridge: Cambridge University Press, 1971), 18.
82. Moshe Lewin, *Russian Peasants and Soviet Power: A Study of Collectivization* (London: George Allen and Unwin, 1968), 85.
83. Male, *Russian Peasant Organization before Collectivisation*, 89.
84. Lewin, *Russian Peasants and Soviet Power*, 90.
85. Lewin, *Russian Peasants and Soviet Power*, 87.
86. Lewin, *Russian Peasants and Soviet Power*, 93.
87. Male, *Russian Peasant Organization Before Collectivisation*, vii.
88. Harold J. Berman, "Soviet Property in Law and in Plan," *University of Pennsylvania Law Review* 96, no. 3 (1948): 324–53.
89. As Vladimir Gsovski pointed out, "a non-Soviet jurist would look in vain for a new concept of ownership in the Soviet Code Civil." Cited in Asya Ostroukh, "Russian Society and its Civil Codes: A Long Way to Civilian Civil Law," *Journal of Civil Law Studies* 6, no. 1 (2013): 385.
90. On the false Soviet narrative of the crisis of the agricultural system of rural societies in order to justify their destruction, see Michael Kopsidis, Katja Brutish, and Daniel W. Bromley, "Where Is the Backward Russian Peasant? Evidence Against the Superiority of Private Farming 1883–1913," *Journal of Peasant Studies* 42, no. 2 (2015): 428–49. The authors show that between 1861 and 1911, there was a constant increase of agricultural output based on communal tenure.

91. G. M. Armstrong, *The Soviet Law of Property: The Right to Control Property and the Construction of Communism* (The Hague: Martinus Nijhoff, 1983), 22–40; John H. Hazard, "Soviet Property Law," *Cornell Law Review* 30, no. 4 (1945): 466–87; Boris N. Mamlyuk, "Early Soviet Property Law in Comparison with Western Legal Traditions," in *Research Handbook in Political Economy and Law*, ed. Ugo Mattei and John D. Haskell (Northampton, MA: Edward Elgar, 2016), 454–80.
92. Sherron Nay Acker, "Maria Spiridinova and the Struggle for the Social Revolution," PhD diss., Rutgers University, 1999, 214.
93. Keep, *Debate on Soviet Power*, 132.
94. Keep, *Debate on Soviet Power*, 177–78.
95. Acker, "Maria Spiridinova," 312.
96. Viktor Mikhailovich Chernov at the second PSR Congress in Imatra, 1906; in Ettore Cinnella, *1905: La vera rivoluzione russa* (Pisa-Cagliari: Della Porta Editori, 2008), 221.
97. Chernov, in Cinnella, *1905*, 221.
98. Chernov, in Cinnella, *1905*, 221, 223.
99. Lenin, *What the 'Friends of the People' Are and How They Fight the Social-Democrats* (1894), in *Collected Works* (Moscow: Progress, 1960), 1:330–31.
100. V. I. Lenin, "The Economic Content of Narodism and the Criticism of it in Mr. Struve's Book" (1895), in *Collected Works* (Moscow: Progress, 1960), 1:361–79.
101. V. I. Lenin, *The Development of Capitalism in Russia* (1899), in *Collected Works* (Moscow: Progress, 1960), 3:314–25. The legacy of modernizing and the stagist conception of history of the Second International Marxism remained the outlook of the Bolshevik Party in power. In order to implement Russian development, wrote Eric John Marot, the Trotskyist :eft, the Bukharian Right, and the Stalinists agreed to destroy the peasant way of life: Eric John Marot, *The October Revolution in Prospect and Retrospect: Interventions in Russian and Soviet History* (Leiden: Brill, 2012), 11. See Loren Goldner, *Revolution, Defeat and Theoretical Underdevelopment: Russian, Turkey, Spain, Bolivia* (Chicago: Haymarket, 2017), 8–51.
102. Steinberg, *Voices of Revolution*, 143.
103. Steinberg, *Voices of Revolution*, 242.

104. On the *usus modernus Pandectarum*, see Franz Wieacker, *A History of Private Law in Europe*, trans. Tony Weir (Oxford: University Press, 1997).
105. Anton Friedrich Justus Thibaut, *System des Pandekten-Rechts* (Jena: Mauke, 1818). See Schwab, "Eigentum," 75–76.
106. Steven A. Grant, "Obshchina and Mir," *Slavic Review* 35, no. 4 (1976): 636–51.
107. "Russian intellectuals invented the obshchina about the year 1840." See Grant, "Obshchina and Mir," 651. Roger Portal, *Le statut des paysans libérés du servage* (The Hague: Mouton, 1963), 35–37.
108. Alexander Herzen, "The Russian People and Socialism: An Open Letter to Jules Michelet" (1851), in *Selected Philosophical Works*, trans. L. Navrozov (Moscow: Foreign Language, 1956), 486.
109. Georg Ludwig von Maurer, *Geschichte der Markenverfassung in Deutschland* (Erlagen: F. Enke, 1856).
110. Marx to Engels, March 14, 1868, in *Marx and Engels Collected Works* (London: Lawrence & Wishart, 1987), 42:547.
111. Karl Salomo Zachariä, *Der Kampf des Grundeigenthums gegen die Grundherrlichkeit* (Heidelberg: A. Osswald. 1832), 6; Georg Friedrich Puchta, *Cursus der Institutionen* (Leipzig: Breitkopf und Härtel, 1851), 2:579.
112. Anna Taitslin, "The Commune Debates on the Eve of Peasant Emancipation: The Long Shadow of Russian Paternalism," *Review of Central and East European Law* 4 (2015): 2–39.
113. T. K. Dennison and A. W. Carus, "The Invention of the Russian Rural Commune: Haxthausen and the Evidence," *Historical Journal* 46, no. 3 (2003): 561–82.
114. August von Haxthausen, *Studies on the Interior of Russia*, ed. S. Frederick Starr, trans. Eleanore L. M. Schmidt (Chicago: University of Chicago Press, 1972), 292.
115. Macpherson, *Political Theory of Possessive Individualism*, 269.
116. Steinberg, *Voices of Revolution*, 242.
117. Macpherson, *Political Theory of Possessive Individualism*, 275.
118. Nikolay Gavrilovich Chernyshevsky, *La possession communale du sol*, trans. E. Laran-Tamarkine (Paris: Marcel Rivière, 1911), 65–67.
119. Chernyshevsky, *La possession communale du sol*, 13.

120. Chernyshevsky, *La possession communale du sol*, 70.
121. Vera Zasulich to Karl Marx, February 16, 1881, in Teodor Shanin, *Late Marx and the Russian Road: Marx and "The Peripheries of Capitalism"* (New York: Monthly Review, 1983), 98–99.
122. Shanin, *Late Marx*, 129.
123. Shanin, *Late Marx*, 124.
124. Shanin, *Late Marx*, 121.
125. Shanin, *Late Marx*, 121.
126. Shanin, *Late Marx*, 134.
127. Shanin, *Late Marx*, 136.
128. Shanin, *Late Marx*, 136.
129. V. Zenzinov, "Propavshaia gramota," *Sovremennie Zapiski*, book 14 (Paris: 1925), 401, cited in Haruki Wada, "Marx and Revolutionary Russia," in Teodor Shanin, *Late Marx and the Russian Road: Marx and "The Peripheries of Capitalism"* (New York: Monthly Review, 1983), 42.
130. V. M. Chernov, *Konstruktivnyi Sotsializm* (Prague: Volia Rossii, 1925), 128, cited in Wada, "Marx and Revolutionary Russia," 42.
131. Marx was interested in the forms of communal possession in different historical and geographical contexts: "It is a laughable prejudice, spread abroad recently, that naturally arisen communal property is a specifically Slavic, or even an exclusively Russian form. It is the original form (Urform) that can be found among the Romans, Teutons, and Celts, and which indeed is still in existence in India, in a whole collection of diverse patterns, albeit sometimes only vestiges of them." Karl Marx, *Grundrisse*, trans. Viktor Schnittke, in *Marx and Engels Collected Works* (London: Lawrence & Wishart, 1987), 29:275.
132. Karl Marx, *Capital*, trans. David Fernbach (London: Penguin, 1981), 3:911.
133. John Riddell and Ma'mud Shirvani, eds., *To See the Dawn: Baku, 1920 – First Congress of the Peoples of the East* (London: Pathfinder, 1993), 158. See Robert J. C. Young, *Postcolonialism. An Historical Introduction* (Malden: Blackwell, 2000), 134–39.
134. Riddell and Shirvani, *To See the Dawn*, 232.
135. Riddell and Shirvani, *To See the Dawn*, 232.
136. Riddell and Shirvani, *To See the Dawn*, 107.
137. Riddell and Shirvani, *To See the Dawn*, 219.

138. "Pilaff and Palaver: Communist Farce at Baku," *The Times*, London, October 6, 1920.
139. "The Red Flag in the East," *The Times*, London, September 23, 1920.
140. Stephen White, "Communism and the East: The Baku Congress, 1920," *Slavic Review* 33, no. 3 (1974): 501–502.
141. Alp Yenen, "The Other Jihad: Enver Pasha, Bolsheviks, and Politics of Anticolonial Muslim Nationalism during Baku Congress 1920," in *The First World War and Its Aftermath: The Shaping of the Middle East*, ed. Thomas G. Fraser (Chicago: University of Chicago Press, 2015), 287–289.
142. Riddell and Shirvani, *To See the Dawn*, 262.
143. G. W. F. Hegel, *Philosophie des Rechts nach der Vorlesungsnachschrift K.G. von Griesheim 1824-25*, in *Vorlesungen über Rechtsphilosophie 1818-31, Vol. 4: Edition und Kommentar in sechs*, ed. Karl-Heinz Ilting, (Stuttgart-Bad-Cannstatt: Fromman-Holzboog, 1974), 735.
144. Carl Schmitt, "The Age of Neutralizations and Depoliticizations" (1929), trans. Matthias Konzen and John P. McCormick, in *The Concept of the Political* (Chicago: University of Chicago Press, 2007), 95.
145. Riddell and Shirvani, *To See the Dawn*, 332. See Matthieu Renault, *L'Empire de la Révolution: Lénin et les Musulmans de Russie* (Paris: Éditions Syllepse, 2017); Ian Birchall, "The Communist International and Imperialism," *Viewpoint Magazine* 6 (February 2018).
146. Riddell and Shirvani, *To See the Dawn*, 332.
147. Riddell and Shirvani, *To See the Dawn*, 333.
148. Riddell and Shirvani, *To See the Dawn*, 337.
149. Riddell and Shirvani, *To See the Dawn*, 337.
150. Zinoviev, quoted in Riddell and Shirvani, *To See the Dawn*, 77.
151. Michael Kemper, "Red Orientalism: Mikhail Pavlovich and Marxist Oriental Studies in Early Soviet Russia," *Die Welt des Islams* 50, nos. 3–4 (2010): 467.
152. Riddell and Shirvani, *To See the Dawn*, 164.
153. Riddell and Shirvani, *To See the Dawn*, 232.
154. Bibinur, quotred in Riddell and Shirvani, *To See the Dawn*, 235.
155. Riddell and Shirvani, *To See the Dawn*, 308.

156. Riddell and Shirvani, *To See the Dawn*, 201.
157. Nikolay G. Chernyshevsky, *What Is to Be Done?*, trans. Nathan Haskell Dole and S. S. Skidelsky (New York: Thomas Y. Crowell, 1886), 387–388.
158. Richard Stites, *Revolutionary Dreams: Utopian Vision and Experimental Life in the Russian Revolution* (Oxford: Oxford University Press, 1989), 55.

Chapter 5

1. José Carlos Mariátegui, *Seven Interpretative Essays on Peruvian Reality*, trans. Marjory Urquidi (Austin: University of Texas Press, 1971).
2. Clandestine Revolutionary Indigenous Committee-General Command of the EZLN, "Votán Zapata lives in our dead," *La Jornada*, April 10, 1994, in *Zapatistas! Documents of the New Mexican Revolution* (New York: Autonomedia, 1994), 270. The Spanish versions of all the Zapatista documents and texts cited are available at http://enlacezapatista.ezln.org.mx.
3. Morelos Declaration, March 1994, in *Zapatistas! Documents*, 272.
4. First Declaration of the Lacandona Jungle, January 1, 1994, in *Zapatistas! Documents*, 49.
5. "Declaration of Quito, Ecuador" July 1990, http://unpfip.blogspot.com/2012/09/declaration-of-quito-1990.html.
6. "Before 1994 there was no respect for women. . . . We joined the struggle and that's when things started to change and we stepped being oppressed"; Hilary Klein, *Compañeras: Zapatista Women's Stories* (New York: Seven Stories, 2015), 47–48. See Márgara Millán, "Zapatista Indigenous Women," in *Zapatista! Reinventing Revolution in Mexico*, ed. John Holloway and Eloina Perez (London: Pluto, 1998), 64–80; Sylvia Marcos, "The Borders Within: The Indigenous Women's Movement and Feminism in Mexico," in *Dialogue and Difference: Feminisms Challenge Globalization*, ed. Marguerite Waller and Sylvia Marcos (New York, Palgrave Macmillan, 2005), 81–112; Guiomar Rovira, *Women of Maize. Indigenous Women and the Zapatista Rebellion* (London: Latin America Bureau, 2000).

7. On the reference to tradition in Zapatista politics, see Enrique Rajchenberg and Catherine Héau-Lambert, "History and Symbolism in the Zapatista Movement," in *Zapatista!: Reinventing Revolution in Mexico*, ed. John Holloway and Eloina Perez (London: Pluto, 1998), 19–38. On indigenous tradition, see Laura Carlsen, "Autonomía indígena y usos y costumbres: la inovación de la tradición," *Chiapas* 7 (1999): 45–91, http://indigenas.bioetica.org/not/PDF/Carlsen.pdf.
8. E. P. Thompson observed that folklore has been discredited by both Marxism and the Left in general, which, being interested in "innovative, rationalizing movements," have abandoned folklore in the conservative field and, finally, to Fascism. E. P. Thompson, "Folklore, Anthropology, and Social History," *Indian Historical Review* 2, no. 2 (January 1978): 247–66.
9. John Womack, *Zapata and the Mexican Revolution* (New York: Vintage, 1968), 226–34.
10. Clandestine Revolutionary Indigenous Committee-General Command of the EZLN, "On the Opening of the Dialogue," February 16, 1994, in *Zapatista! Documents*, 194.
11. Clandestine Revolutionary Committee,, "Votán Zapata," 270.
12. Clandestine Revolutionary Indigenous Committee-General Command of the EZLN, "We want all who walk with the truth to unite in one step," January 20, 1994, in *Zapatista! Documents*, 112.
13. John Holloway, *Change the World Without Taking the Power: The Meaning of Revolution Today* (London: Pluto, 2003).
14. Press Conference with Subcomandante Marcos on February 24, 1994, published in *La Jornada*, February 25, 1994, in *Zapatista! Documents*, 224.
15. Press Conference with Subcomandante Marcos, in *Zapatista! Documents*, 224.
16. Constitución política de los estados unidos mexicanos (1917), most recent revision by the DOF on January 29, 2016: http://www.ordenjuridico.gob.mx/Constitucion/cn16.pdf
17. Interview with Marcos by reporters from *Proceso, El Financiero*, and *New York Times*, February 1994, in *Zapatistas! Documents*, 207.
18. Press Conference with Subcomandante Marcos, in *Zapatistas! Documents*, 224.

19. Press Conference with Subcomandante Marcos, in *Zapatistas! Documents*, 224.
20. Womack, *Zapata and the Mexican Revolution*, 227.
21. Press Conference with Subcomandante Marcos, in *Zapatistas! Documents*, 224–25.
22. The cargo system is made up of an entire hierarchy of positions whose counterpart is the community assembly, which is the place where political decisions are made; see Kara Zugman Dellacioppa, *The Bridge Called Zapatismo: Building Alternative Political Cultures in Mexico City, Los Angeles, and Beyond* (Lanham, MD: Lexington, 2009), 94–95.
23. Press Conference with Subcomandante Marcos, in *Zapatistas! Documents*, 225.
24. Interview with Ramon Vera (1999), expert on indigenous issues and editor of *La Jornada*'s supplement on indigenous matters; cited in Dellacioppa, *Bridge Called Zapatismo*, 99.
25. Sylvia Marcos, "Deconstructing Captivities. Indigenous Women Reshaping Education and Justice," in *Indigenous Education and Empowerment*, ed. Ismael Abu-Saad and Duane Champagne (Oxford: AltaMira, 2006), 75–76.
26. Ana Esther Ceceña, "El mundo del nosotros: entrevista con Carlos Lenkersdorf," *Chiapas* 7 (1999): 191–205.
27. Hobbes, *Leviathan*, chap. 16.
28. Max Weber, *Complete Writings on Academic and Political Vocations*, ed. John Dreijmanis, trans. Gordon C. Wells (New York: Algora, 2008), 157.
29. Adelfo Regino Montes, "La autonomía fortalice la democracia," *Perfil de La Jornada*, March 29, 2001.
30. Dellacioppa, *Bridge Called Zapatismo*, 100, interview with Ramon Vera.
31. According to Iroquois principles of equality and participation, "male chiefs were chosen by women leaders, who also had the power to impeach and replace them"; see Iris Marion Young, "Hybrid Democracy: Iroquois Federalism and the Postcolonial Project," in *Political Theory and the Rights of Indigenous Peoples*, ed. Duncan Ivison, Paul Patton, and Will Sanders (Cambridge: Cambridge University Press, 2000), 241–245.

32. Émile Benveniste, *Le Vocabulaire des institutions indo-européennes* (Paris: Minuit, 1969), 2:148–51.
33. Myriam Revault d'Allonnes, *Le pouvoir des commencements: essai sur l'autorité* (Paris: Éditions du Seuil, 2006), 13: "le temps est la matrice de l'autorité comme l'espace est la matrice du pouvoir."
34. This is what Benjamin called the "inaccessible realm of reconciliation and fulfillment of languages." Walter Benjamin, "The Task of the Translator," trans. Harry Zohn, in *Selected Writings, vol. 1:1913–1926*, ed. Marcus Bullock and Michael W. Jennings (Cambridge, MA: Harvard University Press, 2002), 253–63.
35. Interview with Subcomandante Marcos, May 11, 1994, in *Zapatistas! Documents*, 294.
36. Leandro Vergara-Camus, *Land and Freedom: The MST, the Zapatistas, and Peasant Alternatives to Neoliberalism* (London: Zed, 2014), 273.
37. Carlsen, "Autonomía indígena y usos y costumbres," 45–91.
38. *La Jornada*, May 18, 1995. See John Holloway, "The Concept of Power and the Zapatistas," *Common Sense* 19 (1996): 20–27.
39. Comandante David, in *La Jornada*, May 17, 1995.
40. "Declaration of War from the Lacandona Jungle [First Declaration]," December 31, 1993, in *Zapatista! Documents*, 50.
41. Zapatista National Liberation Army, "Letter to Rigoberta Menchu," in *Zapatista! Documents*, 84.
42. Karl Griewank, *Der neuzeitliche Revolutionsbegriff: Entstehung und Entwicklung* (Wimar: Böhlau, 1955); Reinhart Koselleck, "Historical Criteria of the Modern Concept of Revolution," in Koselleck, *Futures Past*, 43–57.
43. Immanuel Kant, "On the Common Saying: This May Be True in Theory, but It Does Not Hold in Practice," in *Toward Perpetual Peace and Other Writings*, ed. Pauline Kleingeld, trans. David L. Colclasure (New Haven: Yale University Press, 2006), 54–55.
44. Second Declaration of the Lacandona Jungle, in *Zapatistas! Documents*, 348.
45. Press Conference with Subcomandante Marcos, February 23, 1994, in *Zapatistas! Documents*, 219.
46. On the structure of the Juntas de Buen Gobierno, see Martínez Espinoza and Manuel Ignacio, "Las juntas de buen gobierno y los caracoles del movimiento zapatista: fundamentos analíticos

para entender el fenómeno," *Revista de Investigaciones Políticas y Sociológicas* 5, no. 1 (2006): 215–33.
47. "Iniciativa de Ley enviada al H. Congreso de la Unión por el Presidente Fox" December 5, 2000, 3, http://www.diputados. gob.mx/comisiones/asunindi/Iniciativa%20de%20%20 Presidente%20VFox.pdf.
48. Luis Hernández Navarro, *Chiapas: La nueva lucha india* (Madrid: Talasa, 1998), 122–28.
49. Fifth Declaration of the Lacandon Jungle, July 1998, in *¡Ya Basta! Ten Years of the Zapatista Uprising*, ed. Žiga Vodovnik (Oakland, CA: Akpress, 2014), 675, available online at http://enlacezapatista.ezln.org.mx/1998/07/17/v-declaracion-de-la-selva-lacandona/.
50. "Iniciativa de Ley enviada al H. Congreso de la Unión por el Presidente Fox," 3.
51. "Iniciativa de Ley enviada al H. Congreso de la Unión por el Presidente Fox."
52. See "Mexico's Constitution of 2017 with Amendments through 2015," trans. M. Fernanda Gomez Aban for the Comparative Constitutions Project, https://www.constituteproject.org/constitution/Mexico_2015.pdf?lang=en.
53. "Modificaciones del Senado a la ley Cocopa," *Perfil de La Jornada*, April 28, 2001.
54. Comandanta Esther y María de Jesús Patricio, "La ley actual, no la de la COCOPA discrimina a las mujeres," in *Triple Jornada*, April 2, 2001.
55. María de Jesús Patricio, "La mujer frente a los usos y costumbres" in *Perfil de la Jornada*, March 29, 2001, 7.
56. Sylvia Marcos, "We Come to Ask for Justice, Not Crumbs," in *Indigenous Peoples and The Modern State*, ed. Duane Champagne, Karen Jo Torjesen, and Susan Steiner (Walnut Creek, CA: Altamira, 2005), 97–108.
57. "Zapatista en el Congreso," *Perfil de la Jornada*, March 29, 2001.
58. Juan Álvaro Echeverri, "Territory as Body and Territory as Nature: Intercultural Dialogue?" in *The Land Within. Indigenous Territory and Perception of the Environment*, ed. Alexandre Surrallés and Pedro García Hierro (Copenhagen: IWGIA, 2005), 232–234.

59. Sixth Declaration of the Selva Lacandona, June 2005, http://enlacezapatista.ezln.org.mx/sdsl-en/.
60. Jeff Conant, *A Poetics of Resistance: The Revolutionary Public Relations of the Zapatista Insurgency* (Oakland, CA: AK Press, 2010), 283.
61. Carlos Antonio Aguirre Rojas, *Chiapas, Planeta Tierra* (Bogotá: Ediciones Desde Abajo, 2007), 148.
62. James Clifford, *Return: Becoming Indigenous in the Twenty-First Century* (Cambridge, MA: Harvard University Press, 2013), 24–27; Raquel Gutiérrez Aguilar, *Rhythms of the Pachakuti: Indigenous Uprising and State Power in Bolivia* (Durham, NC: Duke University Press, 2014).
63. Sixth Declaration of the Selva Lacandona.
64. Mariana Mora, "Zapatista Anticapitalist Politics and the 'Other Campaign': Learning from the Struggle for Indigenous Rights and Autonomy," *Latin American Perspectives* 34, no. 2 (2007): 66.
65. Interview with Subcomandante Marcos, May 11, 1994, in *Zapatistas! Documents*, 292.
66. EZLN, "Popular Love in the Chiapaneca Jungle," February 16, 1994, in *Zapatista! Documents*, 193.
67. Interview with Subcomandante Marcos, May 11, 1994, in *Zapatistas! Documents*, 299.
68. Sian Lazar, *El Alto, Rebel City: Self and Citizenship in Andean Bolivia* (Durham, NC: Duke University Press, 2008), 140–43.
69. Lazar, *El Alto*, 63. James Holston, *Insurgent Citizenship: Disjunctions of Democracy and Modernity in Brazil* (Princeton, NJ, and Oxford: Princeton University Press, 2008), 252. Sergio Tischler, "Detotalization and Subject: On Zapatismo and Critical Theory," *South Atlantic Quarterly* 113, no. 2 (2014): 327–38.
70. I borrow the idea of trans-locality from the conversation that took place with the friends and colleagues of the Committee on Globalization and Social Change at the Graduate Center, CUNY. In my understanding, it expresses a network of close relations between different places and people, a network in which no node is the center.
71. Courtney Jung, *The Moral Force of Indigenous Politics: Critical Liberalism and the Zapatistas* (Cambridge: Cambridge University Press, 2008), 87–92; Linda Green, "What's at Stake? The Reform

of Agrarian Reform in Mexico," in *Reforming Mexico's Agrarian Reform*, ed. Laura Randall (Armonk, NY: M.E. Sharpe, 1996), 267–70.
72. Vergara-Camus, *Land and Freedom*, 20, 49–59; Luin Goldring, "The Changing Configuration of Property Rights Under Ejido Reform," in *Reforming Mexico's Agrarian Reform*, ed. Laura Randall (Armonk, NY: M.E. Sharpe, 1996), 271–87.
73. Neil Harvey, *The Chiapas Rebellion: The Struggle for Land and Democracy* (Durham, NC: Duke University Press, 1998), 211.
74. Hilarion Noel Branch, *The Mexican Constitution of 1917 compared with the Constitution of 1857* (Philadelphia, PA: American Academy of Political and Social Science, 1917.) The original Spanish text of the 1917 Constitution can be found at http://www.diputados.gob.mx/LeyesBiblio/ref/cpeum/CPEUM_orig_05feb1917.pdf.
75. Article 3 of the Agrarian Law (1915) stated: "The Nation recognizes the traditional and historic right which the pueblos, ranchos, and communities of the Republic have of possessing and administering their fields of communal distribution and communal use (*ejidos*) in the form which they judge proper." Womack, *Zapata and the Mexican Revolution*, 406.
76. James J. Kelly, "Article 27 and Mexican Land Reform: The Legacy of Zapata's Dream," *Columbia Human Rights Law Review* 25 (1994): 541–70.
77. "Mexico's Constitution of 1917 with Amendments through 2015."
78. Press Conference with Subcomandante Marcos, in *Zapatistas! Documents*, 223.
79. Interview with the Clandestine Revolutionary Indigenous Committee-General Command, February 3–4, 1994, in *Zapatista! Documents*, 135.
80. Constitución política de los estados unidos mexicanos (1917), http://www.ordenjuridico.gob.mx/Constitucion/cn16.pdf
81. Elvira Pulitano, ed., *Indigenous Rights in the Age of the UN Declaration* (Cambridge: Cambridge University Press, 2012).
82. Audra Simpson, *Mohawk Interrupts: Political Life Across the Border of Settler States* (Durham, NC: Duke University Press, 2014), 7, 183.

83. Glenn Coulthard, *Red Skin, White Masks: Rejecting the Colonial Politics of Recognition* (Minneapolis: University of Minnesota Press, 2014).
84. Henry Sumner Maine, *Ancient Law, Its Connection with the Early History of Society and Its Relations to Modern Ideas* (New York: Henry Holt, 1906), 165.
85. Georg Wilhelm Friedrich Hegel, *Philosophy of Mind*, trans. Michael J. Inwood (Oxford: Clarendon, 2007), 159.
86. Pedro García Hierro, "Indigenous Territories: Knocking at the Gates of Law," in *The Land Within: Indigenous Territory and Perception of the Environment*, ed. Alexandre Surrallés and Pedro García Hierro (Copenhagen: IWGIA, 2005), 248–76.
87. Andrés Aubry, "Tierra, terruño, territorio," *La Jornada*, June 1, 2007.
88. Hierro, "Indigenous Territories," 267.

In Lieu of a Conclusion

1. Karl Marx, *Capital*, trans. Ben Fowkes (London: Penguin, 1976), 1:171 n32 (translation modified).
2. Stuart Banner, *How the Indians Lost their Land: Law and Power on the Frontier* (Cambridge, MA: Harvard University Press, 2007), 188–189; Lindsay G. Robertson, *Conquest by Law: How the Discovery of America Dispossessed Indigenous Peoples of their Lands* (Oxford: Oxford University Press, 2005).
3. Paul Nadasdy, "'Property' and Aboriginal Land Claims in the Canadian Subarctic: Some Theoretical Considerations," *American Anthropologist* 104, no 1 (2002): 247–61.
4. John Locke, *Two Treatises of Government*, ed. Ian Shapiro (New Haven, CT, and London: Yale University Press, 2003), 111.
5. Georg Wilhelm Friedrich Hegel, *Elements of the Philosophy of Right*, ed. Allen W. Wood, trans. H. B. Nisbet (Cambridge: Cambridge University Press, 1991), §44.
6. Hegel, *Elements of the Philosophy of Right*, §§ 34–35.
7. Locke, *Two Treatises of Government*, 119.
8. Hegel, *Elements of the Philosophy of Right*, §44.

9. Hegel, *Elements of the Philosophy of Right*, §44.
10. Hegel, *Elements of the Philosophy of Right*, §37 Z.
11. William Thomas Stead, *The Last Will and Testament of Cecil John Rhodes* (London: Review of Reviews, 1902), 190.
12. Gerrard Winstanley, *The Law of Freedom and Other Writings*, ed. Christopher Hill (Cambridge: Cambridge University Press, 1983), 100.
13. Winstanley, *Law of Freedom*, 104.
14. Winstanley, *Law of Freedom*, 105.
15. Tom Scott and Bob Scribner, eds., *The German Peasants' War: A History in Documents* (New York: Humanity, 1991), 252–57; Blickle, *Die Revolution von 1525*, 321–27; Rudolph, "Thomas Müntzer Sozialökonomische Konzeption," 562.
16. Gracchus Babeuf, *Manifesto of the Equals*, in *The Spectre of Babeuf*, ed. Ian Birchall (Chicago: Haymarket, 2016), 193.
17. Aguilar, *Rhythms of the Pachakuti*, 16, 58–59.
18. Mariátegui, *Seven Interpretative Essays on Peruvian Reality*.
19. José Rabasa, *Without History: Subaltern Studies, the Zapatista Insurgency, and the Specter of History* (Pittsburgh, PA: University of Pittsburgh Press, 2010), 271–80; Javier Sanjinés, *Embers of the Past: Essay in Times of Decolonization* (Durham, NC: Duke University Press, 2013), 24–25.
20. Paolo Grossi, *Il dominio e le cose: Percezioni medievali e moderne dei diritti reali* (Milan: Giuffrè, 1992), 733.
21. Paolo Grossi, *L'inaugurazione della proprietà moderna* (Naples: Guida, 1980).
22. Blaufarb, *Great Demarcation*; Schwab, "Eigentum."
23. Simpson, *Mohawk Interrupts*, 70.
24. Lewis Henry Morgan, *Ancient Society, Or Researches in the Lines of Human Progress from Savagery through Barbarism to Civilization* (London: Macmillan, 1877), 552.
25. Morgan, *Ancient Society*, 552.
26. Marx, *Drafts of the Letter to Vera Zasulich*, 350.
27. Marx, *Capital*, 3:911 (translation modified).
28. Mahatma Gandhi, *Satyagraha Ashram*, in *The Collected Works of Mahatma Gandhi* (New Delhi: Publications Division Government of India, 1999), 42:109, http://gandhiserve.org/cwmg/VOL042.

PDF; Nehal A. Patel, "Mindful Use: Gandhi's Non-Possessive Property Theory," *Seattle Journal for Social Justice* 13, no. 12 (2014): 289–318.
29. *La sociale*, no. 23, April 22, 1871.
30. Chief Arvol Looking Horse, "Letter to Barack Obama," November 12, 2016, excerpt at https://oneearthsangha.org/statements/stand-with-standing-rock/.

INDEX

Aguirre, Carlos Antonio 208, 276n61
American Revolution 34, 151
Arendt, Hannah 64–65, 151, 250n113, 250n114, 261n159, 265n59, 265n60, 265n63
Arnould, Arthur 81, 82–83, 90–91, 98, 101, 110–11, 253n25, 254n35, 254n38, 254n39, 256n65, 258n97, 260n133
associations viii, 26–27, 29, 56, 58–60, 69–70, 78–79, 83–85, 86–87, 90–92, 95–98, 104–5, 108–10, 115–16, 117–18, 126–27, 132, 138, 158–59, 209, 215, 227, 232
authority viii, 15, 25–26, 32, 48–49, 56, 58–60, 91–92, 98–100, 132–33, 138, 140–42, 158–59, 168, 195, 196–98, 206–7, 220–22
  plurality of authority viii, 19, 22–23, 77–79, 84–85, 88–89, 95–96, 101–2, 191–95, 196–98, 246n61

Babeuf, François-Noël 51–52, 226, 246n59, 279n16
Baku Congress of 1920 131, 176–79, 180–82, 183–84, 269n133
Balibar, Étienne 66, 250n114
Benjamin, Walter viii–ix, 1, 5–7, 11, 12–13, 71, 235n1, 236n11, 236n12, 237n27, 238n32, 252n1, 274n34
Billaud-Varenne, Jacques-Nicolas 100–1, 257n94
Blanqui, Louis-Auguste 81, 254n36
Bloch, Ernst viii–ix, 5–7, 30–31, 121–22, 236n10, 242n4
Bloch, Marc 108–9, 258n103
Bolsheviks 122–24, 128, 133, 134, 137, 142, 145–46, 153, 155, 156–57, 158–59, 161, 162, 163, 165, 178–79, 180–83, 211

Bonaparte, Napoleon 7–8, 19–20, 46, 84–85, 103–4, 112–13, 118–19, 237n20
Bonaparte, Napoleon Luis 62, 258n100
Bordiga, Amadeo 137
Brissot, Jean-Paul 40, 44
Bulach (Baku Congress) 176–77

Chakrabarty, Dipesh 10–11, 237n18
Chernov, Viktor 167–68, 175–76, 267n96
Chernyshevsky, Nikolay 6, 168–69, 170–72, 175–76, 185, 268n118, 268n119, 269n120, 271n157
chronotones. *See* temporalities
Cicero 104, 258n109
Cieszkowski, August von 3–4, 235n4
Cloots, Anacharsis 37, 114–15, 260n146
Cocopa Law 202, 205–6, 207–8, 275n53, 275n54
Comandanta Esther (Zapatistas) 205–6
Comandanta Kelly (Zapatistas) 222
(Sub)Comandante Marcos (Zapatistas) 198–99, 201–2, 272n14, 272n17, 272n18, 273n23, 274n35, 276n65, 277n78
Comandante Tacho (Zapatistas) 198–99
constitution
  1789 French Constitution 19, 32
  1791 French Constitution 56, 57, 248n81
  1793 French Constitution 37, 38–41, 50, 56, 57, 120–21, 134, 244n27, 244n30, 249n94

  1795 Thermidorian Constitution 40–41, 56, 57, 76–77, 246n55
  1801 Constitution of Haiti 17–19, 46–48, 239n47
  1848 French Constitution 76–77, 78, 93, 101–2, 253n23
  1857 Federal Constitution of the United Mexican States 213, 277n74
  1917 Political Constitution of the United Mexican States 2–3, 191–93, 201–2, 204–5, 213, 215, 220
  1918 Constitution of the Russian Socialist Federated Republic ix–x, 13–14, 120, 125, 126, 127–28, 131–33, 134, 135–36, 137–38, 139–40, 141, 142, 144, 147–49, 166, 182–83
  1936 Constitution of the USSR 129–30, 134, 137–38, 139–40, 141, 158–59, 160
  1958 French Constitution 93
  Amendments to Article 27 of Mexican Constitution 210, 213, 215, 277n76

Declaration
  1649 Declaration from the Poor Oppressed People of England 225–26
  1776 US Declaration of Independence 34
  1789 Declaration of the Rights of the Man and of the Citizen 17–19, 20–21, 30, 31, 32, 33, 34–35, 41–43, 62, 63, 66, 86–87, 132, 232, 250n111
  1791 Declaration of the Rights of Woman and the Female Citizen 14–15, 37, 41–43

INDEX | 283

1793 Declaration of the Rights of the Man and of the Citizen 30, 31, 32, 33, 35–41, 43–44, 57, 62, 114–15, 131, 132
1795 Declaration of Rights and Duties of Man and Citizen 46–48
1804 Haiti Declaration of Independence 22–23
1871 Declaration to the French People 79, 83–84, 93, 95, 152, 253n24, 265n64
1871 Declaration of *La Commune de l'Algérie* 72
1918 Declaration of the Rights of the Toiling and Exploited People 120, 126, 128–29, 130–32, 147–48, 149–50, 152, 166, 176–77, 178, 181–82
1948 Universal Declaration of Human Rights 62–63, 242n9
1994 Zapatista 1st Declaration 187–89, 199–200
1994 Zapatista 2nd Declaration 274n44
1996 Zapatista 4th Declaration 28, 186–87, 190–91
1998 Zapatista 5th Declaration 207–8
2005 Zapatista 6th Declaration 207–8, 209, 210, 275n49
Diggers 26–27, 225–26, 227–28
Dmitrieff, Elisabeth 109
dominium (right to property) 98–100, 106–7, 160–61, 221–22, 227–28, 229, 233–34, 258n108
Droysen, Johann Gustav 11–12

Enragés 17–19, 22, 26–27, 37, 40, 51–52, 53–54, 60–61, 67, 226, 241n67, 244n27, 244n29

Gaillard, Napoleon 80–81
Girondins 37–40, 44, 50–51, 54–55, 57–61, 67, 244n29, 247n68
Gortari, Carlos Salinas de 200, 213, 215, 219, 220
Gouges, Olympe de 37–38, 41–43, 69, 252n130
Guyomar, Pierre 22, 65, 67–68, 240n55

Hanum, Najia (Baku Congress) 176–77, 183
Haxthausen, August von 168–69, 268n113
Hegel, Georg Wilhelm Friedrich 3–4, 14–15, 23–24, 79–80, 121–22, 124–25, 170–72, 179–80, 221, 225, 226, 238n37, 245n41, 254n27, 261n3, 270n143, 278n85
Herder, Gottfried 4, 236n6
Herzen, Alexander 166–67, 168–69, 170–72, 268n108
Hobbes, Thomas 26–27, 34–35, 42–43, 74, 88, 168–69, 196, 242n12, 255n59

imperative mandate 10, 13–14, 17–19, 22–23, 27–28, 39–40, 52, 53–56, 57–60, 89–93, 95–97, 98, 100–1, 105–6, 140–41, 195, 226, 247–48n80, 248n90, 248n91, 249n103, 256n69, 257n80, 263n35

jacobins 37–39, 40–41, 48–49, 54–55, 57–61, 65–66, 69, 114–15, 120–21, 147, 241n62, 251n119
James Cyril Lionel Robert 30, 46, 241n1
Jefferson, Thomas 151, 265n62

Kant, Immanuel viii–, 4, 15–19, 23–24, 74–75, 121–22, 200–1, 236n5, 238n38, 238n39, 274n43

Kirchheimer, Otto 125–26, 136–37, 262n12
Koselleck, Reinhart 5, 11–12, 235n2, 236n7, 238n30, 257n89, 274n42
Kun, Béla 184

Lambert, Alexandre 72–73
Larin, Yu 157
Leclerc, Théophile 51
Lenin, Vladimir 79–80, 123–24, 133, 141, 143–44, 156–57, 162, 164–65, 172, 185, 263n43, 264n47, 266n75, 266n77, 267n99, 270n145
Locke, John 105–6, 168–69, 224–26, 278n4, 278n7
Louverture, Toussaint 19, 37, 46, 245n42, 245n51

Machiavelli, Niccolò 88–89, 256n60
Macpherson, Crawford Brough 170, 259n119
Madison, James 142–43, 264n54
manifesto
  1793 Manifesto of the Enragés 26–27, 67, 226, 241n67
  1796 Manifesto of the Equals 226, 279n16
  1871 Manifesto of the Twenty Arrondissements 86–87, 93, 255n50
  1848 Manifesto of the Communist Party 51–52
  1920 Manifesto to People of the East 179–80
Marcos. *See* (Sub)Comandante Marcos
Mariategui, Jose Carlos 186, 271n1, 279n18

Martynov, Semyon 166, 169–70
Marx, Karl viii–ix, 5, 6–7, 12–13, 51–52, 62, 80, 81, 101–2, 167–68, 170–72, 173–76, 206–7, 223–24, 229–31, 236n13, 236n14, 236n15, 238n33, 253n16, 268n110, 269n121
Mensheviks 135–36, 142
Michel, Louise 73–74, 88, 112–13, 253n14
Mill, John Stuart 7–8, 169–70, 237n22
mir 13–14, 153–54, 155, 157–59, 160–61, 163–64, 165, 166–67, 168–69, 185, 228–29, 268n106
Morgan, Lewis Henry 230, 279n24
multiversum, multiverse viii, 5–7, 27, 223–24, 228
Müntzer, Thomas 26–27, 168–69, 226, 241n65

narodniks. *See* Russian populists
natural rights
  insurgent natural rights 26–27, 31, 33, 42–44, 50–51, 54, 56, 84–85, 249–50n106
  liberal tradition of 116, 133, 138
New Economy Policy (NEP) 123–24, 161–62

Obshchina 152, 153, 166–69, 170–72, 174–76, 228, 265n65, 265n66, 268n106, 268n107
Oswald, John 100, 115–16, 257n96

Pashukanis, Evgeny 149, 264n55
Pavlovich, Mikhail 181–82, 270n151
Plekhanov, Georgi 165, 172, 173–74, 175–76
Portalis, Jean-Etienne Marie 103–4

INDEX | 285

possession
  apariagraha
    (nonpossession) 231–32
  collective 27, 101–3, 107–8, 149–
    50, 155, 160–61, 166, 187–88,
    215, 220–22, 223–26, 227–28,
    233, 269n131
  individual 102, 104–5, 107–8,
    160–61, 168–69, 170, 182–83
  medieval conception 228–29
Pothier, Robert Joseph 103–4,
  258n106
property
  common property (right of
    use) 26–27, 104–6, 108–9, 152,
    154, 155, 158–59, 166–68, 170–
    72, 208–9, 223–24, 231–32
  private property viii, 7–8, 9–10, 15,
    19, 22, 26–27, 48, 50–51, 61–62,
    76, 79, 98–100, 101–5, 107–8,
    110–11, 125, 126–27, 138, 148–
    50, 151, 153, 160, 161–62, 166,
    168–69, 190, 204–6, 210, 213, 215,
    221–22, 223–25, 226, 230, 231
Proudhon, Pierre-Joseph 103–5,
  258n104
Putchta, Georg Friedrich 168

Ranke, Leopold von 11–12
Reisner, Mikhail 146
Robespierre, Maximilien 2, 22–23,
  37, 38–39, 40–41, 50–52, 54–
  55, 60–61, 79–80, 114, 121–22,
  243n17, 243n22
Romano, Santi 75–76, 239n50
Roux, Jacques 26–27, 51,
  226, 241n67
Russian populists 2–3, 6, 164–65,
  168–69, 173, 174–76, 185
Ryazanov, David 173–74, 175–76

Schmitt, Carl 92–93, 126, 134,
  179–80, 182–83, 242–43n14,
  244n31, 248n89, 250n116,
  256n73, 262n15, 270n144
Shabanova (Baku Congress) 176–77
Sieyès, Emmanuel Joseph 24–25,
  34–36, 48–49, 60–61, 69, 212,
  241n61, 250n107
Skachko, Anatolii 124, 178, 183
Socialist-Revolutionaries (SRs) 2–3,
  146, 150, 152–54, 155, 156–58,
  160–61, 162, 163–64, 165, 175–
  76, 265n58, 265n72
  Left Socialist-Revolutionaries
    (Left SRs) 133, 145–46, 153,
    155, 157, 162, 163
Sorlin, Pierre 71–72, 252n2
Stalin, Josef 122–24, 129–30,
  137, 261n7
Standing Rock protests 232, 280n30
Steklov, Yuri
  Mikhailovich 143, 261n2
Stuchka, Peter 149, 264n55

temporalities
  anachronism 10, 14, 19–20, 24,
    27–28, 55, 165, 172, 175–76,
    185, 187–88, 224–25, 228
  chronotones 10, 24, 46–48, 184,
    185, 213, 228, 230
  synchronization 9–10, 101–2,
    122–24, 220, 254n32
Tocqueville, Alexis de 7–8,
  151, 237n20
Trotsky, Leon 143, 163, 263n38

Vaillant, Édouard 82–83
Varlet, Jean-François 37–38, 54, 57–
  58, 247–48n80, 248n83
Varlin, Eugène 90–91, 256n64

White, Hayden 11–12, 238n29
Winstanley, Gerrard 26–27, 168–69, 226, 279n12

Zachariä, Karl Salomo 168, 268n111

Zapata, Emilio 13–14
Zasulich, Vera 6, 172, 173–76, 236n13
Zenzinov, Vladir 175–76, 269n129
Zinoviev, Grigory 178–79